D1154910

MIRIAM ADAHAN

Living with Difficult People

(INCLUDING YOURSELF)

gefen גפן
publishing house בית הוצאה לאור

Although the examples contained in this book are all true, the names have been changed to protect the privacy of those involved. Any similarity to people with these names is purely coincidental.

The royalties from this book are dedicated to impoverished families in *Eretz Yisrael*.

First published 1991

Copyright © 1991 by Miriam Adahan

Published by Feldheim Publishers Ltd. in conjunction with
Gefen Publishing House Ltd.

Feldheim Publishers Ltd.
POB 35002
Jerusalem, Israel

Philipp Feldheim Inc.
200 Airport Executive Park
Spring Valley, NY 10977

Library of Congress Cataloging in Publication Data

Adahan, Miriam.
    Living with difficult people — including yourself / Miriam Adahan.
    p. 306 cm. 23
    Includes bibliographical references.
    ISBN 0-87306-518-2
    1. Mental illness — Popular works. 2. Interpersonal relations.
I. Title.
RC480.515.A33 1990   90-35019
616.89–dc20   CIP

Typesetting by Gefen Publishing House Ltd.

Printed in Israel

This book is dedicated
to my sister, Yehudis Karbal,
who was the first one
to help me out of the darkness
in which I was immersed for so many years,
and
to my EMETT family — all the women who have attended EMETT groups
over the past thirteen years and who have shared their joys and woes with
me, who have sustained me with their love, have encouraged me with their
examples of determination and courage, and have been an ongoing
inspiration for me to do this work.

1710 BEACON STREET
BROOKLINE, MASSACHUSETTS•02146

Although we are living in a world of seeming plenty, there is much that is lacking. The problems people face in coping with the immense challenges of life—striving for achievement in the physical and the spiritual realms—are often difficult to deal with.

A support system is important to guide us through the journey of life so that we can be better people, so that we in turn can lead a better family life, and so that we can affect the community we live in.

Living with Difficult People (Including Yourself) by Miriam Adahan, is, I believe, a good means through which one can gain better insight into oneself.

When Hashem confronted Adam after his failure to deal with the one prohibition he was faced with, He asked him: *"Ahyeka?—Where are you?"* In the most literal sense, this is a question we ought to ask ourselves at all times and at all stages of life.

Where are you? Are you fulfilling the will of Hashem in the manner that God wants you to? Are you providing the emotional support for your family and your friends that you have the potential for?

The authoress, Mrs. Adahan, tries to put a better perspective on *"Ahyeka?"* in order to help those who need help and this may be good reading also for those who don't think they need help.

May her efforts to help people "locate themselves" be blessed with *hatzlachah*.

בברכת התורה ממני דוד שלמה אליעזר ושמו בן ציון ע"ה

CONGREGATION BETH PINCHAS • NEW ENGLAND CHASSIDIC CENTE
GRAND RABBI LEVI I. HOROWITZ • ת המדרש בית פינחס של אדמו"ר מבאסטאן
1710 BEACON STREET • BROOKLINE, MASS. 02146 • RE 4 510

KIRYAT NACHLIEL · קרית נחליאל

RABBI NACHMAN BULMAN   הרב נחמן בולמן

Even among those who strive to live in accord with Torah thinking, emotional stress inflicts wounds not easily healed. Especially among "late beginners" in Torah observance, the unconscious remains resistant to the impact of Torah behavior. Nor does the negative influence of their surroundings leave Torah observant Jews unblemished, whatever their background.

Without access to counseling based on Torah, while also expressed in a familiar idiom, many turn to secularist oriented counseling and therapy.

Miriam Adahan is one of the few whose faithfulness to Torah, and whose professional competence as a counselor and therapist, have reflected unfailing harmony. Her written works and the EMETT movement she leads, have won her the gratitude of thousands, and the warm approval of the Torah community.

Another work is about to appear from Mrs. Adahan's pen: *Living with Difficult People — Including Yourself*. Emotional disorder, manifestations, effects, and possible healing are her theme.

In the book's twelve chapters, the authoress blends wide-ranging Torah knowledge with rich experience; unflinching truthfulness with unlimited compassion; and total reverence for Torah guidance.

What are the roots of emotional disturbance? Are we to be either paralyzed by guilt or deny its reality? How are we to balance humility and pride; fear and love; aggressiveness and passivity? How are we to react to compulsive or oppressive behavior of others towards us? How shall we channel suffering into refinement of spirit rather than bitterness? How shall insight into the causes of our own failings be transformed into freedom of will and moral strength?

On all of the above topics, Miriam Adahan's latest work sheds penetrating light. It is the hope of this writer that many will find in its pages the healing power of David Hamelech's teaching: **תורת ד' תמימה משיבת נפש**, "The Torah of Hashem is perfect; it restores the soul."

נחמן בולמן

Rabbi Zelig Pliskin
14 Panim Meirot
Jerusalem
372-773/372-110

Living with Difficult People (Including Yourself) is a
book which addresses painful topics in an extremely
constructive manner. It contains a treasury of tools
and techniques for coping with one's own journey toward emotional and spiritual health, and gives an approach for dealing effectively with difficult people.

Every life situation is an opportunity to elevate
ourselves spiritually. We create our world and ourselves by how we react to our life tests. This guide-
book will give many readers, who recognize themselves
in these pages, the courage, insight and information
to handle their personal obstacle course in a wise
manner.

As a consultant, I feel that this book will serve
as a sourcebook for people in the helping professions.
It will enable them to recognize patterns of behavior
with greater efficiency and thus be more empathetic
and compassionate to those who seek their counsel. It
will supply them with practical techniques that have
proven themselves to be beneficial.

One major point raised in this book is the long-
term harm of *ona'as devarim*, harming people with words.
This Torah prohibition is dealt with at length in my
book, *The Power of Words*. It is crucial for parents
and educators to master positive communication ap-
proaches in order to have a positive influence on
children. This will prevent many problems from aris-
ing. Someone who has been guilty of condemning and
verbally abusing others can do *teshuvah* by spreading
the concept of using positive speech.

I have already heard from readers of the first edition of this book how it has greatly helped them.
Hopefully, the ideas and tools in this book will lead
to much healing and positive character traits.

Rabbi Zelig Pliskin
Consultant
(specializing in tools for
improving relationships,
reaching goals, and mastering
positive emotions)

Acknowledgments

> The true service of God is built on a foundation of gratitude. (STRIVE FOR TRUTH! vol. I, p. 153)

I thank God for being with me even when I felt most alone and despairing and for having brought me to the light of Torah, a light which sustains me every moment of my life. I am very grateful to Rabbi Zelig Pliskin, whose ongoing encouragement and advice have helped me to achieve a more positive attitude.

I thank Bracha Steinberg, of Feldheim Publishers, whose painstaking analysis of the manuscript and hundreds of revisions and comments helped make this book.

I am grateful to my dear husband, Carmeli, who has encouraged me and given me the freedom to pursue my goals, and to my four wonderful children, whose love and laughter have helped me endure the heartbreak which is an inevitable part of my work as a psychologist.

I sincerely thank all those who have caused me pain, for in doing so, they forced me to work on my *middoth* and to turn to the ultimate Source of strength and love.

...You refined us as if refining silver. You brought us into the prison...we entered fire and water and You brought us out into abundance.

(TEHILLIM 66:10-12)

This is the day which God has made. I will be glad and rejoice in Him.

(TEHILLIM 118:24)

Contents

Introduction

The impetus for this book was threefold. First, my desire to make people aware of what emotional health is so that they can set healthy goals for themselves, get the help they need in their struggle for health, and protect themselves from those who refuse to do so.

To simplify a very complex matter, the measure of a person's mental health is the degree to which he imitates God's attributes. This means having a good heart (*Avoth* 2:9), being slow to anger (Ibid. 2:10), being forgiving, compassionate, merciful and *abounding* in kindness and truth. Other disciplines which are necessary for mental health are summarized in *Avoth* 6:5-6, and include: studying Torah, expressing awe and love of God, modesty, humility, cheerfulness, being generous to others, associating with the wise, avoiding sin, accepting pain with love of God, loving all His creations, loving rebuke, claiming no credit for our achievements, helping others to improve, sharing others' pain (empathy), judging others favorably and giving them the benefit of the doubt, etc.

Many people think that mental health is a matter of luck or ease. What the above list implies is that mental health requires constant self-discipline, for our entire lives.

Second, I wanted to share what I have learned in my own struggle for emotional health in order to help others with similar problems. A friend once told me, "Bloom where you're planted," and some of us have bloomed only by pushing through concrete and finding cracks in rocks. Despite many painful times, I do not regret anything I have gone through. Every person I have met and every event I have encountered has taught me something, has brought me a message to help me understand why I am here and what I am meant to do with

1

my life. If I had had a different upbringing or had a secure, confident nature, perhaps I would have less ability to understand the pain which others live with.

My third impetus is my desire to help people overcome the effects of spirit-crushing criticism and overcome their addiction to this devastating habit. We are told that *lashon ha-ra* (speaking contemptuously of others) is comparable to murder (*Arachin* 15b). Sadly, this prohibition is all too often applied only outside the home. Yet it is no less murderous to speak *lashon ha-ra* to our immediate family members and about our own selves as it is to speak ill of outsiders!

This point is illustrated in the beginning of the book of *Devarim*, where Moshe, close to death, rebukes *B'nei Yisrael*. Rashi (1:3) states that he learned this from our forefather Ya'akov, who refrained from rebuking his sons until he, too, was on his deathbed. Because Ya'akov did not want to alienate his son, Reuven, he held his tongue, "So that you should not leave me to go and join my brother Esav." Two other reasons which Rashi brings are that he did not want to have to rebuke again and again and cause his sons to be embarrassed in future encounters with their father.

Unfortunately, few parents show such self-restraint. Most think that they must continuously criticize, threaten, scold, punish, lecture, nag, beat and otherwise coerce their children (and often their mates as well) into improving their *middoth*. Such people think they are being loving, protective and responsible. But careless criticism does not feel like love to the recipients.

Millions of people feel that they are worthless, unlovable and incompetent because they were programmed to think this way by various people in their past or present environments. They think that the only way they can motivate themselves or others to improve is through incessant criticism. Yet the Torah prohibits causing pain with words (*Vayikra* 25:17).

Many people think that words, lacking concrete visible form, also lack power. They deny that the negative emotional vibrations which they emit when they even think hostile thoughts, let alone say them, have a harmful effect on themselves as well as the objects of their contempt. Often, we can do little to stop them, other than maintain emotional and physical distance. But there are other times when we can and must assert our right to be treated with respect. And we can certainly wean ourselves away from the compulsion to put ourselves and others down. We can refuse to allow chronic fault-finders into our homes, just as we refuse to put unkosher food into our mouths.

The widespread campaign to stamp out *lashon ha-ra* has had a tremendously positive impact on the Orthodox community. My hope is that this book will spark the same kind of revolution in homes and schools where the "private" *lashon ha-ra* between husbands and wives, parents and children and teachers and pupils produces so much emotional trauma. I hope people, especially religious leaders, will recognize the need to speak out forcefully against the unbridled fault-finding which many people think is an inescapable part of school and family life.

We have a mitzvah to rebuke others (*Vayikra* 19:17) and to be conscious of our most minor imperfections and sins. Parents are obligated to make children aware of their misbehavior and, like orthodontists straightening teeth, apply gentle, but steady pressure during their early years to keep them on the proper path. But it is no mitzvah to criticize people whenever we feel like it, to obsess about our faults to the point of self-loathing, or to condemn people's entire character with negative labels. Rebuke, when done properly, is a sign of love and strengthens relationships. But reckless criticism cripples the spirits of the criticizer and the one criticized. We can see the Godliness in this world and in others only if we are aware of the Godliness within ourselves. Constant criticism can blind people to their Godliness and engender feelings of inadequacy and a dread of emotional closeness which may last a lifetime.

Third, one of the most important messages in this book is how essential it is for parents and teachers to create a nurturing environment in the home and the school and encourage people to take action against those who poison the minds of young children with insults and physical abuse.

Dealing with emotionally wounded people

Emotionally wounded people make insatiable demands on others and make impossible demands on themselves. The result is chronic negativity, anxiety and hostility. We may wonder, "How do I go on

when I'm so depressed that I have no will to live? I'm such a failure."
"I have a healthy need to feel loved. So how can I avoid being angry
all the time at my spouse who is so unaffectionate and uncommunicative that it's like living with a freezer!" "How do I stay
calm when my parents visit? They're so critical that they make me feel
like I'm crazy!" "My oldest son just lies around doing nothing with
his life. How do I get him to be more ambitious?" "A neighbor beats
her children, but won't go for help. How can I help?" "How can I get
along with a boss who is a tyrannical bully?" "My son's teacher is
hot-tempered and critical. Talking to him is like talking to a stone
wall. My normally happy son is miserable. What can I do?" It would
take an entire book to answer these questions. So, here it is!

I hope this book will help readers see how complex emotional
disturbances are, how difficult it is to become self-aware and
overcome negative habits, and how damaging it can be to live with
someone who is immersed in negativity. I hope it will help readers
feel less alone, as they see how common emotional problems are.

I hope this book will help readers be more sympathetic toward
those who must live or work with people who are chronically negative
and critical. Such people suffer from "cancer of the spirit," which has
the same devastating effect on relationships that cancerous growths
have on bodies.

When people refuse to improve their behavior, then the answer to,
"What do I do?" is to be very courageous, as courageous as someone
living with a serious physical disease. We cannot always influence,
heal or communicate with those who cause us pain. But we can learn
to focus on our own growth, which is our greatest source of joy in
life. By focusing on the daily miracles of life, we are able to bear pain
with good will. After all, "No man dies with even half his heart's
desires fulfilled" (*Koheleth, Midrash Rabbah* 1:34). This may include
not achieving the caring relationships we want with certain people.

The importance of counseling

To live with a disturbed person who refuses to behave
responsibly is like living with a chronically painful, degenerative
disease. Pain clinics teach people how to manage chronic physical
pain. Therapists teach people how live with emotional pain.

Counseling can be tremendously helpful if the therapist is a truly compassionate Observant person, who is a model of Torah values, and who uses a goal-oriented approach to help clients build self-esteem and faith. No one should be ashamed of wanting help. In fact, it takes maturity, courage and inner strength to be able to admit to one's shortcomings and actively do something to correct them. Everyone needs help in this lifelong process. After all,

> Wisdom is the consciousness of self.
> (GUIDE FOR THE PERPLEXED, p. 74)

Counseling is especially helpful in marriage, where it is essential to develop sensitivity to one's partner's needs and feelings. Unfortunately, husbands are often resistant to seeking outside help, for they see this as an admission of weakness and failure. However, a husband and wife are like one body. If half the body is sick, the other half suffers too. Successful treatment requires that the family be dealt with as a unit.

However, since women are often more willing to take responsibility for problems in relationships, they are often the ones who must insist on getting help and may have to go alone initially. They must have the courage to face opposition from mates who ridicule them as crazy or protest that money should be spent only if there is physical pain. Relief from the pain of a lonely or abusive relationship is a legitimate need. Counseling can bring about tremendous growth if both are willing to become more appreciative and understanding of the other. However, if one spouse is seriously disturbed, counseling may have little or no effect.

Unfortunately, those who are most disturbed are often the most resistant to seeking therapy or applying what they learn when they do go. It is impossible to help a person get well who does not want to be helped, any more than a doctor can help a patient who refuses to come for treatment or throws away the prescribed medication. No one can change another person. People do not change unless they sincerely want to. Emotional health requires constant self-discipline and self-awareness. Many people do not want to put forth the effort to do so. We can demonstrate Torah values, but we cannot force others to follow the disciplines necessary to become loving human beings.

When one partner refuses to seek counseling, it is even more important for the other to have an understanding person to turn to.

I also hope that this book will give hope to those who feel hopeless, for there are many who give up too quickly on themselves. Even those who go to numerous doctors, rabbis and therapists often do not believe that they will ever achieve mental health. They often say, "The lofty ideals of Torah sound wonderful, but they don't apply to me. I'm too sick. I just can't control myself. My problems are too overwhelming." There is hope — for anyone willing to put forth the effort to learn to become self-respecting and to honor others, irregardless of their talents, backgrounds or social status.

On the other hand, the power of therapy should not be overestimated. Therapists don't heal people. Scars from emotional traumas never disappear completely. Nor can therapists completely eliminate the unavoidable pain which is part of being alive. Therapists can only facilitate the growth process by teaching the skills necessary to become loving human beings. But it is up to their clients to actively practice them. If one's therapist isn't providing these skills, a different one should be consulted. It is important to choose a therapist wisely, for some therapists are themselves poorly trained and severely disturbed. University degrees do not guarantee compassion, good *middoth* or good judgment.

Good mental and physical health requires work

When a person asks how he can stop being so depressed, anxious, hot-tempered or critical, he often expects some quick solution which will transform him by the next day. But being stuck in a negative emotional state is like being overweight. There is no quick or easy way to lose weight. A whole new way of thinking and behaving must be adopted.

This reprogramming process of the mind and muscles takes effort, both mental and physical. I compare the recovery process to that of a friend who recently underwent an operation to repair a congenital heart defect. She spent her entire life thinking of herself as a sickly invalid. Although doctors have assured her that she can now live a normal life, one can only imagine how difficult it is for her to integrate this fact into her daily life! She still hesitates before climbing stairs, worries about not getting enough sleep, and thinks and behaves in thousands of other ways as if she still has a heart defect. It will take time for her to readjust to a new reality.

So, too, for each of us. Unfortunately, there are few therapists and almost no institutions which provide the two factors which are most essential for mental health, i.e., opportunities to give and receive love and involvement in confidence-building, soul-satisfying activities. In fact, most institutions provide the exact opposite!

Ideally, recovery from emotional wounds could best be accomplished by surrounding oneself throughout the day with people who are unconditionally loving, who model Torah values, and who teach that self-worth must come from within, from one's relationship with God, and not from external sources. Yet, all too often, the wounded person must live or work with people who also suffer from emotional problems and crush others as they were crushed. Even with a helpful support group or class once or twice a week, each person is left to struggle for self-acceptance and self-worth pretty much on his own, often in the same judgmental atmosphere which made him feel inadequate and insecure in the first place.

Legacies from childhood

Some people may object to the parts of this book which recommend getting in touch with childhood wounds. They may believe it is unnecessary to dredge up painful experiences from the past. But the past is our personal storehouse, containing information about our negative programming from childhood which is still producing negative behavior in the present. Those who cannot honestly face the painful events of the past end up repeating the same destructive acts which were done to them. Examining our emotional heritage is as important as knowing our spiritual heritage. We become stuck emotionally at the age when our greatest traumas took place. From then on, almost any sound, smell or sight in the present can instantly flip us back into reacting as we did then. When we look to the past to discover how our negative attitudes and behaviors were formed, we have taken the first step toward healing ourselves.

On the other hand, although many psychological problems can be traced to childhood traumas, this does not in any way provide an excuse to engage in destructive behavior today or waste time blaming one's parents, speaking *lashon ha-ra* about them or being disrespectful toward them. Those who cannot accept and forgive their parents can never accept or forgive themselves. Our parents did the best they could with their own imperfections, just as we now do with our own. Blame is useless. The focus must be on our own healing. And that takes an entire lifetime.

If one's parents were abusive, overcontrolling or inattentive, one may suffer from strong feelings of loneliness, inadequacy and insecurity. Yet it is by overcoming these handicaps that we bring the light of holiness into our lives. And no one appreciates light like one who was once blind.

Surrender or fight?

It is said that when the Ten Martyrs were informed that they were to be brutally tortured and slaughtered by the Romans, they asked Rabbi Yishmael to ascend to heaven and ascertain if this was the decree of God. If not, they would not allow themselves to be slain, but would use the ineffable name of God to turn their captors into ashes. Rabbi Yishmael did as he was requested. He returned with the answer that it was a Divine judgment that they die at the hands of the Romans. Immediately, they delivered themselves to death with total acceptance of God's will (*Lev Eliyahu*, vol. I, p. 24).

This story illustrates, among other things, that even our greatest Sages did not always know what attitude to adopt toward painful situations. Those who live with disturbed people face the same predicament. Emotionally wounded people are dishonest, untrustworthy and abusive toward themselves and those around them, although they usually do not think that what they are doing is wrong or abnormal. The recipients of the abuse often wonder, "How much abuse should I endure for the sake of my job or this relationship? Is it cowardly or courageous to leave or to stay? Do I need more *gevurah* or more *chesed*? Will my spiritual growth be enhanced by staying or leaving? If I leave, does that mean I'm a selfish quitter who didn't try hard enough, or a realistic pragmatist who is simply being self-protective? Do I surrender and let God take over or do I take charge and get tough? What demands are reasonable? What is the line between foolish romanticism and healthy realism?" No matter what the choice, there are risks and losses. We are often in the dark, with no Rabbi Yishmael to turn to.

There is always a berachah there — somewhere

Each of us is like Columbus, sailing on uncharted waters to discover a new world. That world is ourselves. Each difficult situation, each irritating person, is like a wind which urges us onward toward health.

We cannot cope positively with a burden which we think is unfair. And that includes our own and other people's emotional handicaps. Once we see these handicaps as the ones deemed necessary by God in order to heal our own defects, we can accept them with love and will eventually come to appreciate how painful events can refine and balance us. This trust in God's wisdom is what gives us the strength to grow spiritually, no matter what the outer circumstances may be.

Every painful event provides us with an opportunity to practice responding in a God-like manner. Each time we do so, we strengthen our ability to hear that inner Godly voice which calls on us to resist our destructive impulses. In moments of weakness, this inner voice tells us, Don't be submissive, withdrawn and despairing. Be hopeful, loving and generous. Or, Be tough, strict and unyielding — you can control yourself. Behave in accordance with what you know to be Godly. Don't let that person crush you. Your worth comes from God, not man.

Thus, when we wonder, Why, God? Why me?, we might consider:

First, God gives us various painful events in order to bring about greater understanding and sensitivity. We really understand only what we have experienced personally. For example, most parents with deaf children learn a great deal about deafness and also connect at a deeper level with those who share similar difficulties. Of course, they could also reject the child and become immersed in bitterness. Thus, any painful event offers us the opportunity to understand situations and people which we would not have been sensitive to otherwise, or to become mean, bitter and resentful. It's our choice.

Second, painful events provide opportunities for us to develop inner strengths. It is as if God is saying to us, "I'm going to give you a difficult test. If, despite the pain, you do your utmost to imitate My attributes, the result is that you will forge a relationship with Me, will be able to bear the pain and will gain tremendous spiritual awareness."

Whether our suffering is physical or emotional, God knows that this was exactly what we need in order to force us to turn to Him for solace and guidance and to give us the opportunity to grow. Yet this intellectual awareness does not mean that acceptance will be instant. Making our will one with His will is a life-long struggle.

No one is born with an indomitable spirit or a high degree of *emunah* and *bitachon*. These qualities need to be developed. There is potential greatness in each of us which is waiting to be revealed through our own tests of faith. God knew the potential greatness of our forefather Avraham, but Avraham didn't. It was only his numerous trials which enabled Avraham to see his own ever-increasing levels of courage and faith.

Third, suffering can force us to forge an attachment with God. To suffer in isolation, without a sense of this attachment, is to miss the Divine purpose of the event.

The Talmud states that it is an obligation to bless God for suffering just as we bless Him for the good we experience (*Berachoth* 54a and 60b). Faith is an art. It must be practiced day in and day out. From our first words of *modeh ani* and the washing of our hands, we orient ourselves to an attitude of faith and gratefulness.

To overcome the tendency toward defeatism and despair, we must practice our Torah disciplines when they are most difficult, and even when they feel most insincere and absurd, such as when we want to return an insult with an even bigger insult or lie around in apathy, feeling cheated by man and God. It is when we feel most crushed that these disciplines have the greatest power to elevate us.

A final note

This book is for both male and female readers. Rather than burden the text with "he/she" throughout, I arbitrarily selected one or the other pronoun for different situations. The reader should not think that a particular problem is more prevalent among men or among women. The disturbances discussed here know no sex discrimination.

As with my other books, this one is a product of my own personal struggles of a lifetime and my counseling experiences over the past twenty-six years. The examples are representative of the problems most commonly mentioned by the people who attend EMETT groups and who talk to me privately. If this book does not address your particular problem, it is probably because it is not typical of the people I meet. If you wonder why I have not written more about how to cope with mean, bossy people, the answer is that there is not much that can be done except to disengage emotionally and sometimes physically as well. Such people are rarely interested in working on their own *middoth*, but they certainly force us to work on our own!

I wish all my readers much growth in faith and love as they find positive ways of dealing with whatever God has decreed for them.

Miriam Adahan
Jerusalem, 5750

CHAPTER 1:
What Is Our Mitzrayim?

Each and every day, every person is obligated to see
himself as having personally left Egypt.
(PESACHIM 10:5)

Mitzrayim (Egypt) literally means a "place of narrowness." It was a place where people were enthralled by flashy materialism, were fascinated with death and were lacking in reverence for life. It was a society which believed that only those people in the most exalted positions were deserving of honor and that they were justified in their arrogant disregard of and cruelty toward those who were beneath them. It was a place in which we lived in physical slavery and bondage.

Within each of us there is also a spiritual *Mitzrayim,* from which we must extricate ourselves daily. This *yetziath Mitzrayim* is accomplished by breaking out of our narrow boundaries and demonstrating our reverence for God, for the Godliness within man, and for the lasting values of Torah. As we will see, this is a difficult transition.

Our *Mitzrayim* begins during childhood, in which our view of life is distorted by the limitations of our mental capabilities. For example, young children often perceive love in terms of how much they get, both emotionally and materially. In reality, mature love is based on a desire to give, not receive, as hinted at in the Hebrew word for love, *ahavah*, whose root means "give" (see *Bereshith* 30:1). Children also misunderstand the meaning of power. They think it means simply having control over others, not realizing that true power is the ability to master and control our own impulses (*Avoth* 4:1).

Because children are dependent on others for their sense of worth and security, they try to control the people and events around them.

Yet they often feel deprived and afraid, since they are dependent on people whom they cannot really control. They often blame others (usually their parents) for their unhappiness and try to coerce them into giving them what they want by acting mad, sad, bad, sick or crazy. They scream, cry, beg, criticize, cling, sulk, act helpless, withdraw, complain, overfunction or underfunction, and use a whole arsenal of other tactics to manipulate their parents into being and doing what they want, because they think that the source of their own happiness lies with others.

Thus, children grow up alternating between what may be called a "Pharoah-mode" and a "slave-mode" type of thinking. There are times when they feel enormously powerful, almost omnipotent, as they exercise their ability to manipulate their parents in order to get what they want. There are other times, though, when they feel inferior and powerless, like resentful slaves forced to submit to oppressive forces beyond their control.

In order to reach emotional maturity, a child must leave this *Mitzrayim*-mentality. He must learn to look within himself for his sense of worth and joy, must develop tolerance and respect for his fellowmen, not just those at the top or those who agree with him, and must stop using manipulative control tactics to force others to change. Most people never make the transition. They remain enslaved in a spiritual *Mitzrayim*, constantly condemning those who don't measure up or compulsively seeking approval to make themselves feel loved and successful, while feeling like losers deep inside. They alternate between an angry Pharoah-mode (i.e., oppressing others in an attempt to feel superior) and a depressed slave-mode (i.e., allowing themselves to be oppressed and stifled, because they feel helpless, hopeless and inferior).

Love and power

What we choose to love, value and control determines whether or not we leave *Mitzrayim*. This transition requires that we (1) recognize that all people deserve love and respect, regardless of their status or accomplishments, by virtue of having been created in God's image (*Bereshith* 1:26-27); (2) give up the attempt to control people out of a desire to feel worthwhile or powerful, and (3) rid ourselves of the winner-loser mentality which is based on an attachment to things which have no real value and which provide only an illusion of love and power.

Those who remain in a spiritual *Mitzrayim* can never be truly loving because their love is conditional and is restricted to those people who are in complete agreement with them and are exceptionally brilliant, wealthy or powerful. They can never be truly content because they are constantly running after external signs of love, status and success. Their view of people is epitomized by a kind of Hitlerian mentality expressed in the belief that, "You deserve to live and be treated with respect only if you come from the 'right' family, have the right looks and agree with me."

Only by forming lasting bonds of love for God, man and Torah will one be able to bring oneself out of this darkness.

The spiritual journey

The transition from a materialistic value system to a spiritual one is not accomplished without great effort. This is why the concept of spiritual growth is often depicted as a journey in which one is painfully wrenched away from one's old attachments. For example, when Avram was commanded to break his ties with his past, God said,

> Go away from your country, your kindred and your father's house to a land that I will show you.
>
> (BERESHITH 12:1)

A spiritual journey requires awareness and separation: to become aware of our Godly essence, we must separate from all that is false, in particular our selfish, personal desires ("country," in Hebrew, is *aretz,* which hints at the word *ratzeh,* meaning "desire"), our inborn tendencies to various extremes ("kindred," in Hebrew, is *molad,* which denotes that which one was born with), and the erroneous beliefs which we acquired during our formative years in "our father's house."

To leave our childlike view of the world is as difficult — and as joyous — as the original Exodus. As we develop the wellspring of love, joy and faith from within ourselves, we free ourselves from our need for status and approval, from our illusory sense of ourselves as winners or failures, from our craving for material possessions and the need to control those around us.

To begin the process of disengagement from Mitzrayim, we first need to know what we must separate from.

The childhood checklist

What is each person's *Mitzrayim*? It is the sum of erroneous beliefs and destructive habits which he adopted early in life and which must now be discarded in order to feel loved and loving, and experience joy in life.

If you have been immersed in negative feelings about yourself or your family members for months or years at a time, you may have first adopted this negative "theme song" quite early in life, because of the way you were treated as a child. Perhaps you think: "No one could ever really love or respect me because I'm not perfect"; "I can't respect people who don't agree with me"; or "People who show their feelings are weaklings."

To get a better idea of your characteristic emotional patterns, look at the following list of feelings and circle the ones which were highly characteristic of you in relation to your parents and/or significant siblings during your first seven years of life. Next to each emotion, write the initial M for Mother, F for Father, and the first initial of the names of the siblings who had a significant influence on you, such as D for David or R for Ruth.

PLEASURABLE FEELINGS

___accepted   ___secure
___capable   ___trusting
___competent   ___trustworthy
___confident   ___understood
___loved   ___validated as an individual
___respected   ___other

PAINFUL FEELINGS

___abandoned   ___anxious   ___ashamed of
___afraid   ___ashamed of my   myself
___angry   family   ___betrayed/tricked

___conflicted	___inferior	___untrusting
___deprived	___jealous	___treated unfairly
___disappointed	___left out	___unappreciated
___exploited	___misunderstood	___unheard
___guilt-ridden	___overprotected/	___unimportant
___hateful	stifled	___unloved
___helpless/powerless	___rejected	___unwanted
___hopeless	___sad	___weak
___humiliated	___stupid	___vulnerable
___hurt	___suspicious/	___other

Now, go back and put a check mark by the feelings which are dominant in your life today. Chances are that these same feelings are probably still with you, affecting all your present behavior. Probably the same emotional theme song is still playing in your mind today, so that any stress, no matter how minor, sparks the same feelings. For example, suppose someone mentions that you are disorganized, or you feel that you are lacking in intelligence because you didn't grasp a concept as quickly as your learning partner did, or someone ignores you when you try to say something. Instantly, you may revert back to feeling like a vulnerable, rejected, helpless child, desperately wanting to gain control by raging at others or stewing in silent hostility or despondency.

Now, think about some of the ways you coped with pain, tension, abuse and rejection as a child. Check the ones which you used quite often:

PASSIVE-AGGRESSIVE BEHAVIOR:
___procrastinating
___not bathing
___being sloppy and disorganized
___being lazy
___sulking in self-pitying depression
___giving up easily
___compulsive approval-seeking and people-pleasing
___oversleeping
___being forgetful
___"spacing-out"

___being cold and aloof
___not standing up for yourself
___allowing yourself to be abused and exploited
___retreating in hostile silence
___undereating
___biting your nails
___others:_____

ACTIVE-AGGRESSIVE BEHAVIOR:
___screaming
___hitting
___criticizing
___slamming doors
___lying
___stealing
___excessive overeating or dieting
___damaging property
___running away
___throwing things
___others:_____

Now, study the responses you have checked and ask yourself if, as an adult, you are still responding in the old familiar way. If you grew up in a shame-bound family, in which parents constantly criticize and insult their children, then you most likely assume that the negative messages you received were true, and reflected an accurate picture of yourself. Circle the messages which you adopted as true:

> *"No one could ever love me. After all, I'm stupid, lazy, overly emotional, selfish, incompetent and a pest."*
>
> *"I have nothing worthwhile to contribute to the world."*
>
> *"There's something terribly wrong with me."*
>
> *"If I don't get what I want, I must get very sad and mad."*
>
> *"I must mold myself to be what others want me to be."*
>
> *"Only conceited people accept themselves as they are."*
>
> *"If I'm not outstanding, I'm a failure."*
>
> *"Having feelings is a sign of weakness."*

"Only successful people deserve love and respect."

"I can't control myself."

"If something bad happens to me, it's because I'm bad. I don't deserve to have anything good in life."

"Life is too much for me. I can't handle being alive."

The Child within you constantly strives to recreate the same feelings which were dominant in your earliest years, because that atmosphere is the most familiar and because, unconsciously, you want to succeed in the present at what you failed to do in the past, i.e., to win the unconditional love of your parents. Unfortunately, if you grew up in a nonnurturing environment, it is likely that you abuse yourself in similar ways and surround yourself with people who are somewhat similar to your parents or who provide the same level of tension and pain which were familiar to you as a child. Or, if you do have loving people in your environment, it is likely that you do not view them as such and that you sabotage their efforts to create a more positive atmosphere because you are mistrustful or believe you are unworthy of love. You may still be creating tension and trauma because that is what you learned to expect from life and from relationships, and this is the only emotional pattern you know.

However, once you have identified your individual *Mitzrayim*, you know what you need to leave behind. Previously, you might not have even realized that it was possible to do so, since these negative moods and behaviors seemed to be a part of your very nature. By recognizing how you reacted to painful events in the past, you can identify your inappropriate responses and unrealistic expectations today. This awareness can then help you to adopt more positive responses.

Reducing the mountain of shame

You shall love your fellowman as yourself.

(VAYIKRA 19:18)

God commanded us to love people unconditionally — as they are. He did not say, "Love only perfect people, and withhold your love and respect from all other people until they reach that level of perfection." Yet this is how many people behave. They justify hurting others by thinking, "When my standards are met, then I will be respectful and loving." We see this particularly in the treatment of children, who are often subjected to unrelenting criticism because they have not reached their parents' or teachers' standards.

Because humiliation is so painful, it is successful, and therefore it is the most frequently used method of getting children to conform and cooperate in the home and in the classroom. However, excessive shame creates a thick psychological barrier, blocking one's sense of inner Godliness. And it is this connection with our own *neshamah*, the part of us which is in direct contact with God, which enables us to truly love others as ourselves.

It is only when we reduce that mountain of shame — so that we feel shame and guilt only when they are appropriate (when a halachic issue is involved) — that our natural ability to love both ourselves and others is able to flourish. Since shame is stockpiled in the mind from our earliest years, it cannot be eliminated until we face its existence.

Think back to your childhood and the various reasons you were shamed by yourself, parents, teachers, siblings and peers.

COMMON REASONS FOR SHAME
Check what you felt shame about as a child:
___your weight
___your height
___being female (or male)
___not being as intelligent as other children
___being too emotional
___being poor
___not getting good grades
___your personal appearance
___lack of bladder control
___being shy and unaggressive
___being too wild and aggressive
___thumb sucking
___being moody
___being sickly
___being disobedient
___talking too much or too little
___having physical handicaps
___being disorganized

___being awkward and clumsy
___not having the clothes, possessions, or furnishings you would have liked
___being unpopular among peers
___not fitting in religiously
___having parents who didn't fit in
___others: _____

Did marriage or parenthood add to your shame about your intelligence, appearance, possessions, ability to manage money, food, home, or relationships? Specify: _____
_____.

Do you shame your children or mate for any of the above reasons? Specify: _____
_____.

Has growing older added new shame about your deteriorating physical or mental abilities, your hearing, eyesight, memory, looks? Specify: _____
_____.

To reduce this mountain of shame, we must rid ourselves of the false values and beliefs which keep us from loving unconditionally and living fully.

The sensory belief system vs. the neshamah belief system

A small child perceives reality strictly through his senses. To him, whatever he senses is what is real. For example, the world is flat and it revolves around him. It is hard for him to believe that God really exists because he cannot see Him. Likewise, if his parents are unhappy with him, he concludes that he is unloved and unlovable, because that is what feels true. If he is frequently criticized and punished, he assumes, "I'm bad. No one loves me. I should be able to be perfect." These conclusions feel like absolute truth.

Without realizing it, our emotional pain today often stems from the fact that we still harbor childhood beliefs and still rely on what we see and feel to tell us what is true. We cannot free ourselves from our personal *Mitzrayim* by using the beliefs of our senses because the senses cannot grasp anything which is transcendent, infinite or unconditional. The infantile Sensory Belief System can only inform us about an inferior form of love, which is conditional and transitory (*Avoth* 5:16):

> *"I can't have a real relationship with God because He is distant and out there somewhere. I'll try to pretend."*
>
> *"I feel God's love only when He gives me what I want."*
>
> *"I can love people only if they do what I want."*
>
> *"I can love myself only if I am successful."*
>
> *"If you're not at the top, you're at the bottom."*
>
> *"People who have more than I have (e.g., more money, brighter children, greater intelligence, better looks, etc.) are more loved by God."*

In addition, the infantile belief system equates pain with failure:

> *"If an event causes me pain, it must be bad."*
>
> *"If something bad happens to me, it means I am bad."*
>
> *"I can only be happy if I succeed in getting what I want."*
>
> *"Because I am bad, I must be punished by having bad things happen to me. Therefore, it is wrong to think well of myself or be happy."*

It is concerning this limited, sensory-bound view of the world that we are told:

> Do not follow after your heart and after your eyes which you lust [*zonim*] after, so that you may remember and fulfill all My commandments and be holy to your God.
>
> (BEMIDBAR 15:39-40)

The use of a strong word like *zonim* (prostitute) implies that our infantile belief system has no stable commitment to the ultimate truth. It is attracted to external appearances. Our flesh-and-blood senses and our cause-and-effect minds are imprisoned within a very limited and simplistic framework.

Thankfully, there is a second way of perceiving truth which is not based on the senses. This is accomplished by seeing the world from the point of view of the *neshamah*, the soul. The *neshamah* allows us to experience the spiritual truths which may seem absurd to our limited sensory grasp of the world.

> ... the desert was the only proper environment for *mattan Torah*....By giving us His Torah in the desert, Hashem taught us that devotion to Torah is never compatible with belief in 'nature.' A person who sees the world only as the arena of natural forces will inevitably consider any attempt to live a spiritual life as doomed to failure. The Torah demands from us faith in a Power Who is above nature and Who directs nature in accordance with spiritual purposes. (STRIVE FOR TRUTH! vol. 2, pp. 258-9)

To make the transition from a *Mitzrayim*-oriented, Sensory Belief System to a Transcendental Belief System is not easy. They are two different worlds. From the point of view of the *neshamah*, God is not distant, "out there" somewhere. There is no outside or inside. He is within us and we are within Him. In the Transcendental Belief System, giving is getting. In the Transcendental Belief System, we are not victims of an unfair fate. No matter where we are, we can experience spiritual freedom by imitating the attributes of God. According to the *neshamah*, outer trappings of success have no significance. What matters is only the degree of our attachment to that which is Godly.

When the past is the present

It is the most natural thing in the world for babies to scream when they are unhappy in order to get what they need. So, it is no wonder that many people grow up thinking that screaming is the trick to getting their wishes fulfilled. A person may think that what happened "back then" has nothing to do with how he reacts now, but it is likely that that infantile "scream response" continues to spark his undesirable behavior in the present. When he is hungry, tired or not getting the attention, respect or control he wants, he might feel just as helpless and endangered as he did in childhood. And, just as in childhood, he might "scream," lashing out angrily at the people around him or, failing to get what he wants, turning his anger against himself in chronic self-criticism and depression. Such responses may seem irrational to the Adult in us, but it is perfectly logical to the Child in us which still believes, "Being mad, bad, sad, sick or crazy is the only way to get what I want."

However, we do not have to remain enslaved to these patterns of the past. From our awareness of the past, a new richness of insight and understanding can come.

Legacies from childhood

Just as a car accident can leave a person with permanent physical disabilities, traumatic events from the past can leave emotional scars which influence our present behavior. Thus, a minor rebuff or failure today can trigger memories of all the past rejections, betrayals and failures we ever experienced. When present traumas, however minor, evoke what are called "reminder symptoms," we are filled with the cumulative pain of these unresolved conflicts and unexpressed feelings. This is why a seemingly minor event can arouse emotions which seem completely out of proportion to the present situation.

Take Sara. Sara's mother-in-law, a very caring woman, innocently remarked that it was not a good idea to let the baby sleep with a bottle of juice because this could cause tooth decay. Sara felt devastated and retreated to her room, feeling like a total failure. She has the same response whenever her husband mentions even the most minor change he would like her to make or fails to give her the attention she craves. She says, "I bend over backwards to please people, but I always feel anxious and overwhelmed. I have no confidence. The smallest thing shatters me. I'm so emotional. I must be crazy."

Sara's parents fought a great deal when she was a child. Her world was full of chaos and confusion. She was constantly tense, wondering when the next explosion would occur. When feeling especially hurt, she would pull out her hair or hurt herself in other ways. She felt abandoned emotionally and physically by her parents. She decided that when she married, she would always give in and make peace, no matter what the cost, in order to avoid all conflict.

All this happened a long time ago, but Sara continues to feel out of control, tense and insecure as an adult. In her mind, criticism is still associated with abandonment. Because she assumes that people are certain to reject her eventually, she interprets the most minor expression of displeasure as proof that her worst fear has been realized. Because she feels she can never do enough to win her husband's or children's love, she is often rejecting and defensive with them, afraid to really be trusting and close. She never lets them know what she is thinking or feeling except when she loses control, which is when they cannot really hear her. She feels like a child, trying to take care of children, totally inadequate to the enormous responsibilities she faces as a wife and mother. She often sinks into passivity and dysfunction.

The influence of early childhood rejection also affects Sharon. Sharon also grew up with a strong "I'm not okay" message. Not only was her mother very critical, but she also had an older sister who was far more successful in school than she was. At home the atmosphere was excessively strict: spilled juice was a major catastrophe, putting the milk back in the wrong place in the refrigerator brought a stern reprimand, any act of disobedience brought a quick slap, the children had to finish all the food on their plates or receive a punishment, etc. No matter what she did, it was never good enough to win the love she craved.

Now, as an adult, Sharon is a perfectionist and an overfunctioner, taking too much control and responsibility for everybody and everything. She thinks that by being perfect, she will win the approval she never had as a child. She cannot allow herself to be an average wife or mother, nor can her children or husband be average. Everyone has to be a star. Her self-esteem goes down to zero unless she is doing ten things at the same time, all perfectly. She panics if anything is out of place and spends so much time cleaning and cooking that she never has time to create nurturing relationships with members of her family. She relates to her children and husband as objects which must be pushed into accomplishing more and more. To her, only perfect people deserve love. At the same time, her secret sense of being defective and not being able to measure up to her own perfectionist standards, put her in a constant state of anxiety, making it more and more difficult for her to control her urge to scream at and hit her children as well as criticize her husband constantly.

Sam is another example of how early childhood rejection influences a person in adulthood. Sam constantly criticizes his wife and children. Everything they do seems wrong in his eyes. He is always on the defensive and quick to lash out, accusing people of not respecting him. However, because he does not respect himself, he constantly feels that others do not respect him either.

Sam's father was extremely controlling and critical, constantly telling him that he wasn't smart enough, fast enough or good enough. Overcontrolled as a child, Sam sees even the most minor request for help as an attempt to control him now and attacks angrily in an attempt to protect himself. If his wife asks him to get something from the store or diaper a child, he feels she is trying to dominate him.

Because Sam's mother was very nervous and required frequent hospitalization, he often felt abandoned. His way of coping with the pain of his loneliness and rejection was to suppress all desire for closeness with people and to make himself feel better by putting everyone else down. Like his father, he controls people through anger and bullies his family members into giving him the power he never had as a child.

For example, whenever his wife goes out to a class or to visit a friend, he gets furious. He doesn't realize that she unwittingly pushes his old "abandonment button" when she leaves, and that his anger stems from the fear of being rejected. When the house is messy, it pushes his "failure button." He doesn't realize that his rage stems from the fear that others will think he is a failure for not having a brilliant mind and for being "just a teacher." He responds irrationally, with the same fury he felt when his mother abandoned him as a child or his father punished him for accidently breaking or dirtying something.

One can observe these childhood beliefs being formed in many families. For example, nine-year-old Deena is a kind of family "dumping ground." She is the target of the family's frustrations and anger. Her mother absolves herself of responsibility for doing the difficult work of healing this child's psychological wounds by defining Deena as "hopelessly bad." This view allows her to treat the child according to that label. The mother explains, "Right from the beginning, she was difficult. She had trouble nursing and she cried all the time." Because the mother never really "bonded" to the baby, she did not give her the attention she needed. That made the baby even more terrified and insecure. Not wanting to feel like a failure, the mother defined Deena as the failure, and gave up on her. Deena was probably suffering from a combination of slight neurological dysfunction called Poor Sensory Integration (see *Raising Children To Care*, ch. 13) which was made worse by the lack of cuddling and rejection she experienced. The family members are convinced that if they treat her kindly, she will only get worse.

In defense, Deena has become very hostile and untrusting. She needs love desperately, but people avoid her because she is so angry and unreliable. The more hostile she becomes, the more rejecting others become toward her, and the more destructive she becomes in return. The few times when she had a loving teacher who provided the closeness and warmth she craved, she was very cooperative in school. Otherwise, she misbehaved. Most of her experiences in life have convinced her that she is bad. How is she going to think any differently?

Deena has already contemplated suicide. She said, "Maybe if I die, people will see how much they've hurt me. No one wants me around anyway, so it would be a relief to them if I died." She feels that the only way to end her pain or get through to people is to hurt herself. Will self-abuse become a lifelong behavior pattern, to get what she wants? Will she always feel that she has no value and that no one will ever really care?

Even the most abusive parents vehemently protest that they do love their children. But a child cannot possibly feel loved if his parents are unhappy with him as he is. The parents might think of themselves as loving, but the quality of that love is so inferior as to appear nonexistent to the child.

Furthermore, in a child's mind, the face of God has the face of his parents. Thus, when a child from a nonnurturing home turns to God for comfort, he gets, instead, a feeling of frozen indifference, helplessness, cruelty, or the dry recital of impersonal rules and regulations.

Note: If you see yourself in these descriptions, don't panic. Honesty is the first step to change. The exercises in this book will help you to heal yourself and your relationships.

Erroneous interpretations which keep us mentally enslaved

Deeply rooted negative attitudes and behaviors take time to overcome. Since we interpret present events in light of whatever we experienced in the past, the first step in this process is to become conscious of our thinking patterns, or cognitions.

The mental process of cognition is a process of perceiving reality and also interpreting what you perceive. For example, if your only experience with dogs was being bitten, you won't like dogs much. If you were forced to eat certain foods, you may still hate them. If you failed to do well in certain subjects in school, you may still be convinced that you cannot possibly succeed in those areas. Likewise, if you were brought up with a great deal of tension and torment, then you probably continue to respond to people and events in a way which brings you further tension and torment. By understanding these connections, you begin to see how much of your present anger, depression, and anxiety is based on limited experiences of the past which can be consciously changed today.

People who come from nonnurturing backgrounds interpret events differently than those from more loving homes. For example, insecure people interpret minor upsets, such as differences of opinion, spilled juice, and social blunders as being threats to their fragile sense of security and self-esteem. It is not the specific events themselves which are so disastrous, but rather the catastrophic conclusions which they infer from these events. Their subjective interpretations convince them that these minor frustrations indicate some major threat to their relationships, independence, or security, or point to inevitable physical or mental collapse.

Note how the following insecure interpretations reinforce and maintain the same feelings of anger, shame, anxiety and betrayal which many people experienced in childhood:

Event: "My wife didn't pick up my suit from the cleaners."

Catastrophic conclusion: "She doesn't give a hoot about me. I'm not important to her. I have no value in her eyes."

Constructive conclusion: "I'll give her the benefit of the doubt. I'm sure she's had a busy day, and didn't realize how much I was counting on it."

Event: "My husband forgot our anniversary."

Catastrophic conclusion: "He doesn't really love me. I have no value in his eyes."

Constructive conclusion: "I don't have to take it personally. He shows his love in other ways."

Event: "My daughter was disobedient."

Catastrophic conclusion: "I'm a failure as a parent. I can't do anything right." "She did this on purpose. She'll grow up to be uncaring. No one will ever marry her. And I'll be to blame."

Constructive conclusion: "I can help her to learn better communication skills by modeling them myself."

Event: "I'm high-strung and get emotional very quickly."

Catastrophic conclusion: "I'm immature. I must be cracking up. I certainly can't cope with life."

Constructive conclusion: "I'm not crazy, I'm just undisciplined. Because I have this handicap, I have to be more assertive about creating a more protective environment for myself."

Event: "I do nothing all day but cook and clean."

Catastrophic conclusion: "My brain is turning to mush. I'm nothing but a stupid and boring person. My life is a waste. No one could ever respect someone like me."

Constructive conclusion: "Being a homemaker is the most creative and challenging job in the world. And when I need to take a break, I can find the time to get out of the house at least two hours a week."

Event: "My spouse said something nasty."

Catastrophic conclusion: "It will always be like this. I'll never be loved." "If I don't have everybody's approval all the time, it means I'm a total failure."

Constructive conclusion: "He's going through a very hard time now. I'll reassure him that I love him and I'm sure he"ll respond more lovingly."

Event: "I don't feel good."

Catastrophic conclusion: "I'm going to die soon."

Constructive conclusion: "It's probably nothing, but even if it is something major, I can bear the pain and make my life meaningful nonethless."

Event: "I lost control."

Catastrophic conclusion: "I'll never have control. I'm going to destroy myself and everyone around me."

Constructive conclusion: "I will try harder. I know I can do it. Discipline will give me self-respect."

As we saw in each of the above situations, the person could just as easily have taken a secure thought such as, "Oh, he just forgot," or "I'll manage somehow," etc. But the insecure person chooses the interpretation which maintains the familiar atmosphere of tension and torment which he grew up with.

Other cognitive errors which maintain negative beliefs from the past are:

Overgeneralizations and exaggerations: Insecure people draw all-inclusive conclusions from minor mistakes or disappointments. For example, a spouse will see that the kitchen sink is full of dishes and say, "This place is a total pigsty." Or, after asking someone to do something and finding that it has not been done, she might say, "I can *never* rely on you. You're *totally* unreliable." Upon hearing of a minor accident, the same person might comment, "You cannot be trusted at all." When such a person can't figure out the instructions on a newly purchased item, he concludes, "I can't do *anything* right. I'm a *total* idiot."

Labeling people (e.g., stupid, incompetent, lazy, selfish) is a common form of destructive generalization which we must be careful to avoid.

Thinking *davka*: This is the tendency to asume that people intentionally, and with premeditated malice, meant harm to us — before establishing whether or not this is true. For example, if the wife sings in the kitchen and the husband thinks, "*Davka*, she's doing this *purposely* to irritate me." Or, if the husband doesn't bring back the exact items the wife wanted from the store, she thinks, "He *purposely* forgot, just to punish me for something I said this morning." Or, when the small child wets his bed, the mother thinks, "*Davka*, he's doing this to drive me crazy and manipulate me into giving him attention which he doesn't need or deserve."

"*Davka* thinking" is the primary source of all anger, for it makes us see people, even small babies, as enemies who are purposely trying to drive us crazy, deceive us, manipulate us, or drain us of our finances. If we think *davka* every time a family member doesn't agree with us, or doesn't give us the attention or help we want, we will be furious quite often.

It is common for children to think *davka*. If a parent is late in picking a child up, she thinks, "She didn't come to get me on purpose." If a parent doesn't have the money to buy a child a new outfit, the child says, "You just don't want to buy me something new. You don't care about me." The parent asks for help, and the child thinks, "*Davka*, he wants to keep me from having any fun in life."

While it is natural for children to think *davka*, we can overcome this powerful habit only by constantly heeding our Sages, counsel to give others the benefit of the doubt (*Avoth* 1:6). It is also important to get in the habit of verifying our suspicions before jumping to conclusions. If we are insecure, we can learn to ask others for reassurance that we are loved and that they had no deliberate intention to harm us, although this can happen occasionally, due to human imperfection.

The power to choose our thoughts and words gives us power over our actions. In order to develop this power, we must know when we are responding according to our irrational, childhood belief system and not according to a more mature reality. One clue which lets us know that we are probably in the former mode is our use of exaggerated, temperamental lingo, such as "always" and "never" in accusations, or the use of "I can't," when what we really mean is "I really don't want to." For example:

"*You always put me down.*"

"*We never have any fun.*"

"*You never help me with anything.*"

"*She's always yelling.*"

"*I can't stand the mess.*"

"*I can't stand having company.*"

"*I can't cope with having to put the kids to bed.*"

The use of "total" and "complete" (as in "total disaster" and "complete idiot/failure/slob," etc.) also fits into this category.

This is not to deny the existence of real tragedies, overwhelming stresses, and deliberately destructive people. However, the majority of mistakes and upsets which we encounter are merely distressing, not dangerous, and the majority of people who hurt us are not consciously evil, but are merely annoying and lacking in sensitivity, good manners, intelligence or self-control. By identifying our erroneous conclusions, we can understand the source of much of our present unhappiness. In so doing, we feel less hostile and anxious, which enables us to respond to present-day disappointments and failures more constructively than we responded in the past.

Using daily events as opportunities for growth

The Child within us never disappears completely. However, it can be educated. To free ourselves from the temper-producing patterns of the past, we must constantly discipline ourselves and practice the following guidelines, none of which we were capable of doing as children:

Distinguish between a phony sense of threat as opposed to real danger. To avoid excessive emotionalism, we can ask ourselves, "On a scale of zero to ten, how dangerous is this?" "Is this situation merely unpleasant, or is it actually dangerous to my physical or emotional health?" "Is my sense of danger a feeling or a fact?" By taking away the danger, we calm down.

Distinguish between trivialities as opposed to major life-changing events or crimes. Major or minor crimes, actual dangers, and major life changes call for a strong emotional response. Minor upsets, losses, and changes do not. Most of the situations in life are trivialities. Using the word "triviality" puts minor irritations in the proper perspective.

Distinguish between acts of deliberate cruelty as opposed to negligence or unintentional accidents. We can avoid excessive anger toward others by asking, "Did this person hurt me deliberately?" By taking away the thought of deliberate malice, we can respond in a loving manner and be more forgiving of others. If the act was deliberate, we need to use a reasonable amount of shaming to awaken a desire for *teshuvah* without crushing others' self-esteem.

Distinguish between averageness as opposed to true exceptionality. We can lessen our feelings of isolation and estrangement from others by asking, "Are my thoughts, responses, feelings, problems, and flaws shared by many other people, perhaps even the majority of mankind? If so, then I am average." By accepting our averageness, we are released from the paralysis of perfectionism and the fear that rejection and mistakes are proof that we are dismal failures.

Distinguish between temporary moods as opposed to serious personality disturbance. We gain objectivity by avoiding the use of "always" and substituting "sometimes" when speaking about character traits. Almost no one is *always* selfish, withdrawn, stingy, uncooperative, childish, insensitive, depressed or lazy. But all of us manifest these traits at times. If a family member is generally caring, then an occasional uncaring act can be ignored or dealt with calmly. This is a lot different than living with someone who is almost always selfish, uncaring and insensitive. By viewing negative traits as minor and temporary, we feel more capable of handling them successfully.

Distinguish between realistic as opposed to unrealistic expectations of yourself and others. When upset, we can ask ourselves, "Am I expecting perfection from myself or another? Do I think I should always know what to do and always be able to make others happy? Do I expect my family members to always be cooperative and sensitive to my needs?" Romanticism excites the imagination, but realism enables us to act more rationally.

It is by disciplining ourselves with these steps that we gain maturity and we overcome the tendency to respond to events with child-like impulsiveness. Our initial response to many stressful events may harken back to our childhoods, but we can learn to quickly substitute a more mature reaction.

Power to the positive: nurturing through endorsement

Another important element of discipline in the journey away from the bondage of *Mitzrayim* and toward the freedom of a positive attitude, is to focus on the good in God, ourselves and others. This means constantly expressing appreciation and gratefulness and avoiding doing or saying anything which will deprive us or others of a sense of dignity and worth. Any act which obliterates our contact with our *neshamah* is an indirect profanation of God, since it is a part of Him.

We can train ourselves to be more positive through the simple act of "endorsing": applauding the good in ourselves and others. We already know how to do this from our prayers in which we praise God. We can do the same with ourselves, praising and acknowledging — endorsing — our every act of *chesed* or self-control, even small things like smiling when we feel grouchy or for learning one line of Torah. We can also endorse others for their most minor act of cooperation and helpfulness. It is extremely important for parents to endorse each other in front of their children. The foundation of *shalom bayith* is for parents to avoid criticism and to constantly mention each other's good points.

Endorsing is like strengthening a muscle. The excercise may feel insincere and awkward at first, but it gets easier and more powerful with time.

The Endorsement Principle: If we endorse ourselves for the steps we are taking toward emotional health today, no matter how small they may be, we will take bigger steps tomorrow. Likewise, if we berate ourselves continuously for not doing more, we will do less tomorrow.

Acceptance: when release brings relief

There are only three things which we can control: our thoughts, speech, and actions. Everything else is beyond our control: our basic nature, other people's *middoth*, external events which we did not deliberately cause (including the past and the future), and those initial negative emotional responses to various people and occurrences which we have not yet succeeded in modifying or changing.

Trying to control what is beyond our control makes us feel out of control. We then feel either enraged or discouraged. To avoid wasting precious energy trying to combat that which cannot be changed, we can make it an active mental exercise to remember that everything is in God's hands except our *middoth*. The following guidelines can help us avoid trying to control that which is beyond our control:

Do not fight painful feelings directly once they are already aroused. Instead, identify the spiritual work which needs to be done, such as to be more grateful, forgiving, or disciplined, or to find positive sources of fulfillment. *Gateway To Happiness*, by Rabbi Zelig Pliskin, can help us adopt a positive attitude.

◆ EXAMPLE: "I was eating myself up with jealousy after I heard that my sister-in-law was pregnant again, while I am still trying to conceive. My grief is legitimate, but the hostility is destructive. I've learned that when I feel so heartbroken, I must strengthen my trust in God."

◆ EXAMPLE: "When I heard that a number of teachers would be laid off at the school where I teach, I panicked. I could barely eat or sleep. So I began to focus on the spiritual work which I needed to do, which for me was to avoid giving up in despair so easily, and to decide to aggressively look for a new job if necessary."

Do not fight uncomfortable physical sensations. Nervous symptoms — anxiety, headaches, heart palpitations — cannot be forced away. Instead, when we feel nervous, we can divert our attention, keep busy with positive activities, and think calming, hopeful thoughts until the symptoms fade on their own.

◆ EXAMPLE: "I was working for a very critical person. The tension was making me physically sick. I kept putting myself down, thinking that I should be able to take the criticism and be so filled with compassion that his grouchy moods and nasty comments wouldn't bother me. All this self-talk didn't work because I'm just not at the level of being able to take abuse and not be adversely affected by it. When I stopped putting myself down, I found the courage to change jobs."

Give up trying to change people by using hostility. Hatred arouses hatred. In a hostile environment, people become more defiant, irresponsible and disrespectful. We can disengage by acknowledging and accepting people as they are.

◆ EXAMPLE: "One of my children was always difficult to handle. The first expert I consulted said that she was a very manipulative child and that I had to punish her by taking away the things she enjoyed most and locking her in her room when she misbehaved. But she only became even more hostile. I then consulted another psychologist who diagnosed a learning disability and told me that my child was in desperate need of affection and a calm, structured environment. The new psychologist taught me how to rebuild our relationship and provide experiences which would help my daughter feel better about herself. When she acts up, I tell myself, 'Don't judge; accept,' which reminds me to love her as she is. She has improved tremendously."

Do not fight that which cannot be changed in your personality. We must accept our limitations with humility, not shame.

♦ EXAMPLE: "After many years of hating myself for being so emotional, I finally just accepted that I am insecure and do overreact sometimes. Only then was I able to use specific mental exercises to help me tone down my response whenever I become overwrought. It's really no different than having to do exercises to correct the curvature in my spine. Once I stopped being ashamed of what I was and accepted myself, I could deal with painful incidents more constructively without having the extra agony of being ashamed of my emotional reactions. Ironically, acceptance calms me down and makes it easier to control my tendency to overreact!"

When we stop trying to control what is beyond our control, we free ourself to invest our energies where they can do some good. When we stop disliking ourselves and resenting others, we begin to blossom spiritually. We become more self-respecting and more able to assert our legitimate right to be treated with respect.

Responding with love

When we were children, we often had no positive way of handling criticism. Nor could we express our pain with words. Instead, we lashed out or withdrew in silent resentment. Now, as adults, we can protect our *tzelem Elokim* by calmly but firmly letting others know when they have stepped on our Godly image:

"I am sure you did not mean to hurt me. But I felt hurt by what you said. When can we talk about it?"

"I am sure you can say the same thing respectfully." "I am as precious as a *sefer* Torah. *It is a* chillul Hashem *to treat me disrespectfully."*

"To me, being loved means being listened to and having my feelings and opinions valued. Are you willing to take the time to do that in order to have a healthy relationship?"

When these responses would be inappropriate or ridiculed, we can repeat to ourselves mentally, "I have infinite value, no matter how others treat me. My worth is not dependent on the opinions of human beings."

Similarly, if we have hurt someone, we can allow them to share their pain with us and can respond nondefensively, i.e., without attacking them back:

> *"I hear you. You have a point. Tell me specifically how I can improve things."*
>
> *"I'm very sorry I hurt you. How can I help you to forgive me?"*
>
> *"Our needs and values are different. We have to work out some compromises so that we don't hurt each other. For example, you have trouble planning ahead and making decisions, while I value closure. You are laid-back, while I value order and neatness. You value the disclosure of feelings, while I find that difficult and even boring."*

Every once in a while, during a calm and happy time, it is extremely helpful to ask each family member, "What can I do to improve our relationship?" Such honesty can break the cycle of shame and hostility which afflicts many families.

If we know, deep within, that we have intrinsic worth, then we feel intense shame whenever we think, say, or do something not in keeping with our *tzelem Elokim*. But we also recognize that it is senseless to torture ourselves forever for our mistakes. Acceptance creates the climate in which forgiveness and growth can take place.

We leave our personal *Mitzrayim* by honoring ourselves and others. Whether it is a matter of avoiding thoughts or words which we know are harmful to us or others, we always have the choice of deciding to honor and appreciate what is best in ourselves and in our lives, or to turn around and go back to the place where false values and destructive control tactics reign.

Three thoughts which bring mental health

The bridge between the Sensory Belief System and the Transcendental Belief System is a language of the spirit, or "*neshamah* language." It is a language of unconditional love and hope. It forces us to focus on the positive. Although it may sound insincere and even silly to those who are not used to hearing it, it becomes internalized with practice. We strengthen ourselves spiritually every time we think or speak this positive language. Even if the phrases seem like lies at the moment, they become truths when we see how effective they are.

Thus, during times of stress, we can:

(1) Strengthen our trust in God when we are feeling bitter about life and distant from God, by repeating: "*I will it to be this way for my spiritual growth. Since it is Your will that this be happening, I make it my choice, too.*" On a personal level, we might not like what is happening, but we can *choose* to have these events occur on a higher level, because we know that they are part of the perfection of God's will. According to our Sensory Belief System, some event or relationship may seem terrible, but by choosing to experience it, we immediately become aware that there is a Divine purpose to it. This helps us to respond constructively.

(2) Strengthen our trust in ourselves when we are feeling down, by repeating: "*I have infinite, intrinsic worth* which is independent of human judgment." Even if people insult us or treat us as if we have no value, our worth is determined by God. No one can take it away. We can also repeat, "I trust my basic strengths to pull me through this difficult time," until the phrase becomes a reality.

(3) Strengthen our love for those who have disappointed us by repeating in our minds or saying out loud: "By hurting me you have given me the opportunity to demonstrate the values of Torah, such as giving the benefit of the doubt and not returning an insult with an insult."

By repeating them over and over again, no matter how much they seem to contradict our inner reality, these phrases enable us to leave behind our negative thinking patterns of the past and enter a world of transcendent truths. They are the bridge which allows us to go from slavery to freedom.

It is especially important for people from nonnurturing backgrounds to use this language frequently, for it helps to dispel the negative beliefs they grew up with. With these phrases, such people can disentangle their image of God from that of their parents. This then creates the potential to develop a positive relationship with a loving God, and a more caring, accepting, forgiving relationship with others (including their parents) — and with themselves as well.

These mental gymnastics might seem quite difficult at first. But each time we practice them, we take another step away from the mentality of *Mitzrayim.*

CHAPTER 2:
Emotional Addictions and Mental Health

> *God in His lovingkindness created each human being*
> *with a completely different combination of powers*
> *and faculties, thus ensuring that each has a different*
> yetzer ha-ra *[evil inclination] and thus a mode of*
> *spiritual struggle different from every other human*
> *being who has ever existed or ever will exist.*
>
> (STRIVE FOR TRUTH! vol. I, p. 89)

As has been shown in the previous chapter, it is every Jew's task to leave the *Mitzrayim* of his negative childhood attitudes and adopt the values and behavior of a Torah-true way of life. This requires that we free ourselves of our addiction to the negative values and habits of our personal *Mitzrayim*. There are many definitions of the word addiction. The one which best fits the context of this book is a very broad one: an addiction is whatever thoughts, moods or activities a person habitually engages in which keep him in a chronic state of tension and torment and which isolate him from God and man. Addictions start off as a quest for a quick "high" and end up paralyzing one's ability to generate true states of love and joy from within oneself. To be addicted means to be in *Mitzrayim* — to lose one's sense of Godliness and to give up one's freedom of choice. Addictions prevent one from fulfilling the obligation to love God and man.

Addictions, as we all know, are very difficult to break, because they provide certain pleasures and powers which many people are unwilling to give up. Addictive substances are so alluring because they give their users a temporary escape from the responsibilities, pains and frustrations of life. They also provide an illusory feeling of power, security or self-confidence which many people believe they cannot obtain in any other way.

Over the past fifty years, a plethora of support groups have sprung up to help people break just about every addiction one can imagine. There are groups that fight substance addictions to alcohol, food and drugs (both legal and illegal). There are also groups that fight behavioral addictions, such as overworking, binge buying and the inability to respond assertively to abusive people.

This book examines a more subtle form of addiction — the addiction to harmful thoughts and emotional states. In most cases, emotional addictions begin as primitive attempts to protect oneself from pain. But they end up causing far more pain than they were supposed to prevent. If you often find yourself "intoxicated" with defeatism and hostility, or feel stuck in destructive habit patterns which you find difficult or impossible to discard, this book will help you: (1) to become aware of your addictive patterns, and (2) to apply the Torah disciplines which will help you overcome them.

If you do not have this type of addiction, this book can help you to understand and deal with those who do.

The ultimate choice

> I have put life and death before you…and you shall choose life, so that you may live…
>
> (DEVARIM 30:19)

It would seem like such an easy choice. Doesn't everyone want to "choose life"? Obviously not:

> "The Lord God formed man" (*Bereshith* 2:7). In this verse, the word "formed" (*vayitzer*) is written in Hebrew with two yuds, to show that God created two inclinations, one good and the other evil. (BERACHOTH 61a)

The term *Beth Ha-Bechirah*, an alternative term for the Holy Temple, is usually translated as "God's chosen house." But it can also be translated as "house of choice." We enter a spiritual *Beth Ha-Mikdash* each time we make conscious, pro-life choices which deepen our sense of connection to God and man. To be addicted means to allow oneself to be driven by passions which do the exact opposite.

An addict acts as if he has no freedom of choice. When the thought pops into his mind, "I'm so inadequate," he doesn't challenge it. Instead, he automatically agrees and allows the thought to bring him down. If he is angry, he doesn't examine his motives or take the time to find a constructive solution. He simply explodes or stews in resentment. If he's depressed, he sulks and wallows in pain, thinking "I'm hopeless." He experiences himself as a prisoner of his anger and despair. He does not even realize that the door to his prison cell can be opened simply by opening his mind.

The lack of free choice is, according to Rabbi Shimshon Rafael Hirsch, the essence of *tumah* (impurity). *Taharah* (purity), on the other hand, is "a condition of moral free will, of mastery of oneself" (*Vayikra* 7:20). Exercising freedom of choice is the source of our real power. When a person denies his ability to choose, he denies a fundamental precept of Torah. Yet addicts resist acknowledging the truth, because if they acknowledged that they do have the power to behave differently, they would have to take responsibility for their destructive behavior. It is easier to delude oneself into thinking that one has no choices:

◆ EXAMPLE: "I went into the kitchen to make myself some coffee, and when I opened the refrigerator to get out the milk, I saw the chocolate cake. I knew, intellectually, that I must lose weight because of my heart problems, but something came over me. My mind went blank. Before I knew it, I had eaten half the cake. I just can't control myself."

◆ EXAMPLE: "I knew I shouldn't have responded so angrily, but when my teenager gave me that defiant smirk, something came over me and I started to yell at him like a maniac, berating him for being a selfish brat and an idiot. I know I shouldn't react like this, but I'm hot-tempered. That's my nature. It's something I can't control."

◆ EXAMPLE: "The principal of the school where I teach made a comment about how I could improve. It was constructive criticism and made with the best intentions, but I sat there consumed with the feeling I've felt my whole life — of total inadequacy. No matter what I do, the slightest thing crushes me and I plunge right back down into the dumps again. It's not something I have any power to control."

◆ EXAMPLE: "After a certain relative hurt my feelings, I was burning with resentment. She's so selfish and inconsiderate. I can't let go of my anger toward her! I remember every little hurt forever. That's the way I am."

Addicts are so used to the tension and torment they create, that they think it is normal and the only way to be. If told that they could behave more rationally and lovingly, they react as if the person is trying to sell them a bogus bill of goods. In contrast to the drama and excitement of an all-out binge, the agitation of an impending nervous breakdown or an explosive quarrel with one's mate, being nurturing to oneself and others may not even seem like a worthwhile goal.

> Man is made up of diverse entities, natures conflicting and mutually antagonistic.   (DUTIES OF THE HEART, vol I, p. 195)

No one is free from the obligation to fight this inner battle. "Choosing life" means honoring our Godly essence even in the midst of strong passions and deep pain. It means not returning a hurt with a hurt even when the impulse to do so seems overwhelming. It means doing a *chesed* for someone when we'd rather not or don't like the person all that much. It means being grateful for what we have instead of bitter about what we lack, and talking respectfully to others when we are feeling impatient and annoyed with them.

It is even harder to discipline our minds than it is to discipline our bodies! We sometimes want to be selfish and destructive. We crave immediate pleasure and release. We may want to speak *lashon ha-ra*, rant and rave at some family member, ignore someone who needs help or sink into despair. However, if we want to grow spiritually, we must constantly sacrifice our personal impulses in favor of doing God's will, because that is what our own higher will really wants.

> Fulfill His will as you would your own will...nullify your will because of His will.
>
> (AVOTH 2:4)

Tension between the two wills — our self-indulgent will and our Godly will — is inevitable. However, there are moments when we win a battle and feel, with heartfelt sincerity, that our personal will is really in full agreement with God's. These are our moments of true inner serenity. This is what happens each time we overcome a negative impulse. The strength to do so comes only from knowing who we really are.

The most important spiritual exercise: to remember who we really are

Our perception of reality is not always a reflection of absolute truth. We see this clearly in the tragic episode of the spies, who were sent by Moshe to scout out the land of Canaan. All twelve spies looked at the same external reality. Ten of them brought back a report so negative in its outlook that almost the entire nation was thrown into rebellion against Moshe and Aaron. They suffered a loss of trust in God and lapsed into complete discouragement.

The ten spies rationalized their report by saying that they were simply stating the truth when they said that the inhabitants of Canaan were so enormous in stature that, "We were in our own sight as grasshoppers, and so we were in their sight" (*Bemidbar* 13:33). However, by thinking of themselves as grasshoppers, they were sure that others saw them in that light as well. It is said in the name of the Kotzker Rebbe that because they projected an image of inferiority, they were actually seen as inferior by others. Their "grasshopper mentality" then made them feel totally inadequate and incapable of waging war to conquer the land.

Yet Kalev and Yehoshua looked at the same land and the same "giants" and, by coming to a completely different conclusion, were filled with optimism and courage. In other words, it is not external events which necessarily cause us to feel discouraged and depressed, but rather the meaning we give to them. Like the spies, we always have the choice to react to every person or event with a defeatist, grasshopper mentality, or in a way which strengthens our faith in God and ourselves.

Within each of us is a microcosm of God called a *neshamah*. To forget this fact is to feel like a grasshopper, i.e., inadequate and inferior. When we adopt a grasshopper frame of mind, we become blinded to our true nature and cut off from our inner source of strength and wisdom. Then, like the spies, we feel incapable of doing battle against our destructive impulses.

Our *neshamah* is the part of us which is in direct contact with God. Without that contact, we feel lost and alone. It is then that we turn to addictive substances or abusive relationships in an attempt to escape from the pain of those feelings and the inner emptiness which engulfs us. Not only that, but when we lose touch with our *neshamah*, we lose all sense of our purpose in life. We become dazzled by external signs of love, beauty and success and easily angered or despondent when they are absent. Love which is not based on an awareness of our *neshamah*, is temporary and illusory, collapsing with any minor disappointment or failure. It is said in the name of Rabbi Solomon of Karlin, *z.l.* that the worst of the evil impulses is to forget that one is a child of the King.

However, forgetting is quite easy, especially when we look around and see those who are more talented, intelligent, "luckier," richer, more competent, poised and successful and think that, in comparison, we are failures. We look at ourselves and see that we have many flaws. Our condemnations of ourselves leave us feeling inadequate and unworthy of love and respect from others, which then leads to chronic anger, despair and jealousy.

Both the fundamental cause, as well as the most harmful effect of addictions, is the loss of contact with our Godly nature. Thus, the first and most important spiritual exercise is to always remember that, no matter what our imperfections, our inner essence is Godly. Man's soul is nothing less than the breath of God (Ramban on *Bereshith* 2:7). If we find this difficult to accept, we must realize that the ultimate purpose of the evil inclination (the *yetzer ha-ra*) is to keep this truth hidden from our awareness. The only way it can be revealed is by thinking or acting in a way which honors God, ourselves and others.

Recognizing our choices:
I am the program director

> ...freedom of choice is granted...
>
> (AVOTH 3:15)

No matter how wounded we may have been in the past or how difficult things may be in the present, we are capable of making choices which will help us grow spiritually. We can, like the ten spies, look around us and focus on the negative in the world, in people, and in ourselves. Or, like Yehoshua and Kalev, we can look at the same people and events and find some opportunity for growth. The following is an example of how we can use even the most petty incident as a reminder of our holy responsibility. "A pious man...passed by the carcass of a dog that gave forth an offensive odor. His disciples said to him, 'How terrible this carcass stinks!' He said to them, 'How white are its teeth.' The pupils then regretted the disparaging remark they had made concerning it. If it is reprehensible to make a disparaging remark concerning a dead dog, how much more so is it to do so concerning a live human being. And if it is proper to praise a dog's carcass for the whiteness of its teeth, how much more so it is our duty to praise an intelligent and understanding human being. In fact, the object of this pious teacher's rebuke was to instruct his pupils not to accustom their tongues to speak evil, so that self-restraint should become natural to them and they should accustom their tongues to speak good of others so that this would become a fixed and natural habit..." (*Duties of the Heart*, vol. II, p. 99).

Most people are not aware of the fact that we are in a constant state of choosing one thought over another. Yet our minds are very much like the news room of a radio station. Thousands of pieces of information filter in throughout the day. Like the program director of that station, we construct a certain view of reality according to the items we choose to emphasize in our mental "broadcasts" to ourselves.

If we choose to continually "broadcast" what is wrong with ourselves and the world, it is not surprising that we feel angry or hopeless after having listened for so many hours to the "Voice of Danger and Defeatism." If we have been "hooked" on negativity for many years, we might feel that it is impossible to change. Looking for the good can be harder than jogging ten miles if we are unfit. But with countless repetitions, it becomes an easy, automatic habit. With practice, each of us can learn to program our minds to focus on thoughts that build a sense of love, gratitude, confidence, and hope. It is a question of what we, as program directors, choose to emphasize.

Becoming a warrior

To those who are sick in body, the bitter tastes as if it were sweet and the sweet as if it were bitter. Among sick folk, some long and yearn for things unfit for [unwholesome] food...and have an aversion to wholesome foods. Similarly, human beings whose souls are sick...love evil dispositions and hate the way that is good and are too indolent to walk therein, and find it exceedingly irksome because of their sickness.

(RAMBAM, HILCHOTH DEOTH 2:1)

To those brought up in a nonnurturing environment, abuse of their own and others' bodies and spirits seems natural, while good health seems strange and even threatening. To a person who has been used to eating junk food all his life, stomach upsets, headaches and chronic fatigue may seem normal. No doubt, he will find healthy foods to be neither attractive nor tasty.

The same is true of those who have been ingesting harmful thoughts for many years. To such a person, being grouchy, discouraged and resentful seems normal. To one who is "sick in spirit," the "duties of the heart" prescribed by Torah (e.g., reverence for God, love of man, cheerfulness, giving the benefit of the doubt) may seem absurd, or something which may be fine for others but not for himself. In fact, to such a person it seems more honest and effective to complain bitterly about life's unfairness and to stew resentfully against those who have caused him pain.

It is a struggle to change that frame of mind. A story is told about a pious man who met a group of soldiers returning from a particularly fierce campaign against their enemies. "You have come back from a small conflict," he told them. "Equip yourselves for the great war." When they asked what war he was talking about, he said, "The war against the evil inclination and his armies" (*Duties of the Heart,* vol. II, p. 23).

The major goal of the *yetzer ha-ra* is to keep us from experiencing a sense of closeness with God, man and our higher self. It is only by reversing this tendency that we acquire true emotional health. The ability to love unconditionally is the result of constant effort to imitate His attributes under the most difficult circumstances (*Sotah* 14a). In particular, to feel close to God we must imitate Him by being givers rather than receivers, for God is the ultimate Giver.

In contrast, addictive behavior is always selfish, despite the fact that addicts sometimes deceive themselves into thinking that they are giving. For example, the smoker deceives himself into believing that he is giving himself relaxation and comfort. The criticizer deceives himself into believing that his chronic fault-finding is a way of showing concern or "just being honest." This kind of "giving" is a giving in to the worst destructive forces within them.

Breaking out of this pattern requires the "breaking of one's [personal] will" (*Shaarei Teshuvah* 1:30-34). One must become a dedicated warrior. To have been "created in His image" (*Bereshith* 1:26) means that each of us has the power to do so.

Mental health and our level of shame

> Shame, kindheartedness and charitable acts are the signs of a Jew.
>
> (YEVAMOTH 79a)

> Intelligence is a sense of shame and a sense of shame is intelligence. A person [should be] ashamed before God alone...for anything wrong he does publicly or privately.
>
> (THE WAYS OF THE RIGHTEOUS, pp. 77, 81)

Shame can bring us closer to God by making us aware of when we are not acting in accordance with our Godly image. But shame can also distance us from God if it blinds us to the fact that our true nature is Godly. Thus, spiritually aware people often suffer from low self-esteem, because they are so aware of their faults that they feel constantly ashamed. Less aware people tend to be smugly self-satisfied and do not even admit to the need to change themselves in any way.

Emotionally wounded people suffer from an imbalance of shame. At one extreme are those shame-filled individuals who are robbed of all joy in life because they believe that their inability to measure up to the demands of their perfectionistic inner tyrant means they don't deserve happiness, love or respect. Instead of feeling ashamed of their improper thoughts and actions, which is appropriate, such people feel ashamed of who they are in general, which is devastating.

At the opposite extreme are those shameless, arrogant types who go around trying to induce shame in others. They feel no anxiety, remorse, or guilt over their most outrageous acts of immorality, irresponsibility or cruelty. They think they should be adored no matter how they act and they are oblivious to or uncaring about how their behavior effects others.

Many people feel incorrect shame. For example, a mother might feel ashamed that she does not have a fancier house, yet feels no shame about neglecting her children. Or, a man might feel ashamed that he does not have a bigger bank account, yet feel no shame about abusing his employees.

Shame over sins which we have committed consciously and deliberately is appropriate and necessary. But it must never blot out the light of our *neshamah*. It is impossible to love God or anyone else while feeling like a failure because the barrier of shame prevents true closeness. Both excessive shame and an absence of it are emotionally crippling. Thus, we are told:

> Do not consider yourself wicked in your self-estimation.
>
> (AVOTH 2:13)

> Do not regard anyone with contempt.
>
> (AVOTH 4:3)

To maintain mental health, we must discriminate between appropriate and inappropriate shame. It is senseless self-torture to allow oneself to be filled with shame and guilt over Divinely-willed aspects of our lives which are beyond our control, such as innate predispositions or personality traits, unavoidable accidents and illnesses and the behavior of other people. Even when shame is appropriate, we should do *teshuvah*, make the necessary changes and go on with our lives with joy and love. If not, the temptation to indulge in abusive, addictive behavior becomes strong.

Shame: a major method of control

When someone says, "Shame on you!" to a young child, he usually looks stunned, as if he has just been hit. He has — on an emotional level. While this is sometimes a necessary means of behavioral control, and is appropriate when a child has deliberately transgressed *halachah*, its overuse is psychologically crippling.

Most parents have seen how their previously happy children suddenly become depressed or hostile within days of being in a classroom with a highly critical, punitive teacher. A child's fragile connection with his *neshamah* is easily broken, sometimes forever, by excessive shame. Yet many children grow up and go to school in an atmosphere which induces self-loathing.

Children who grow up in a shaming environment believe:

> *"If I shame myself constantly, I'll be transformed into being all I want to be and all that others want me to be."*
>
> *"If I shame the people around me enough, I can force them to be what I want them to be."*

So it is no wonder that emotionally disturbed people have little or no *joie de vivre*. Their beliefs make them think they are *obligated* to beat themselves and others emotionally with constant condemnations in order to get what they want. In their minds, shame is a kind of magic genie which will make their dreams of perfection come true. So they go around condemning themselves and others for being "crazy idiots," "nudniks," "selfish brats," or for being fat, stupid, ugly, slow, etc., as if this is going to produce change. And if change doesn't occur, they think they need heavier doses of shame. This is the same old "scream response" at a more destructive level. Like a scream, shame sometimes works to motivate people to shape up temporarily. But its overuse leads people to feel isolated and inferior, which sets the stage for shame-arousing addictions.

A highly sensitive person is shattered emotionally, and often physically as well, in a shaming environment, whereas a less sensitive person becomes even more obdurate and aggressive. Since addictions are attempts to escape the pain of failure and isolation, it is essential to create an environment in the home and school which enhance a child's sense of self-worth and adequacy.

Rejection, isolation and addiction formation

> [Our] ultimate goal [is] joy and ecstatic attachment to God in love. (STRIVE FOR TRUTH! vol. I, p. 145)

The first experience of "ecstatic attachment" is in infancy with one's parents. This relationship forms the basis for future relationships with God and man. When a baby reaches out to his mother and is met with warmth and love, he learns what it means to care and be cared about. However, if he is met with rejection, indifference or cruelty, the "reach out" reflex becomes damaged. Either the desire for closeness atrophies and dies, so that the person becomes withdrawn and uncommunicative, or the need for contact is so great that the person is always begging for more and never satisfied with what he gets.

Thus, it is no surprise that emotionally wounded people tend to either run away from relationships or demand more than others can give. They may be surrounded by people most of the day, but they feel essentially alone. Unfortunately, such isolation feels normal and deserved because it mirrors the same kind of relationship which many people had with their parents. If a child's parents were excessively critical, overbearing, neglectful, or simply very unhappy much of the time, he probably thinks that's how relationships are supposed to be, including his relationship with God. Instead of "ecstatic attachments" he protects himself from further hurt by not bonding. This inability to bond manifests itself in three main ways:

(1) *Excessive distance.* These unresponsive, essentially autistic people starve others emotionally by being impersonal, distant and often physically unavailable as well. They are rarely home, and when they are, they are undemonstrative and generally uncaring and uninterested in family members' needs and feelings. They do not attach themselves to others and resent any attempt by others to bond to them.

(2) *Excessive domination.* These types create an artificial sense of closeness by being critical, pushy, domineering or overprotective. Whether they are well-meaning advice-givers or tyrannical bullies, they allow others no freedom of expression or individuality. To them, loving people means controlling them. They seem to be highly connected to the people they try to control, but there is no true bonding.

(3) *Excessive dependency.* These types seem to be strongly attached to people, as evidenced by their constant demands for physical and emotional closeness and for approval and reassurance. Here, too, such people seem to be strongly bonded, but their attachment springs from desperation and they usually end up alienating people who feel drained and suffocated by their demands.

These are not exclusive types. Many people demonstrate all three disturbances.

As with all addictions, no amount of distance, control, compliance or closeness will make these individuals feel secure or happy. However, because the human drive for relationships is so strong, they turn to objects instead of people to satisfy this need. They create a "love relationship" with objects, such as food, material possessions, money, physical appearance, cigarettes, external signs of status, etc. Or they relate to people as objects to be used to satisfy their own needs.

The pain which results from the inability to relate in a balanced way can be heard in the distraught words of their family members:

> *"My husband gets depressed if I'm not available the second he wants my attention. He's even jealous of the attention I give the children. No matter how much I do, he never feels secure or satisfied that I really care."*

> *"I feel crazy around this relative, even though I know that she's the disturbed one, because she's constantly attacking me and then insinuating that I'm the one who is hostile and is trying to wreck the relationship!"*

> *"My parents never ask me what I think or feel. They only care about my scholastic achievements, but not me."*

> *"My wife doesn't care about me, only the money I provide. We have a business relationship."*

> *"My husband is constantly putting me down, especially because of my weight. The truth is that he doesn't love me. I don't think he's ever loved anyone. I feel so alone."*

Those who do not learn to connect lovingly to their parents early in life end up bonding positively to things and negatively to people.

"Condemnaholism": contempt that kills the spirit

"Condemnaholism" is the term applied to the behavior of people who are addicted to shaming themselves and others. It has two aspects:

(1) *Self-contempt.* In this state, a person shames himself excessively for his mistakes, imperfections, personality, and lack of accomplishments. He feels like a failure. He is jealous of those who have more or who have accomplished more. He swings between two poles, either trying desperately to win approval by striving compulsively to achieve unrealistic goals or withdrawing in passsivity. He feels that he can never measure up. The result is self-abusive behavior.

(2) *Contempt for others.* Here the shaming is directed outwards. The person punishes others with criticism, angry outbursts, scowls and prolonged hostile silences. He makes others

feel bad and inferior for not making him happy or living up to his standards. He insists on controlling others, on having his desires met, on being right, and on making people conform to his idea of what they should be. Others' needs and feelings are of no value. This shaming and blaming leads to physical and emotional abuse of others.

The big lies which the condemnaholic perpetuates are:

"Shame is the only way to motivate myself or others."

"I can't respect myself until I'm perfect."

"I can't respect anyone who falls below my standards."

As a result of such thinking, condemnaholics are chronically unhappy and angry most of their waking hours, because neither they nor most other people are capable of meeting their needs or standards, at least not for long. They are angry at God for the way He runs things, angry at themselves for not being perfect, and angry at people for not making them happy and for being so inept.

Condemnaholics become as addicted to shame and contempt as smokers are to nicotine. After a while, the poisonous substance actually begins to feel good, nourishing and necessary. That is why it is so difficult to get through to a condemnaholic.

Contempt kills: it poisons the spirit of the one who is contemptuous and it poisons the spirits of those who must live or work in the atmosphere generated by this negativity.

To live with a condemnaholic is like living with an alcoholic. In fact, it is worse, because one does not have a particular substance to blame as the source of one's distress. Everything may look fine on the outside. Meanwhile, the poison worms its way into one's consciousness.

The voice of condemnaholism: despair and danger

The emotionally healthy person expresses a broad spectrum of responses to the many situations that arise in the course of an average day, including moments of love, anger, worry, fear and joy. In general, he feels self-confident, resourceful, loving, and experiences joy in being alive. In contrast, condemnaholics become stuck in certain negative states of consciousness. They produce the same nasty faces any time there is a loss or disappointment. Although there can be numerous versions, these are the three basic messages:

(1) *Despair*. The voice of defeatism says: "No use trying. Give up. Your situation is so oppressive, you'll never succeed. You have no real value. People will reject you when they find out what you're really like. You're a helpless victim of circumstances beyond your control."

(2) *Danger*. The alarmist voice of temper sees danger lurking everywhere, whether it be a sleepless night, a minor headache, a social snub, spilled juice, lost keys or a dirty sink. The internal message is: "You're about to collapse mentally or physically. You can't cope."

(3) *Davka*. The angry voice of temper says, "Get angry! Explode! You have the right. After all, this person is out to hurt you deliberately. He purposely wants to make you unhappy." "Don't trust or love anyone because people are no good. They eventually disappoint, betray, or reject you."

The voice of temper (see *EMETT*, ch. 4) broadcasts these negative messages on a continuous basis throughout the day, thereby reinforcing the same negative moods which produced the destructive thoughts and behaviors in the first place! And, since misery really does love company, condemnaholics walk around complaining, criticizing, glowering and sneering, hoping to pull everyone else down into their whirlpool of negativity and make them feel as badly as they do.

While it is normal to get into these states occasionally, someone who is almost always this way is highly addicted.

These mental habits also have behavioral counterparts, such as: work disorders (workaholism or laziness), eating disorders (bingeing or starving), money disorders (over-spending, hoarding, or stinginess), sexual disorders, drug addictions (legal or illegal) and cleaning disorders (compulsive cleanliness or slovenliness).

These external manifestations cannot be eliminated until one corrects the underlying source of the problem, i.e., lack of love for God, man and oneself. As soon as one begins to express true caring in any of these three areas, the urge to hurt oneself or others fades away.

Unhappiness: implied permission to keep on acting destructively

> If a person commits a sin and repeats it, it becomes permitted to him. Permitted? No, it *seems to him* to be permitted.
>
> (YOMA 86b)

Addictive behaviors seem to work in the short run because they bring some measure of relief, control or attention. However, they are ultimately destructive because they destroy trust. In addition, each time one indulges in the addiction, one feels increasingly compelled — and, more important — *permitted* to repeat the behavior. We learn from the Gemara (*Sukkah* 52a) that bad habits start off like a spider web and end up being like the ropes of a wagon. Our bad habits always seem innocuous and controllable at first, but before long they begin to control us.

Because their urges seem uncontrollable, addicts think their behavior is unavoidable and even justified:

> *"You've insulted me by not having dinner ready on time. So of course I have the right to explode at you!"*
>
> *"I must hit this child! It's the only thing the naughty little brat understands."*
>
> *"I'm nervous. I'll binge and then I'll feel better."*
>
> *"Of course I'm depressed! Look at all these bills! Look at all the stress I'm under!"*
>
> *"When my husband bought the wrong thing at the store, of course I yelled at him for being so stupid and always doing the wrong thing. I can't stand it that he's so stupid and ineffectual! Maybe this way he'll be smarter and more careful."*

For an emotional addict, simply feeling nervous or angry is enough of an excuse to indulge in abusive behavior. Many children grow up hearing people say, "Excuse his/her behavior, he's had a bad day." If the person does not admit that he has acted wrongly and apologize and ask for forgiveness, then the child thinks that bad behavior is permissible, excusable and uncontrollable. He naturally assumes, "Whenever I feel bad, I can act bad too!"

So it is no wonder that so many people keep themselves in a state of chronic tension and anger; they think being unhappy gives them the right to do whatever they want and indulge in any harmful impulse which happens to pop into their minds!

(Note: It is normal to have a strong emotional response to any major change or significant loss. At such times people really do need extra consideration and forgiveness. However, most of life consists of trivial losses and frustrations, none of which justify major outbursts of anxiety or anger. The problem with condemnaholics is that they use *any* upsetting event — from batteries wearing out to noodles getting stuck together — as an excuse to indulge in negative behavior.)

From irresponsibility to responsibility

> One mitzvah brings about another, and one transgression brings about another.
>
> (AVOTH 4:2)

Bad habits are like whirlpools, dragging a person into ever-increasing physical and emotional destruction, and dragging down those who live with them as well. Addictions are never self-limiting; they grow worse with time.

Any lust gathers momentum along its destructive path:

> ...as a slight lust overcomes him and he satisfies it, it stimulates within him an even greater craving, and he will now be even more thirsty for the things which he ate or did than heretofore. He will long for bad things which he did not even crave originally.
>
> (DEVARIM 29:18, Ramban)

To break this pattern, one must reassert one's ability to act with conscious deliberation. It does not matter how small the act, such as telephoning a sick person to offer comfort and aid or restraining the impulse to criticize, the important thing is that one is aware of being able to make pro-life decisions.

> Every man was endowed with a free will; if he desires to bend himself toward the good path and to be just...or to a bad path and to be wicked...
>
> (RAMBAM, HILCHOTH TESHUVAH 5:1)

Certainly we all feel nervous, hurt and angry at times. When an emotionally healthy person is upset, he looks for constructive solutions. He might pray, ignore the incident, confront the person involved, take legal action, talk to a rabbi or other professional or share his feelings with a friend. The emotionally mature person does not use pain as an excuse to become abusive. Addicts do.

Yet the addict will absolve himself of guilt for his destructive response by thinking, "I'm not to blame. I'm just reacting to a stressful situation. It's my nerves, my relatives, my job ..." Because an event and the resulting emotions are so closely linked in time, he thinks that the event caused his destructive reaction. This thought process is the only means by which an addict can justify his continual loss of self-control.

Not all people fly into rages if their homes are a mess, if a clerk is slow or if a child is disrespectful. However, when addicts see others handling such situations more sanely, they assume that either their own situation is worse or that they simply are incapable of doing the same.

But the truth is that it is not external events which cause destructive behavior, but rather the wrong attitudes which merely serve to trigger preexisting tendencies, such as to sulk, explode or binge. Emotionally healthy people use stressful events as opportunities to strengthen positive *middoth*, especially faith. By imitating their attitudes and behaviors, wounded people can heal themselves. It is a matter of learning the proper Torah strategies. For example, the Torah tells us that if we immediately give others the benefit of the doubt, we won't be so easily enraged. If we view all those situations which are beyond our control as perfect, God-given opportunities for growth, we won't be so bitter.

Life's irritations provide us with the chance to put the ideals of Torah into practice. Whether it is the overtired child, car repairs, lost sleep, interferring relatives, dirty dishes, phone bill, lost check or noisy neighbors there are endless opportunities to be abusive or responsible. Since life is full of losses and disappointments, one always has a never-ending supply of raw material to work with.

When a person recognizes his true priorities in life, i.e., for a life based on love of man and God, rather than the raging impulses of the moment or the destructive patterns of the past, he automatically begins to resist the urge to hurt himself and others. In other words, healing comes about naturally when we allow our actions to be guided by the truths of the Torah.

Who me?

That requires the honesty to face our deepest fears and faults. Of course, no one wants to think of himself as an addict. "Addict" may be a frightening word which conjures up horrible images of people enslaved by drugs or alcohol. One might think that calling someone an addict is counterproductive, producing even greater feelings of shame, despair and anxiety. After all, "It's a label, and labels become self-fulfilling prophecies. Tell a person he's an addict, and he'll behave like one." One may wonder what a chronic complainer or hot-tempered person has in common with a victim of a more tangible form of addiction, such as alcohol or drugs. Surprisingly, a great deal.

One need not fear the label "addict," for the addiction model is essentially positive, because it implies that the negative behavior was learned and, therefore, can be unlearned by substituting new, healthier behavior. The Torah provides a very precise path to health. Anyone who follows its disciplines can recover.

A model for hope

This addiction model is a hopeful one because it promises recovery if people take responsibility for their moods and middoth by following the precepts of the Torah. An attitudinal change takes place on numerous fronts. For example:

(1) When people finally accept that they have an addiction, they stop blaming others and realize that the problem is internal. Acceptance of this reality of their illness is the first step toward change.

(2) When people realize that there are no quick cures for emotional addictions, they respect how difficult it is to change. This makes them realize that the recovery process will require ongoing effort and guidance for many years.

(3) When people take responsibility for their own growth, they stop looking outside themselves for cures. They realize that nothing "out there" (no therapist, rabbi, loving spouse or medication) will give them joy, self-esteem or self-discipline. People can be of great help. But each person must build himself up and become more disciplined by his own determined efforts.

(4) By thinking in terms of addiction, those who live with emotionally disturbed people can avoid taking excessive responsibility

for the addict's behavior, for they will realize that no one can fight another person's inner battle. Each of us must wage it with our own negative habits.

While it is admirable to help others, one must avoid tying one's sense of self-worth and success in life to being able to change or heal anyone else, for this leads to a destructive addiction of its own called "codependency." Codependents are people who are obsessed with getting people to be different than they are. Codependents become frantic and enraged when they see that their attempts to fix, change or rescue others aren't working. Their inability to change others, or even please them, fills them with a sense of failure and despair. Even if they feel they are motivated by love, they actually want to get something from the other person, even if it is only recognition of and appreciation for their efforts. But codependents end up creating even more hostility and resentment with their efforts, because love cannot exist along with a desire to control the other person.

> When demands begin, love departs...
> (STRIVE FOR TRUTH! vol. 1, p. 132)

Usually, codependents are desperately trying to win the love of certain types of people in the present who are similar to people they could not reach in the past. It is only when they accept their inability to control the will of any other human being and focus on the need to control and nurture themselves, that codependents can then begin the process of healing their own wounds.

People can only model the ideals of Torah. They cannot force others to practice them.

In *The Gates of Repentence* (p.113), Rabenu Yona states, "If one does not awaken himself, how will he be helped by ethical injunctions?" We can give others the ammunition with which to fight the *yetzer ha-ra*, but we cannot do the work for them.

The addictive-personality quiz

(1) Do you have low self-esteem or do you feel ashamed of who you are? Do you feel like a failure, like you do not deserve love or respect? _____

(2) Do you think you are just fine the way you are, and that your problems are all due to other people's flaws? _____

(3) Are your main, most satisfying relationships in life with things (money, food, etc.) rather than with people? _____

(4) Are you a chronic *kvetch* — critical of others, yourself, and life? _____

(5) When you feel bored, upset or lonely, do you quickly become angry, depressed or do you do something destructive? _____

(6) Do you often feel that your life is out of control and that you are powerless to change your negative habits? _____

(7) Are you overly secretive? Has your fear of exposing your problems led you to avoid seeking professional help? _____

(8) Have you lost trust in God, yourself, and people? _____

(9) Do you have a hundred excuses for your negative behavior? _____

(10) Do you feel excited, "high," and powerful when you "act out" (i.e., when you indulge in the addiction)? _____

(11) Do you feel impotent, lifeless, or empty when you are not engaging in your addictive mood or behavior? _____

If most of your answers to the above questions are yes, and you suspect that you might have an emotional addiction, you probably do. Do not be ashamed of this fact; awareness is the first step toward growth. And awareness requires facing your past honestly and objectively.

The dysfunctional family

A baby born to a drug-addicted mother is addicted from the womb and goes through all the agony of withdrawal upon birth. Similarly, as explained earlier in this chapter, if someone came from a highly dysfunctional family, then he could not help becoming just as addicted to negative behaviors as that baby. This does not mean the person has to stay addicted; it just means that his road to health will be rougher than others.

Characteristics of a dysfunctional home are:

1) *The continual use of shaming* in the form of teasing, sarcasm, negative labeling and criticism. A child in this home grows up feeling "I'm no good," or "I'm not good enough." He believes, "If only I

were perfect, then my parents would love me." Since they don't seem to, the child assumes there must be something terribly wrong with him.

(2) *No honest communication.* There is no opportunity to honestly express what is really bothering a child in this home. Questions are brushed aside and feelings ridiculed or ignored. Consequently, the child has no real sense of being cared about.

(3) *Chaos.* There is no predictable structure, no set place for his possessions, no calm, private space for him to retreat to. Because of the high level of emotional drama and tension, things seem out of control much of the time.

(4) *Unreliability.* The child does not feel he can really depend on anyone to be there for him physically or emotionally.

(5) *Inconsistency.* There are no consistent rules or schedules to give the child a sense of security.

(6) *Lack of humor.* There is little humor to relieve the seriousness, tension and gloom. Whatever humor does exist is usually at someone else's expense.

It is important to remember that *in a dysfunctional family, addictions are survival weapons and protective mechanisms.* For example, the only way some children ever get any attention or a sense of control is when they act helpless, crazy, furious or depressed. The only way they can protect themselves from the pain of rejection is to become untrusting, withdrawn or overcontrolling. In the absence of a truly loving atmosphere, these children must do something to make themselves feel better, and that "something" is probably their addictive pattern in adulthood.

Remember, understanding the past is no excuse for leading an undisciplined life in the present. God wants us to want a relationship with Him. He gives us the precise circumstances which will maximize that possibility. Therefore, we should not feel ashamed of our backgrounds or emotional handicaps any more than we would be ashamed of our physical weaknesses, such as nearsightedness or a predisposition to diabetes. However, as with a physical disability, it is our responsibility to take precautionary and corrective measures. The circumstances of our lives are necessary in order to make our *teshuvah* and our closeness to God that much more of a miracle in our own eyes. God gave each of us the upbringing, talents, intelligence and circumstances necessary to accomplish our particular mission in life.

Blame and resentment only delay change because they keep us from taking responsibility for our behavior. Those who blame their parents, or anyone else, for their behavior, haven't yet gotten to the level of taking responsibility for themselves, which is the first stage in the process of growth.

Recognizing your true needs for love and mastery

Human beings have two major non-physical needs — for love and for self-mastery. When these two needs are not met in a healthy manner, the drive to satisfy them degenerates into the indiscriminate lust for attention and approval from anyone and everyone and/or the lust for power over everyone and everything. Instead of real love and real self-mastery, the person looks for the illusion of love and power. For example, a phony sense of power and self-love can come from the power to hurt others or indulge in one's selfish impulses.

> ◆ EXAMPLE: "I enjoy doing the opposite of whatever my parents and teachers say. I'm going to show them that they can't control me. I'll eat what I like, when I like, as much as I like. I'll get up when I want, or not get up at all. No one is going to control me or tell me what to do. I'm going to do what I want, when I want to do it, no matter who I hurt."

The world of emotional addicts is full of shame, chaos and conflict. The one area where they feel they have some measure of control is in their power to hurt themselves or others. They cannot trust people, but they can count on their addiction to give them some sense of control, and there-by, comfort. The anger-prone person can count on "kicking" someone with a critical remark every time he feels frustrated or upset. The depression-prone person can count on "kicking" himself and sulking whenever he feels lonely or hurt. The anorexic gains a feeling of power at being able to overcome the urge to eat. These predictable responses provide an illusion of control and safety in the midst of their emotionally stormy lives.

Spiritual isolation

When people from abusive backgrounds turn to religion, they often do so in an abusive way. Their feelings toward God are so inextricably bound up with how they feel about their parents that they fail to see God as a force of love.

The true level of a person's spirituality is seen in the quality of his relationships, for "Anyone with whom his fellowmen are pleased, God is pleased with him" (*Avoth* 3:10). Those who cannot bond lovingly to people cannot develop true closeness to God either, for deep within, they believe that they are defective and unworthy of respect. They project their negative self-image onto God, certain that "God could not possibly love someone as awful as me." Or, they feel so superior that they cannot bear the thought of a Being which is in control and above them.

This creates enormous problems in their religious practice, for religion is essentially about relationships. The entire goal of Judaism is to provide the structure which enables a person to bond properly to God and man. Without this awareness of the primary importance of relationships, religious observance becomes mindless worship of external symbols and the compulsive performance of duties which seem oppressive and are used to oppress others. People who practice religion this way are filled with intolerance and hate.

Judaism promotes mental health, family unity, and the unity of the nation. Without love in our hearts, the opposite occurs and people become more mistrusting, anxious and intolerant. Whether we avoid eating junk food out of love and respect for our bodies or avoid giving someone a nasty look out of respect for his right to be who he is, the consciousness that we are choosing to act in accordance with His will is what creates a relationship with God. That is the difference between doing a mitzvah with an awareness of God's will as opposed to doing it out of fear of what the neighbors will think or because it's a mechanical habit.

The Torah path to health

The *mitzvoth* which we are most resistant to are the ones we need most for our spiritual growth. Each of us finds that we have more difficulty with certain areas of *halachah* and particular *middoth*. Our resistance shows us where we have to work the hardest (Maharal, *Tifereth Yisrael* 184).

For example, those who are overly hot-tempered and impulsive must wage an ongoing battle to be be restrained and disciplined.

Those who are rigid and compulsive must learn to be less controlling and more relaxed. High-strung and insecure people need activities which help them become more self-confident and assertive. Those with a tendency toward depression must avoid self-preoccupation and seek outlets which enable them to forget themselves in creative endeavors and good works.

We gain self-respect by waging these battles. It is only in an atmosphere of such unconditional acceptance of our limitations that we can break through these boundaries and grow.

God isn't trying to hurt us when He brings various painful people and events into our lives. He is trying to forge a bond with us by showing us where we need to grow and bringing us to the point of crying out for His help. Thus, in overcoming a harmful addiction, we experience not only the joy of the Divine power of free choice, but the joy of a relationship with God.

CHAPTER 3:
The Roots of Mental Illness

The Book of *Mishlei* describes the characteristics common to those who cannot form healthy relationships. They are:

(1) *Lacking self-discipline.* "The foolish despise wisdom and moral discipline" (1:7).

(2) *Argumentative.* "He who loves strife loves transgression" (17:19).

(3) *Oppositional.* "[Men] who leave the paths of uprightness to walk in the ways of darkness; who rejoice to do evil, and delight in the treacheries of evil; who are perverse in their ways..." (2:13-15).

(4) *Negative.* "He who has a perverse heart will find no good" (17:20).

(5) *Lacking insight.* "A fool has no delight in understanding..." (18:2).

(6) *Hostile and inflexible.* "A wicked man hardens his face" (21:29).

How is it that some people come to develop such characteristics while others do not? The best answer also appears in *Mishlei*:

> Train a child according to his way; even when he is old, he will not depart from it.
>
> (MISHLEI 2:6)

There are two implications to be derived from this statement. One is the indelible impact of early childhood experiences. The other is the recognition that each child has his own natural talents and propensities, and that parents must take these differences into consideration when educating him.

Parents should not read this chapter and think that only perfect saints can raise children properly, or that a child's life should be free of adversity. No parent can be a model of perfection at all times or shield his children from pain. Nor would this be desirable. First, it is important for children to learn to be forgiving and loving despite the imperfections they see in their parents. It is good for them to see parents working on their *middoth*, because that teaches them to do the same. Second, learning to deal positively with adversity builds strength of character.

It would be damaging for an adult to read this chapter and then blame his parents for his present lack of self-control. After all, they, too, suffered from their own emotional wounds and did the best they could with whatever limited tools they were given. It is senseless to deny the effect of one's upbringing on one's psyche. However, the Torah teaches that every person is responsible for his actions, no matter what his background or emotional handicaps (*Guide to the Perplexed*, p. 261).

So, the purpose of this chapter will be two-fold. First, to help the reader understand the factors that created the particular *Mitzrayim* he (or someone close to him) grew up in. And second, it will help the reader to avoid creating such an environment for his children.

Childhood deprivation

If someone were to visit Korea and not know a word of Korean, he would not learn the language even if he listened to the radio twenty-four hours a day for weeks on end, since he never had any foundation for understanding what was said. Similarly, emotionally disturbed people lack the foundation to understand what real love is. Even if they were to listen day in and day out to words about the importance of emotional honesty and mutual respect and cooperation, the concepts would have no meaning for them. When it comes to love, they speak a different language, a language of tension and fear, dominance and submission, superiority and inferiority, of disrespect for themselves or others. This is caused by any of a variety of factors prevalent during their childhood, such as:

(1) *Verbal and physical abuse or neglect.* Not only must babies' physical needs for food and shelter be satisfied, but their emotional needs for love and security must also be met. Children subjected to chronic criticism, name-calling or beatings develop deep feelings of inferiority which then show up in hostility toward themselves and

others. For example, stealing by children over the age of eight has often been associated with a desire to steal love.

Many parents do not realize how devastating their humiliating sarcasm is on the psyche of a young child. When a child hears "You're a pest, a lazy brat and a stupid idiot" often enough, he assumes it is true. After all, to a young child the parents are gods, so they must be right. The child sees himself through their eyes and strives to live up to their labels. In a hostile atmosphere, a child's perceptions of life and people become distorted: he views the world as an unsafe place, sees people (and God) as threatening and untrustworthy, and sees himself as defective and bad.

Furthermore, when there is abuse, a depersonalization process takes place in which the child comes to think of himself as an object and treats others the same way.

Many parents do not realize that they are abusive because abuse can be subtle. It can include depriving a child of food or forcing him to eat food that he does not need or want, locking him in his room, ignoring him consistently and depriving him of positive outlets for his energies and interests. Most parents justify both subtle and obvious abuse by saying they are necessary to educate the child. What they are doing is educating the child to equate love with cruelty.

Favoritism is another form of abuse. It is psychologically devastating for a parent to show love towards one child and consistently reject another.

It is during the earliest years in life that a human being establishes a sense of self-worth and trust in the world. Trust is the foundation for all relationships. The ability to trust forms when a baby reaches out to others and is rewarded with food, affection and protective limits on a consistent basis. Successful bonding with parents becomes the foundation for a sense of security and self-esteem, and becomes the model for being able to reach out to others in future relationships, including the ability to relate positively to God.

If a young child is consistently rejected or ignored, he cannot trust man or God. Without trust, relationships never develop. Affection-deprived children often spend the rest of their lives trying to make up for what they never got from their parents, yet they are never able to get it because they are convinced that, "No one really loves or respects me," and "I'll never measure up or belong."

◆ EXAMPLE: "All I heard when I was growing up was phrases like, 'You're driving me crazy'; 'You'll be the death of me'; 'I wish you were grown up and out of here already.' I still can't believe that anyone could ever really care about me."

(2) *Lack of communication.* Children need to feel that someone is there for them, someone with whom they can share their feelings and have those feelings respected and validated, even if those feelings are not always realistic. If, when a child says, "I don't want to eat this," the parent constantly scowls angrily and forces him to eat it anyway, then his needs and feelings are being invalidated. When a child says, "I hate school," he needs empathy and some way of making his world a little brighter, not an angry "Shut up" from his parents.

An ancient saying states that God gave man two ears and one mouth so that he should listen twice as much as he speaks. But many children are ignored or lectured to, instead of getting a listening ear. To be heard makes a human being feel respected and cared about. Children who are not listened to feel emotionally abandoned. Inevitably, they assume, My needs and feelings are of no value. Something must be very wrong with me if no one cares.

3) *Lack of respect for their individual needs and talents.* Another source of emotional crippling is the refusal to recognize that every child is unique and needs to have his uniqueness acknowledged and nourished. Children are enormously different in their intellectual capacities, motor skills and natural talents. To lump all children together and expect them to perform equally well is not only foolish, it is cruel.

For example, children who are mechanically inclined, musical or artistic need opportunities to express these talents. Children who are scholarly and are quick to grasp abstractions usually learn more quickly than sensory learners or those who are less academically oriented. Hitting or scolding the latter type won't make them learn more quickly. Also, independent, adventurous children are less willing to follow rules and regulations than naturally obedient children. Deeply feeling, sensitive children need a different kind of relationship with their teachers and parents than less sensitive children. Saying "Be tough," or "Don't be such a baby," will not make a child less sensitive.

Another important consideration is whether or not a child has PSI, or poor sensory integration. PSI is an umbrella term for a subtle neurological disturbance affecting approximately 30 percent of all children, 80 percent of whom are boys (*Sensory Integration and the Child*). While most of these children are of average or even superior intelligence, many have moderate to severe learning disabilities. They may display a variety of symptoms such as: a high level of insecurity despite their loving homes, poor coordination and clumsiness, hyper- or hypo-activity, difficulty concentrating, perceptual problems, poor impulse control, frequent tantrums, high-need level (i.e., extremely clingy and demanding) and difficulty getting along with people.

Such children must have occupational therapy in order to learn to cope with their handicaps and to avoid feeling like total failures. Such therapy helps these children's brains become more organized, thereby lessening their anxiety and impulsivity. Without such therapy, these children usually end up rejected and severely punished by parents and teachers who simply do not know how to handle them.

4) *Lack of success experiences.* Self-esteem is based largely on the ability to master whatever skills one and his particular culture value. The feeling of accomplishment is one of life's greatest pleasures. Without it, a person feels that he and his life have little value.

◆ EXAMPLE: "I am the grandchild of a famous scholar, so great things were expected of me. However, I have a learning disability. As a child, I had great difficulty reading and concentrating. My penmanship was awful and I couldn't sit still for long. That was before learning disabilities were recognized. I was constantly being told that I was stubborn and lazy. I was hit a lot. Although I pretended that it didn't bother me, I felt terrible. I felt like garbage. And it didn't help that people treated me like garbage, too. I still tend to feel inadequate. The good thing to come out of this is that I am now a teacher and have a lot of compassion for students like myself. Also, I arranged to have a special program in the school for teaching disabled children, and I give them a lot of extra attention and encouragement to make sure that their spirits don't get crushed by insensitive people."

◆ EXAMPLE: "I was always a little awkward and disorganized. People were forever yelling at me for being a scatterbrain, and for forgetting things and dropping things. I got high grades in abstract subjects, but I just couldn't get things together in the physical world. I was also very unpopular. It was awful."

(5) *Lack of parental harmony.* Children learn how to relate to others from how they see their parents relate to each other. When

parents are contemptuous of each other, then no matter how much they love their children, the children are afraid that they will be treated the same eventually. Mates who are disrespectful to each other may not realize that they are instilling in their children deep-seated fears about abandonment and a predisposition to showing contempt for their mates when they eventually marry.

> ◆ EXAMPLE: "My parents disliked each other intensely. I grew up thinking that this is how men feel about women. I didn't think any man could love me either. I was always afraid that they would get divorced, and that they would divorce me, too! As they got older, they didn't fight openly so much, but their sighs, grimaces and nasty remarks left deep scars on me. It still seems natural and normal to me for married people to be nasty to each other. That's what I was used to."

(6) *Lack of fair, consistent discipline.* True discipline is an expression of love. When a person leans against a wall, he doesn't want it to crumble. Likewise, children need parents who are consistent and fair, who explain the rules clearly and enforce them fairly. Wishy-washy and inconsistent parents make children feel as insecure as those who are overly rigid, inflexible and intolerant. Children need boundaries which are broad enough to encourage individuality and self-reliance, yet clear enough to provide a firm sense of morality and values. But they also want more from a relationship than orders like, "Wash your hands!" "Sit up straight!" "Get your feet off the couch!" "Do the dishes!" "Finish your homework!"

Most parents find it difficult to discipline children with a proper balance between firmness and flexibility. In a healthy marriage, there is a natural system of checks and balances so that neither one goes to either extreme. However, in a dysfunctional family, the parents often polarize each other, with one being tyrannical and punitive, while the other is overly passive or indulgent.

Parents from abusive homes may fail to exercise proper control over their children because they mistakenly associate discipline with cruelty. Others are overly punitive and rigid, demanding obedience from young children which would not even be appropriate for older ones and inflicting harsh punishments for minor infractions.

Children who are poorly disciplined usually have difficulty disciplining themselves as adults, becoming overly controlling, punitive and perfectionistic in some areas and the opposite in others.

Children who have been well loved have the strength to cope with adversity. Those who have not, often fall apart at the smallest stress. They often remain emotionally undeveloped, fixated at the level of a three- or four-year-old, if not younger, which makes it very difficult to communicate with them or help them choose healthier patterns of behavior.

Negative behavior begins as an attempt to gain attention and control

Emotionally deprived children get into a negative feedback loop with their emotionally deprived parents. Because the parents feel inadequate, they see their own children in the same light. When their children, like all children, misbehave or have accidents, the event sparks old destructive childhood patterns in the parents. All the rage that these parents could not express toward their own parents comes spilling out at their children, and they respond with an excess of hostility. Feeling rejected, the children then react by adopting unacceptable and often aggressive behavior in order to get back at the parents. But instead of getting what they need — i.e., loving concern or firm guidelines — the children are permitted to run amuck or are scolded and hit, which makes them even more hostile and obnoxious. Before long, the parents' negative image of them ("lazy brat," "unmanageable bully," etc.) becomes a self-fulfilling prophecy. They and everyone around them believe they are hopelessly bad. Thus, what started out as a reasonable desire for attention or a minor discipline problem quickly evolves into a full-blown battle between the parents and the children, day after day.

Yet the child persists in these negative behaviors because to a child, attention is life. To be heard is to exist. If he does not receive this recognition in a positive way, he will act destructively to get attention and power over his universe, the two things which make him feel safe. Others simply lose touch with their need for relationships and become coldly indifferent and noncommunicative.

> ◆ EXAMPLE: "As a child, I felt no one really cared. I smothered my pain with food. It was the only thing that made me feel better. It's still such a strong feeling — that eating sweets is the only thing that will make me feel cared about."

◆ EXAMPLE: "I was the oldest, and consequently given the most work. Since I wasn't allowed to express anger toward my parents, I took it out on my younger sisters. I would tease them and hurt them any way I could. Then my parents would yell at me and hit me. I didn't care. At least it got their attention."

Being screamed at feels bad, but at least the child's existence is being acknowledged. Getting hit provides him with *negative* body contact, but it *is* contact. To a child, such negative attention is better than nothing. In the dysfunctional family, being able to cause pain to oneself or others becomes a source of pleasure and control.

Take eleven-year-old Ariel, whose parents always worked full-time and who left him with indifferent and inexperienced baby sitters or an older brother who bullied him mercilessly. The parents thought they were very loving toward him. After all, weren't they working so hard to provide for their children? Didn't they criticize him constantly to make him improve? But Ariel never felt loved.

Ariel has learned to inflict pain on his parents by inflicting it on himself. He is also something of a hypochondriac, magnifying every ache and pain in order to get their attention. He said, "Knowing how much my parents want me to do well in school, I often refuse to do my homework. I just want to get back at them. Knowing how worried they are about me being skinny, I sometimes go for days without eating much. I don't want to live anymore. I think a lot about suicide. If I died, I wouldn't have to live with my parents."

Nine-year-old Leah is another child who has become addicted to negative behavior in order to punish her parents and gain some feeling of control over her life. Leah's father is a "smack-addict," smacking her if she spills something, makes noise, doesn't finish her food, makes a mess or talks back. Both parents call her nudnik, dummy, selfish, lazy brat, etc. When her mother feels overwhelmed, she screams "I'm going to kill you," or "I wish you'd never been born." Her mother is sure that Leah knows that they really do love her underneath it all, but Leah is just as sure that they mean what they say.

Leah has come to enjoy lying and acting cruel. "I lie to my parents so that they won't be angry with me. I also like getting back at them. I like to see what I can get away with without getting caught. I've been caught stealing, but I don't care. Let my parents punish me. I don't care how they feel."

Lastly, there is twelve-year-old Rachel, whose mother feels overwhelmed with four children in the family. She feels incapable of establishing consistent rules and sticking to them. There are no predictable meal times or set chores in her household. Everything is haphazard and chaotic, accompanied by a lot of screaming and criticism. When her mother is in a bad mood, she screams at Rachel, "I hate you. I wish you were dead."

Rachel tries as much as she can to get the house in order and the younger children in control, in the hope of winning her mother's approval. But her efforts go unnoticed and the situation quickly reverts back to its usual mess. Although Rachel is gregarious and cheerful with friends, she is often gloomy and insolent around her mother. She said, "When I mope, it makes my mother feel guilty. Then she sometimes gives me what I want, like a new dress or time away to play with my friends instead of having to help with the housework. If I act happy, she'll think everything's all right and ignore me or make me do more chores. I have to act miserable and make her miserable, because that's the only way I get any attention."

Unfortunately, these children are right. Their parents' actions confirm their belief that they must act out and make other people miserable in order to get their way. While this gives the child some measure of power and control over the anxiety and pain he feels, it also encourages him to make misery a way of life.

The language of the dysfunctional family

Just as children learn a mother tongue in the home, so, too, do they learn an emotional language of love which teaches them to either be supportive and respectful or fearful and hateful. Children of critical parents learn that:

"I have to get mad (or bad, sad, sick or crazy) to get what I want."

"When people love you, they hurt you."

"My parents are right. I am lazy, crazy, stupid and bad. Who could possibly love me?"

"I'm defective. I have to hide who I am. I have to present an image, a front for the world, in order not to be rejected and live in fear that someone will find out how bad I really am."

"People will always try to control me and take over my life. I must protect myself by being tough and independent."

"Disapproval is disastrous. I must have everyone's approval. I must please everyone. If not, I cannot bear it."

"I can do whatever I want, whenever I want and it doesn't matter who I hurt. Since no one cares about me, I won't care about anyone else."

"Only exceptionally successful people deserve love and respect. To be average is to be a failure."

When children grow up speaking this *mama lashon,* they inevitably seek future mates and friends who speak it, too.

The internalized parent

The Gemara states that just as Yosef was about to commit a sin with Potifar's wife, the image of his beloved father, Yaakov, appeared before him and encouraged him to control himself right at the moment when his passions were about to overwhelm him (*Sotah* 36b).

Everyone carries within himself an internalized parental image. If a child's parents were nurturing and supportive, if they trusted and believed in him, then he is able to respond to people and situations in keeping with that internalized image of love, trust and strength. A child who is cherished and feels successful has inner strengths which will pull him through life's countless challenges and disappointments. This positive self-image becomes stronger and more secure as time goes on.

The emotionally abused child also has a self-image — a negative one which is built on the feeling of inferiority and the certainty of failure, rejection and abandonment. As time goes on, he adds to that foundation of mistrust and inadequacy. Every present loss or mistake brings back "reminder symptoms," with the emotional impact of all the rejections he ever experienced, and makes him feel that his negative perceptions are correct — that he really is a failure, that people will always disappoint and reject him because he is essentially inept and unlovable.

When this person faces a crisis as an adult, he has nothing to fall back on, no inner resources. He turns to his internal parental image and only finds himself being mocked, humiliated or abandoned just as he was as a child. And he may not even be able to think of constructive options, because he may be stuck at the emotional level of a young child.

Shame and the childhood roots of mental illness

Self-mastery and self-acceptance are the essence of emotional health. This is one reason why parents need to remind children to act in a self-respecting manner, and to be ashamed when they do not. However, when children feel ashamed not only of their isolated acts of disobedience, but of themselves as a whole, they begin to show signs of emotional disturbance.

Normal children begin to experience shame very early in life, some of it legitimate, but much of it not. For example, in addition to appropriate shame over actual sins, they feel ashamed if they are in any way different from others, or if they lack popularity, material possessions and academic success. They also feel ashamed of being dependent. To overcome the hostility which often comes with a dependent position, nurturing parents bolster children's self-esteem by providing them with success experiences and allowing them to participate in decisions which affect them whenever possible and practical. They also encourage as much independence as each child can handle.

Since the ability to earn money is one way of strengthening self-esteem, nurturing parents allow their children a degree of control over their own money. This is one reason why the *Pele Yoetz* ("Genevah," p. 48) suggests that parents give children an allowance each week. Unfortunately, in a dysfunctional home, the parents' excessive need for control over their children's thoughts, feelings, bodies and food intake usually extends to a desire for total control over their spending as well.

Young children feel ashamed of themselves if they are ignored or abused, and blame themselves if their parents ignore or abuse them. Young children assume that they deserve whatever they get. They justify their parents' abusive treatment by saying, "It was my fault. I didn't obey." If a parent dies, a young child thinks, "If I was really good, Mommy/Daddy would not have left me. So, I must be bad."

Another almost unavoidable source of excessive shame is living with a very accomplished sibling who is so outstanding that the child feels stupid in comparison. Also, critical teachers can devastate a child's sense of self-worth. Obviously, only one child can achieve the standing as Number One in the classroom. Yet many children grow up feeling ashamed of themselves for ranking below the best when statistically there is no other place for them to be.

In a nurturing home, parents cherish the child for what he is and focus on his strong points. They do not make a child feel guilty for not measuring up to their standards when it is impossible for him to do so. In a nonnurturing home, on the other hand, parents express much anxiety and shame over their children's lack of abilities. They equate "average" with "failure." The result is that their children are either anxiety-ridden perfectionists or underachievers who protect themselves from further failure by not even trying, as shown in their lack of ambition, initiative and curiosity. Many such children become excessively concerned with conformity to the group, material possessions and external appearance in an attempt to cover their feeling of inner emptiness and abnormality.

Many adults promote the myth that "You can be anything you want to be if you just try hard enough." So, they may push a child to excel in something they excelled in or wished they had, forcing the child to be an extension of themselves rather than an individual with his own God-given aptitudes and interests. Then, when a child performs poorly in a particular subject in school, the parents assume that he just isn't trying, rather than realizing that he may lack ability in that specific area. Such parents are not concerned with the child's emotional or intellectual readiness level or his particular abilities, but with their own need for control and social approval. The child knows this intuitively and fights to gain some control over his life by adopting behavior which he knows will infuriate them.

A fundamental sense of unacceptability

In a nonnurturing home, the child feels like an object which is being used and manipulated for the parents' ego satisfaction. But since no child can ever eliminate a parent's feelings of inadequacy, he ends up feeling like a failure. He thinks he can prevent further rejection only by keeping his inadequacies hidden from others with a false image of religiosity, intelligence and normalcy.

The result of this conflict is an inner split between what the child thinks is the defective "real me" and the phony external image which he adopts to fool the world. This produces enormous inner tension which affects children's physical and emotional health. Various nervous habits may develop as a consequence of this tension, such as nail biting, tics and eating disorders. The child may have frequent explosions or seem emotionally deadened much of the time. He may move about anxiously, unable to relax his tight grip on himself for fear of having to face his ugly inner reality or having others see it. Like all human beings, he wants to be accepted for who he is, but he is certain that he is fundamentally unacceptable.

When self-protection becomes self-destruction

People whose homes have been burglarized often say that their lives are not the same afterwards. They put extra locks on their doors and bars on their windows, yet still don't feel safe. They become super-sensitive — sounds that never bothered them before instantly awaken the memory of that trauma. If this is the effect of one traumatic event on an adult, imagine the effect of repeated traumas on the mind of a young child!

The protective locks and bars which the child has installed to protect himself from pain also serve to prevent him from loving or being loved. If the parents do not know how to break through to him with affection, humor and reassurance, the walls of mistrust and hostility become so thick that they become part of the child's very being.

The following behaviors are typical responses to a nonnurturing environment. In each case, the unconscious hopes become understandable when seen in terms of the limited options of a child whose life is full of pain and who wants to have some measure of control over his universe.

Paranoia. The child's unconscious hope is: I can keep people from hurting me by attacking first and being super-suspicious and untrusting of everyone around me.

Dependency. The clingy, dependent child's unconscious hope is: I can get people to take care of me by showing them that I cannot manage on my own. I'll die unless someone takes care of me. I'll avoid rejection by not taking initiative or making my own decisions.

Depression. The child hopes: If I stop trying, I won't be criticized for what I do. If I go dead and give up hope, then I won't be in pain when people disappoint me or I fail.

Schizoid behavior. This child hopes: Since the world is so painful and terrifying, I will cease to be a part of it. I'll create a fantasy world where I'm powerful enough to stop the pain by ceasing to exist or becoming someone else.

Autistic behavior. The child's hope is to avoid the pain of rejection by isolating himself from all meaningful contact. He simply disappears, either emotionally or physically, whenever the threat of emotional involvement arises.

Passive-aggression. This child's hope is: I'll show my parents that they can't control me no matter how hard they try. I'll act stupid and helpless, and then they'll get fed up and won't make me do anything I don't want to do. I'll hurt them precisely in the areas where they'll have the most pain. If they want most for me to get good marks, I won't study. If they want most for me to be pious, I'll scoff at the religious rituals. If they want me to be neat and responsible, I'll be spaced-out, irresponsible and messy.

Obsessions and compulsions. The insecure child hopes: If I can just figure out which specific thoughts or behaviors I must faithfully adhere to in order to ward off disaster, then my parents and God won't punish me. I'll win their approval by being perfect. If I can just get it right, I'll feel secure. If I can just measure up, I'll be admired.

Psychopathic behaviors. The psychopathic child never develops a conscience. His hope is: If I can show people how powerful I am by hurting them, they won't hurt me. They'll admire me. I should be able to get away with murder and not be punished.

Of course, the feeling of pleasure and power these children feel while engaged in these behaviors is never enough to relieve their sense of insecurity and inadequacy.

Lest readers become unnecessarily frightened over their child's lapse into any of the above behaviors, it should be noted that many children go through phases during which they demonstrate some of the major symptoms of mental illness for short periods of time. Thankfully, with interventions such as family therapy, change of schools, vacation time, creative outlets and the reassurance of parental love, the problem eventually fades away. However, if the behavior seems to be intensifying with time, don't kid yourself that it will all work out. Professional help should be sought immediately.

Maintaining the pain level from childhood

Children become very attached to their bad habits. When asked what might happen if they gave up their negative behavior, children with emotional problems could not imagine that anything positive might result.

> *"If I stopped being depressed, no one would pay any attention to me."*
>
> *"When I imagine myself healthy, I imagine being all alone."*
>
> *"It is dangerous and wrong to think well of myself."*
>
> *"If I liked myself, I would be happy with myself as I am. Then I'd become a lazy bum and not do anything with my life."*
>
> *"If I tried harder, I'd fail. So why try?"*

Strange as it may seem, there is a kind of safety in the predictability of knowing that one will always fail, that nothing will ever turn out right, that people will always be rejecting and untrustworthy, that one will always feel depressed, mean or helpless. These beliefs may be the only thing the child has ever been able to count on.

Children will carry their negative beliefs and behaviors into adulthood and pass them along, in turn, to *their* children, unless they have the courage and determination to change. Unfortunately for many such children, the world of good health, love, joy and mutual respect remains foreign and frightening. They do not even know what is normal. They do not even know enough about emotional health to know what to strive for. Recovery means struggling for an entire lifetime to maintain balance and health.

CHAPTER 4:
Recovery through Love and Strength of Will

The *Zohar* states (1:4a) that the greatest satisfaction in life is to fulfill the purpose of our existence, which is "to turn darkness into light." This is the difficult spiritual work which, though often silent and unseen by others, takes tremendous effort.

Very few people ever achieve true unconditional love for God, mankind and themselves, for this requires profound spiritual awareness and maturity. Thus, most people grow up and live in an atmosphere of conditional love, i.e., "I love you according to what you have accomplished and can do for me, according to whether you satisfy my needs and make me happy."

To grow up in a nonaccepting environment is to grow up with a death wish. After all, if a parent keeps telling his child, "I wish you were smarter, less bossy, more confident and orderly, etc.," the parent is, in effect, saying, "I wish you would die and be replaced by someone different. You, as you are, are not wanted." Of course, parents do not actually say such words or mean them, but this death wish is communicated to children as if it were on a flashing neon sign. Children do not have the sophistication to realize that their parents think they are protecting their children by pushing them to be better or that they fear public disapproval and often feel alone, insecure and incompetent. Rather, the children assume that they are simply not good enough to be loved.

Recovery cannot begin unless we develop compassion for our parents, understanding their fears and forgiving them for their limitations. Only when we love and accept our parents with all their imperfections, can we ever accept ourselves with our human limitations and love despite theirs.

The healing journey

We have within us an infinite capacity to heal ourselves. No matter how bad we feel at any moment or how difficult our past may have been, we are born with the power to grow. Recovery means satisfying our need for true closeness to God and man and giving up our immature desire for approval and control over others. It means accepting full responsibility for our present thoughts and actions.

> If man had been created solely for the sake of this world, he would have no need of being inspired with a soul so precious and exalted as to be greater than the angels themselves.
>
> (PATH OF THE JUST, p. 23)

We heal as we learn to make contact with this precious soul within us. Healing requires that we engage in an ongoing struggle to love unconditionally, and by so doing, transcend our limitations of the present moment. This process of self-transcendence does not take place in one giant leap. Rather, we take tiny tortoise steps, plodding forward in sickness and in health, in joy and in sorrow, toward a goal of which we may be only dimly aware. Perhaps this is why, although *Bnei Yisrael* could have traveled from Egypt to Canaan in only eleven days, it took forty years. The same is true when it comes to leaving our own personal *Mitzrayim*.

An act of will: to accept the necessity of enslavement

> The word "redemption" applies only to one who emerges from darkness into light. One who has never experienced the suffering of bondage and oppression cannot appreciate redemption. The very essence of redemption is the freedom which comes from the oppression itself. Had the Children of Israel never been enslaved, they would never have experienced true freedom. Once they were enslaved, the slavery itself gave rise to the redemption and from the midst of the darkness, and only from that darkness, the light burst forth. Thus said our Sages (*Yalkut Hoshea* 533), "The Israelites said to the Holy One, Blessed be He, 'Oh Lord of the Universe, when will You deliver us?' The Holy One, Blessed be He, answered, 'When you will have reached the lowest depths, at that moment I will redeem you'."
>
> (THE BOOK OF OUR HERITAGE, vol. II, p. 121)

This is a beautiful summary of the stages involved in the journey from a selfish, self-centered existence to a God-centered one, from low self-esteem to a sense of value, or from an abusive mentality to a nurturing one: (1) one must first experience enslavement in order to crave freedom; (2) one must accept that freedom is the result of God's grace combined with great courage and determination; (3) the goal of the recovery process is an internalized awareness of God's presence.

> I will take you to Me for a people, and I will be to you a God and you shall know that I am the Lord your God.
>
> (SHEMOTH 6:6)

Once a person has come under the control of a destructive habit, whether it be condemnaholism or a food addiction, it takes a strong-armed approach to release oneself from its grip. Yet it is by doing so that he discovers the Godly power within himself to overcome the isolation and despair which threaten to drag him down again.

As will be shown, the stages of a personal spiritual journey parallel those of the redemption of the Jewish nation from Egypt. Each step of the way requires a strengthening of will and a greater level of *emunah*.

An act of will: to cry out for liberation

> And they cried and their cry went up to God from the bondage.
>
> (SHEMOTH 2:23)

A spiritual journey begins when a person realizes that he is enslaved and cries out for freedom. Without this longing, no outsider can force change.

> God said to Moshe, "I will bring you out from under the burdens of *Mitzrayim...*"
>
> (SHEMOTH 6:6)

The Hebrew word for "burdens" in the above verse is *sivloth*, which may also be translated as "tolerance." The *Chiddushei HaRim* explains [by *derush*] that the most dangerous aspect of exile is when the people become accustomed to it and, beginning to tolerate it, they stop longing for redemption. If they no longer feel that the exile is unbearable, they cease to cry to *Hashem* to redeem them, and without this prayer, they may never be redeemed.

Each person has a different level of tolerance for unhealthy behavior. Some people stop smoking after the first signs of shortness of breath, while others continue smoking even after a heart attack. Some people go on a diet when they are ten pounds overweight, while others become obese before they finally revolt against their enslavement to food. Some people are so refined that they shudder at the mere thought of saying something which would hurt another's feelings, while others are so dense that they do not even acknowledge the damaging effects of their relentless criticism.

No one can determine that point of "crying out" for anyone else. Anyone who tries to get someone to stop smoking, bingeing or bullying others before the person really wants to change, will find that his efforts are useless. One can only help others to the degree that they want to help themselves.

We are told that "A person's nature exercises a strong downward pull upon him" (*Path of the Just*, ch. 6). That "downward pull" will drag us down unless we develop strength of will. And strength of will is developed by implementing the ethics of the Torah throughout all our waking hours, in every stressful event, whether major or minor.

> ◆ EXAMPLE: "I kept saying that I wanted to give up my abusive habits, but I was only fooling myself. Like most people, I wanted to change, but I didn't want to work at it. Finally, I couldn't take the pain anymore. That was the turning point. I accepted that, 'It's either discipline or death.' I finally stopped blaming my parents and God for my misery. It was only then that I was ready to change. I, and I alone, had to work to develop strength of will by demonstrating self-control day in and day out. Until I was ready to put forth that effort, my cries for help weren't really sincere."

An act of will: to have a vision of hope

> We must develop within ourselves great ambitions, mighty aspirations, precise, goal-directed vision, so that we may fill our lives with unremitting striving to attain them.
>
> (STRIVE FOR TRUTH! vol. 1, p. 232)

In their journey toward the land of Canaan, *Bnei Yisrael* suffered numerous setbacks. But they kept going onward. Similarly, no one overcomes an addiction without going through many moments of triumph as well as despair.

We will not always be successful in our attempts to restrain our negative impulses. The healing journey is not an easy one. We take two steps forward and one step back. There are times when we feel we have not progressed at all. That is when we must not lose hope. That is when we need to remember that a truly firm conviction of God's presence comes only after much effort. We start with a vision and an intellectual awareness that with God's help, we can break out of our personal *Mitzrayim*. When the vision and the hope fade, we can still keep moving forward through sheer strength of will.

> ◆ EXAMPLE: "I was feeling terribly discouraged and didn't even want to get out of bed. I wasn't succeeding in anything I tried, not my relationships or my work. As I lay there, a voice in my head kept saying, 'Close off. Don't trust anyone. Everyone abandons you eventually. Give up. No matter what you do, nothing's going to work. You're a failure.' I wanted to lie there and sulk, but I forced myself out of bed, knowing that I would feel better if I fought the urge to withdraw and acted as if I had hope even if I felt discouraged. It was true. As the day wore on, I felt more self-respecting just because I was fighting to put one foot in front of the other."

An act of will: to respect the difficulty of change

With a strong hand has the Lord brought thee out of Egypt.

(SHEMOTH 13:9)

According to the Midrash, only one-fifth of *Bnei Yisrael* left Egypt; four-fifths chose to stay behind. Interestingly, research studies have shown that approximately the same ratio — four out of five — of those who join self-improvement programs eventually drop out because they lack the determination to continue.

There are powerful forces which keep people immersed in negativity. Some are self-satisfied, believing that they don't have anything to correct. Others try briefly to change, but give up in despair, convinced that it is impossible for them to act any differently. Many of them are afraid to face the world without the negative habits which have provided them with some sense of protection against the pain of feeling rejected, inferior and alone.

The major reason why change is so difficult is due to the brain's physiology. The brain, which weighs only about fifty ounces, is composed of a network of some *thirteen trillion* interconnections (called synapses) between billions of nerve cells! Every time we think a thought, we create a neural pathway in the brain. The more times we think that same thought, the deeper the grooves along that same neural pathway become, and the more likely we are to think the same thought again, and, like a magnetic force, attract other thoughts of the same nature (*Psychofeedback*, p. 33).

Take one bad habit, such as the tendency to criticize. How many times have we crushed ourselves or someone else in the last twenty-four hours? In our entire lives? Imagine how many grooves those condemnations have made in our brains over the course of many years and how many positive thoughts and acts are necessary to counteract their effect.

When we decide to make a change in our thinking, we are like a person whose leg has been in a cast for years and now needs to be exercised. It is very painful. The task of building new neural pathways of positivity in our brains takes repetition and perseverance. A lot of people are not willing to make that effort.

Furthermore, there is the pain of separating from those who do not want to be on this spiritual journey. Those who are truly committed to achieving emotional and spiritual health can expect that they will have to leave many people behind, including those close family members who are unwilling to grow or actively oppose anyone else's struggle for health. That, too, is part of God's plan, for the most difficult test of a person's character is whether he can demonstrate his fierce devotion to the ideals of Torah in the presence of those who don't want to do the same and who criticize him for doing so.

An act of will: to practice Torah principles

We cannot really appreciate the profundity of the principles of Torah until we see the wonders which they produce. But first we must put forth great effort, even if we do so insincerely, without much hope that anything will come of them, for "...outer movements awaken inner ones" (*The Path of the Just*, ch. 91).

◆ EXAMPLE: "I get discouraged very easily. One bad thing happens, and I'm ready to condemn everyone and everything. Well, a person I don't like and didn't invite showed up at my daughter's wedding. I was about to say something nasty and ruin the whole evening when I remembered the Torah obligation to avoid hatred, vengeance and grudge-bearing. At the moment, I was experiencing all three. But I decided to be polite and try practicing *ahavath chinam* [baseless love]. Magically, my bad feelings disappeared, and I was able to focus on the positive and enjoy the rest of the evening."

◆ EXAMPLE: "My husband has Alzheimer's Disease and barely recognizes me anymore. It's terribly heartbreaking because we had a wonderful relationship before he became ill. I was very depressed and angry at God for having done this to me. Then I prayed for Him to show me the *berachah* in the situation. Soon after, I began to see that by reaching out to people with similar problems, I felt less alone. I have also strengthened my bond with God, because I see that He is the only one I can give my pain over to when things get really bad, like during those long lonely nights."

◆ EXAMPLE: "I was standing at the kitchen sink feeling sorry for myself because of all the dishes and housework which still needed to be done. I felt like a *shmateh*. All that rhetoric I'd heard about the wonders of motherhood seemed like a lie. But I just felt cold and mean. I started crying and praying to God that He would open my eyes and make me feel grateful for all that I had. A few hours later, I realized that my problem was that I'd been equating success with social status and material comfort, and equating giving with being taken advantage of, so I was resentful all the time. I had been feeling so negative because I was thinking according to a non-Torah value system. If I saw myself as a spiritual teacher, I would understand what it really means to be a mother. My responsibility is to create life not only physically, but spiritually as well, by teaching my children to really love Judaism, not just perform the duties mechanically, and to help them realize that by giving, we get the most. Suddenly, it was okay to be doing dishes. I put on some music and put a smile on my face. Once I got my priorities straight, my spirits lifted."

◆ EXAMPLE: "I was fuming with rage when our refrigerator broke down a day after I had spent so much money getting a repairman to fix it. My usual habit would have been to stew about my rotten luck for days and go around telling everyone how I *always* get gypped and swindled and how *every* repairman is an incompetent liar. Instead, in keeping with my goal of demonstrating good *middoth* no matter what is going on, I disciplined myself to respond in a firm but civilized manner. That was an incredible victory for me."

An act of will: to be willing to make sacrifices

And God spoke unto Moshe...saying...on the tenth day [of Nissan] every man shall take a lamb...and keep it until the fourteenth day...and slaughter it.

(SHEMOTH 12:1-6)

On the day before *Bnei Yisrael* left Egypt, they were commanded to slaughter and sacrifice a lamb. This was an extremely dangerous undertaking, since the Egyptians worshipped the lamb and might have taken revenge on the Israelites for destroying one of their gods. There was also a second type of blood shed that Pesach — the blood of circumcision — another act which also involved possible danger and great self-sacrifice (*Shemoth* 12:6, Rashi).

Similarly, our psychological exodus from the slavery of our personal *Mitzrayim* requires countless acts of self-sacrifice. No word in the English language conveys the true meaning of the Hebrew word for sacrifice [*korban*], which means, literally, "to come close" [to God]. It is essential to keep this in mind — that each time we sacrifice a negative impulse, we are drawn closer to our *neshamah*. However, at the time we may feel as if we are giving up what is most important or pleasurable. It is only afterwards that we experience how much more we get back in terms of greater self-respect and closeness with God. Thus, we are commanded:

Circumcise the foreskin of your heart and be no more stiffnecked...   (DEVARIM 10:16)

And the Lord thy God will circumcise your heart, and the heart of your seed, to love the Lord your God with all your heart, and with all your soul, that you may live.

(IBID. 30:6)

What is this "foreskin of the heart"? It is those beliefs which blind us to our true Divine nature. It consists of inappropriate shame, fear and the hatred of ourselves and others. Removal of this barrier is our on-going spiritual work.

At first we resist, thinking, How will I protect myself if I'm not hostile and angry? / Where will I get love and comfort, if not from food? / Who will take care of me if I become strong and healthy and am no longer sickly and depressed? We have to discover these answers for ourselves.

◆ EXAMPLE: "I used to get so violent when things didn't go my way, maybe because I grew up in an environment where I felt very helpless. Getting angry made me feel powerful. It was my way of saying 'Take me seriously! Respect me.' But my anger ruined all my relationships. So, I decided that whenever anyone caused me pain, I would immediately follow the Torah obligation to give the benefit of the doubt and say either mentally or out loud, 'I'm sure you didn't mean to hurt me.' No matter how insincere it felt at first, the words always calmed me down and helped me stay in control. At first it felt very phony. I still had my old childhood beliefs that if I didn't give back to people whatever they were dishing out to me, it meant I was a weakling and a wimp and that I couldn't respect myself if I didn't shout back. I discovered that self-control was what I needed to feel self-respecting. After months of practice, I actually do feel more sympathy toward people. Even very belligerent people usually calm down if I keep repeating these words in my mind. Even though they have no idea that I am doing this, they seem to get the message! It was incredibly difficult work at first, but it's getting easier."

If we trust that the Torah is "...a tree of life to those who hold fast to it and [that] those who uphold it are happy" (*Mishlei* 3:18), we will be able endure the pain of following Torah ethics even when it is most difficult, knowing that doing so will eventually bring us tremendous joy.

Any and every spiritual effort that we make to raise ourselves from our lowly state becomes all the more precious and valuable in the eyes of God.   (STRIVE FOR TRUTH! p. 107)

We are no longer able to perform animal sacrifices, but we certainly have endless opportunities to sacrifice the animalistic impulses within us and accomplish the goal we pray for each morning in *Birchath HaShachar*: "May the evil inclination have no mastery over us. Make us cleave to the good inclination and good deeds, and compel our will to be subservient to You alone."

An act of will: to use our greatest power wisely

And the children of Israel went up armed out of the land of Egypt.

(SHEMOTH 13:19)

What "arms" do we have in the struggle against our personal *Mitzrayim*? We often feel powerless in the face of painful events and our own destructive urges. However, the one power that always remains with us is our God-like power to create or destroy realities with our thoughts.

We can only have one thought at a time, a secure thought or an insecure thought. Secure thoughts and positive actions produce joy, confidence and inner calm, while negative thoughts and actions produce discouragement, anger and anxiety. Mental health requires that we be as stringent about the *kashruth* of what we think as we are about the food we eat. With our thoughts, we build a reality which either reinforces our *emunah* and *bitachon* or builds fear, despair and resentment. It is our choice of thoughts, not external people and events, which make us feel loving, capable and hopeful, or unlovable, inferior and hopeless. It is our responsibility to generate positive states of consciousness within ourselves and not depend on outside people or events to do this for us.

◆ EXAMPLE: "The week before Pesach, I started having anxiety attacks, wondering how I would manage. The only thing that helped calm me down was to remember that I can either think securely that things will work out, or think insecurely that it will be a total disaster. It is my choice to keep choosing secure thoughts. As I kept moving, cleaning things despite my anxiety, I felt less overwhelmed and more capable."

◆ EXAMPLE: "Because I have a serious illness, I am sometimes gripped with anxiety about being a burden on others and being ruined financially. Whenever I get scared, I visualize myself turning my life over to God and letting Him handle it. This calms me down and enables me to stop trying to control what I can't control, such as the progress of this disease and other people's attitudes toward me."

◆ EXAMPLE: "I was the type of person who was always torturing myself over every decision I made and every defect in myself. I believed that I couldn't control my mind, because the thoughts seemed to just take over. Then, one day, as I was buying apples in the supermarket, the idea flashed into my head that if I have the ability to choose which apples to put in my bag, then I have the ability to choose which thoughts to put in my mind. It's the exact same process! I discard the ones I don't want and pick the ones I do, without torturing myself over whether or not I made the right choice. When I think of exercising my 'confidence' muscles and 'decision-making muscles,' that helps me bear the pain of changing my old self-defeating patterns."

The recognition of our power to adopt or discard beliefs depending on whether or not they serve a Godly purpose, is the most important weapon in our struggle to change. When we get control of our thoughts, we can then get control of our actions. The reverse is also true. No progress can take place without discipline.

Every time we speak disparagingly of ourselves, we deny our potential for growth and our ability to cope effectively with difficult events. For example, every time we think, I'll never change, I can't control myself, or One of these days, I'm going to go nuts, we create a negative self-image which shows in our body posture, facial expressions and speech. This, in turn, leads others to respond to us according to the image we project and encourages more negativity.

Although we all have certain innate characteristics which cannot be changed, our task is to use those predispositions for good (see Rambam, *Hilchoth Deoth* 1:1-3 and *Even Shelemah* 1:7). God gave us the ability to develop any positive or negative personality trait. Our emotional health is largely a matter of which traits we choose to develop. (An excellent list of positive and negative traits appears in *Gateway to Happiness*, pp. 394-398).

◆ EXAMPLE: "A certain neighbor is quite obnoxious. I kept telling myself, 'I can't stand this guy. One day I'm going to punch him out.' And each day, I came closer to making my thoughts a reality. Then, one day I realized that I'd better change my thoughts or I'd be in big trouble. So, whenever I saw him, I would tell myself, 'Here comes my spiritual test of the day.' In time, I was able to actually appreciate the fact that he gave me the opportunity to practice detachment and silence."

◆ EXAMPLE: "I was constantly telling my kids that they were too much to handle and that I was going crazy from all their arguments.

Then I realized that I was programming myself for a nervous breakdown when what I needed most was to program myself for health! So, I started telling myself, 'Every time they argue, I will use it as an opportunity to practice emotional detachment or calm assertiveness. I don't have to feel like a failure and explode each time they fight.' Sometimes I even tell them, 'Thank you for giving me the opportunity to demonstrate self-control to you!' Even if I don't believe what I'm saying at the time, the words calm me down and help me stay in control. So the lie becomes truth. I can control myself if I stop feeling like a failure and become a solution-seeker."

◆ EXAMPLE: "As a divorced mother, I was constantly believing people who told me how my two children's lives were ruined. I ate myself up worrying about their futures until I decided to program myself and my children to trust in our inner strengths and our ability to be more caring and sensitive because of what we've been through."

An act of will: to trust that the sea will part for us

And Israel *saw* the great hand which God used upon the Egyptians. Then the people feared God and trusted in God and in Moshe...   (SHEMOTH 4:31)

True, they trusted when they saw miracles all around them. However, because they had not yet internalized God in their consciousness, they became anxious and felt abandoned and betrayed every time their physical needs were not immediately satisfied. Whenever they felt insecure, they became angry at God and Moshe.

So, too, with us. As long as God remains "out there," external to us, we do not really trust that He is part of our very lives. We demand constant proof of His existence and become bitter and angry when we don't get what we want. It is only when we internalize God's presence within us that we achieve an inner confidence which does not evaporate instantly in times of disappointment and pain.

How do we do this? By seeing God's involvement in every event and seeking his help in overcoming our negative impulses, we internalize a sense of Godliness in our consciousness.

Learning to trust in God's love for us and His desire to help us is especially difficult for those who were repeatedly betrayed and rejected as children, since these experiences teach children to protect themselves by being distant and untrusting. Thus, we must be patient with ourselves and respect our individual rate of growth as we struggle to build our trust in God and relate to Him differently than we related to our parents. Building faith is like building a home; the process takes time and disciplined action.

God did not split the Red Sea until Nachshon, son of Aminadav, walked into it up to his nose (*Sotah* 37). Our bad habits remain just as stubborn as ever until until we make a courageous muscular act to prove our willingness to change. This requires an understanding of the principle of *na'aseh v'nishma* (*Shemoth* 24:7). That is, first we do what God tells us from pure faith that it is the right thing, without any true comprehension of what we are doing or even any desire to do it. Only later do we appreciate the power of these commandments to heal and refine us. Thus, to liberate ourselves from our *Mitzrayim* mentality, we must often engage in acts which may not feel sincere or even rational at the time. Thus, for example, an anxiety-ridden person who decides to replace fear with love must go through precisely the same process as a dieter who gives up rich desserts in order to replace self-indulgence with true self-love.

> ◆ EXAMPLE: "I'm very sensitive and easily intimidated, especially by relatives and people in positions of authority. Well, I got myself involved in a program which wasn't for me. I didn't like the people or their outlook. It was making me physically and emotionally sick. Family members wanted me to continue, and I was afraid to confront the authorities and tell them I was leaving. The compulsive approval-seeking part of me would have suffered through until the end. But I decided to use this as an opportunity to confront my fear of disapproval. As scared as I was, I summoned my courage to talk to the people involved. I armed myself with the Broken Record tactic of repeating what I wanted in as few words as possible, without excuses or defenses. I said, 'The program isn't for me and I'm leaving.' Whenever they objected, I repeated, 'The program just isn't for me.' Then I left. What a victory!"

Faith is the only thing that can overcome the discouragement which keeps many people from making permanent changes in their lives. Faith means doing what is healthy even when we think, "It's too hard. I'm hopeless. Nothing helps." For those who have spent many years immersed in a destructive habit, it is important to realize that the battle for health may never be completely won. One is always "in recovery," i.e., one must always be ready to fight the despair or complacency which will pull one down again so quickly. With each positive act, the "sea" parts. A hundred times a day we can experience a "going out." And each one is a cause for rejoicing.

♦ EXAMPLE: "I was hit a lot as a child, so I always tend to be very nervous around people, as if they, too, are going to beat me up. My only protection was to distance myself from people by adopting a position of superiority or inferiority, thereby cutting myself off from real closeness with anyone. To change this habit, whenever I'm talking to someone, I keep saying over and over, 'Accept, don't judge.' I trust that if God gave us the commandment to love, then He gave me the strength to become a loving person."

♦ EXAMPLE: "I grew up believing that I had to be doing seventeen things at once, and all of them perfectly, in order to be considered worthy of respect. My fear of disapproval made me cringe with terror whenever there was a hint of rejection. I was like a marionette, jumping whenever someone pulled my strings. To overcome this habit, I had to keep reminding myself that I wasn't committing a terrible sin if I couldn't immediately please whoever made demands on me, and that I was no longer a helpless child who would be hit if I wasn't perfect. It was terrifying at first to just be myself. It felt strange to be real and human after so many years of feeling like a wooden doll. Now, it's enough to know that God loves me even if others didn't. Each time I overcome my impulse to please people out of fear, the sea parts and my heart sings!"

♦ EXAMPLE: "My oldest son was hit a lot as a child because I thought that that was the way to educate a child to be obedient. By the time he was ten, he was stealing and enjoyed hurting people. He didn't feel the slightest bit of shame or regret for all the pain he caused. Instead of saying he was sorry, he would deny what he'd done or say the person deserved to be hurt. My husband wouldn't do anything. He kept saying that it was all my fault and if I just ignored him, things would get better. Being a submissive person, I kept waiting for my husband to do something. I didn't want to face the consequences of acting on my own. But I felt I had to save the family. It was so hard for me to seek help, knowing my husband's opposition! Every phone call to a rabbi or a mental health agency took incredible courage. What helped me was trusting that if God gave me this trial, then He would help me overcome my passivity and despair and teach me to fight when fighting was called for."

Just as most back pain comes from not doing physical exercises and most digestive problems come from not eating correctly, most emotional pain is the result of not following the disciplines of the Torah. Once we practice these disciplines, the pain is reduced or even eliminated.

◆ EXAMPLE: "When I first started attending a spiritual support group, I was a victim of my own moods. They controlled me. I went to sleep depressed and awoke depressed. I had zero self-esteem. I thought my group leader, who seemed so calm and strong, was like that by nature. But she kept reminding the group that even after seventeen years of leading, she still had to be very disciplined and repeat certain positive thoughts from the moment she awakened in the morning in order to overcome her tendency toward depression. She said she had to continuously clear anxiety-producing thoughts from her mind just as she had to wash the dirt off her hands throughout the day. At first, I didn't want to do the work necessary to feel good. But stewing in self-pity certainly wasn't getting me anywhere! It helps to remember that my leader, who seems so together, doesn't have it easy either. I now trust that if I follow her example and become more loving yet disciplined, then I will eventually become self-respecting and happier. This hope motivates me to keep doing my spiritual disciplines even though I still often feel worthless and discouraged."

When we take our first halting steps toward emotional health, we feel alone and afraid. We're not sure what will happen if we give up our negative habits. It is only our fragile faith in an as yet unfulfilled promise of health in the future and the threat of death from behind that keep us from going backward to our particular personal *Mitzrayim*.

◆ EXAMPLE: "My mother was extremely critical of my father. As a child, I told myself that I would never do what she did. But I married someone I consider weak. And, guess what? I'm always criticizing him, just like my mother. You can't imagine how terrifying it is to even contemplate what would happen if I stopped being so critical and just accepted him as he is. I feel like I'll lose all my power to make him change and make him get us out of our financial rut. To me, to love someone who is defective means I'm defective and stupid, too. I want to change this pattern. Maybe I'll have to go out to work. The important thing is for me to learn to accept people as they are, including my middle son, who also is not the ambitious go-getter I would like. I want to become a person who can love people no matter what they are like."

Once we have indulged in any negative habit for any length of time, recovery from that habit requires lifelong vigilance. Yet it is through this on-going vigilance that we develop trust in ourselves and God.

Trust can only be tested in the midst of pain and temptation, when the outcome is uncertain. At first we are sceptical, wondering, How can these disciplines work? I've always been unassertive, anxious, depressed and critical! I can't change! If I become more loving, won't people take advantage of me? If I get strong, won't people be threatened and reject me? In the beginning, we don't know that on the other side of fear, despair and resentment is a promised land of love and joy. But it seems so distant. So we need a lot of courage to take those first steps.

Trust does not come easily. Much of the book of *Shemoth* is the story of the Jewish people's struggle to trust in God wholeheartedly despite their recurring fear of abandonment. Even after all the miracles which God performed for *Bnei Yisrael* — leading them out of Egypt, splitting the Red Sea, etc. — they had the audacity to ask:

> Is God in our midst or not?
>
> (SHEMOTH 17:7)

Immediately afterward, we find, "Then Amalek [which has the same *gematria* as "doubt," *safek*] came and fought with Israel" (Ibid. 17:7-8). Their doubts and fears blinded them to God's presence. We, too, will have such setbacks and plunge into darkness, wondering if we will ever gain control over our negative impulses,. We will feel out of touch with God, wondering if He really cares, if He was ever really there for us, and if we have any reason to hope. A part of us may even be curious to find out just how far we can fall!

It is precisely when we feel most hopeless and vulnerable to temptation that it is most important to act in a healthy manner and do our spiritual exercises, even if it feels mechanical or like a lie at the moment. In doing so, we find that our bond with God is suddenly renewed and strengthened.

> If a man consecrates himself in a small measure down below, he is
> sanctified much more from above.
>
> (YOMA 39a)

This is our motto and our reminder: Just one small act of faith or
love, and we are back on the path again.

> From [exile] you will seek the Lord your God, if you search for
> Him with all your heart and with all your soul. In your
> distress…you will return to the Lord your God and hearken unto
> His voice, for a merciful God is the Lord your God; He will not
> fail you…
>
> (DEVARIM 4:29-31)

This is the promise that sustains us and gives us hope.

An act of will: to believe even in the midst of doubt

> God said, 'I will bring you up out of the affliction of Egypt
> unto…a land flowing with milk and honey.'
>
> (SHEMOTH 3:17)

This tells the praise of Israel, for they did not say,

> "How shall we go out into the wilderness without food?" But they
> believed and they went.
>
> (SHEMOTH 12:39, Rashi)

The journey to emotional health begins with much doubt and
hesitation. We try to convince ourselves that we will improve, but
deep in our hearts, we are likely to think, "I'm so messed up. Nothing
will help me get well. I don't have the strength to discipline myself."
We try to convince ourselves that God is with us, but deep within we
feel alone and scared.

We start off like Moshe, feeling awkward and inadequate to the
task before us. As great as Moshe was, he balked at accepting the
mission which God had given to him, saying, "Who am I that I
should go to Pharaoh and that I should bring forth the children of
Israel out of Egypt?" And God said, "Certainly I will be with you"
(*Shemoth* 3:11-12).

Still Moshe protested that he could not possibly take on the job of
leader because "I am of uncircumcised lips" (*Shemoth* 6:12). We, too,
think we are too weak and handicapped to ever become
self-disciplined and self-respecting. At first, the idea that we have

infinite Godly worth is nothing more than a nice theory. But it is meaningless to us. In the beginning, many of the truths of Torah seem like lies. It takes constant repetition for them to become real.

◆ EXAMPLE: "I was stuck in traffic and began fuming silently to myself. Then I started repeating my faith-inducing phrase, which is 'God, You're the Boss. If You want it to be like this, then I will it to be this way, too.' At first, I didn't mean it. But I kept repeating the words until I relaxed and was able to think of how I could make the best of the situation, like doing isometric exercises or reading from my book of *Tehillim*. I use easy situations like spilled juice and traffic jams to build trust so that I can work up to harder ones."

◆ EXAMPLE: "Very few people showed up for a function I had spent a lot of time planning. Ordinarily, my self-esteem would have been crushed and I probably would have given up the idea of ever doing a community project again. But I kept telling myself to be thankful for the opportunity to learn from my mistakes. Obviously, I didn't really feel thankful at first, but the more I repeated the words, the more forgiving I felt. That's when I knew that the lie had become truth."

◆ EXAMPLE: "I had a big fight with my husband and was very depressed. I felt like I just wanted to die. Nevertheless, I went around for a whole day repeating the phrase that I had faith that God would help me out of this darkness and that I would grow stronger. It was a lie at first, but by the end of the day, I felt hopeful again about my ability to cope."

We have been promised that if we sincerely desire to change, God will be there to help us.

The Lord is close to all who call upon Him.

(TEHILLIM 145:18)

But we don't know this is true until we try with all our hearts and all our souls.

An act of will: to accept the rightness of God's will

During the course of their journey, God tested *Bnei Yisrael* in various ways. We, too, need to be tested so that our strengths and weaknesses can be revealed to us and allow us to see where we need to work. This attitude allows us to see the good in all that God does.

And it is this " '...sense of rightness' [which is] identical with faith" (*Strive for Truth!* vol. 2, p. 221).

♦ EXAMPLE: "My oldest daughter is very bossy and we were always getting into fierce struggles. Yesterday, she started screaming at me. I wanted to scream back and slap her for being so insolent. With the utmost of self-control, I looked her in the eyes and said, 'Beneath your anger is pain. You don't have to get angry to get me to listen. Just look me in the eyes and tell me what you want.' Like magic, she calmed down. I realized that by not wanting to control or change her, I was able to act rationally and hear what she had to say. In those moments, I saw clearly that God gives me these painful events so that I have an opportunity to practice loving people as they are. If I can really love her as she is, I will not only calm down, I know I'll feel more loving toward myself and God, too."

When we are small, we want total control over our entire universe. Maturity means realizing that all we can ever control is our own mind and muscles, and even that is difficult! Whenever we try to control that which is beyond our control, we become tense and feel even more out-of-control. But we can recognize this tension, which often manifests itself in anger and anxiety, as a sign that we are over-stepping our boundaries. On the other hand, it is irresponsible to avoid taking control where we should. We cannot always know when to take charge and when to let go and surrender control. By repeating the words, "I accept Your will as perfect," we remind ourselves of our limitations and calm down. Then we see more clearly what can or cannot be controlled in each particular situation.

♦ EXAMPLE: "I wanted to force my children to live up to my image of perfection and felt terribly ashamed when they didn't, which caused me always to be angry and irritable around them. I had the same problem with myself, cringing in shame whenever certain fastidious relatives walked into my home and saw that I'm not perfectly organized. Then I realized that not accepting people as they are is like not accepting that Hashem's will is perfect. There is a perfection in who we are at this very moment. Acceptance creates a positive atmosphere in which I can guide my children assertively without hostility."

When we stop being angry at God for bringing certain events and people into our lives and stop thinking about how awful and unfair these situations are, we can view them as the spiritual challenges which they really are.

◆ EXAMPLE: "Since I am such a sensitive, easily hurt person, with low self-esteem, it seemed terribly cruel for God to have surrounded me with such critical people all my life. But then I decided to thank Him for these people. Sure, it was insincere at first, but then I suddenly became aware that it really is perfect. All my life, I've looked to others for my sense of self-worth. Now I've learned to use every rejection and every critical remark to reaffirm that my value is independent of other people's judgments. Rejection forced me to turn to God as my only source of comfort in my isolation and to discover that He alone gives me value."

Whenever we get tense, we might remind ourselves, "Ooops, there I go, trying to control the universe again!"

◆ EXAMPLE: "My married daughter is a very different personality type from myself. She dresses differently, has a stricter religious outlook and different views on child rearing. Whenever I thought about these differences, I felt depressed, because I felt we could never be close. That, of course, only made our relationship more tense. Then I realized that I wanted to make her into a carbon copy of myself to satisfy my own need for closeness. As soon as I stopped seeing her as wrong for being different, I relaxed and felt more loving toward her. Having a child like this is perfect: it is the only way I could learn how to love unconditionally. Now I have to wait patiently until she becomes more tolerant of me!"

◆ EXAMPLE: "We had huge debts and my husband had no desire to work. I had to go out to work, which was terribly painful because it meant leaving the children for long hours and being overwhelmed with chores when I came home. I work on acceptance, day in and day out. I am developing inner strengths which I would never have known about if I did not have to work. I accept the situation as perfect, because it is His will, even if I don't like it on a personal level."

◆ EXAMPLE: "I came home and saw that, again, my son hadn't done his homework. I was about to explode. But at that moment, I asked for God's help to stop crushing this child with criticism and to help me overcome my habit of always using anger to get what I want. In his case, I want to use my sheer force of will to turn him into a *talmid chacham.* As soon as I accepted the perfection of having this child in my life, I was able to control myself. He must have felt my new attitude of acceptance, because he suddenly became much more cooperative and was willing to learn with me."

An act of will: to be demanding, yet nurturing

In bringing *Bnei Yisrael* out of Egypt, God used a combination of *chesed* (unlimited giving) along with *gevurah* (restraint). Both *chesed* and *gevurah* must be rooted in love, or we will not find the right balance. Without balance, we become too rigid and ungiving or too flexible and generous, too distant or too clingy, too aggressive or too passive. We must be "spiritual orthodontists." Too much pressure destroys, while too little means no change will take place.

> Be of the disciples of Aaron, loving peace and pursuing peace, loving your fellow creatures and bringing them near to Torah.
>
> (PIRKEI AVOTH 1:12)

◆ EXAMPLE: "I hated the thought of going to a marriage counselor. To me, this was a sign of weakness and failure. Despite tremendous inner resistance, I made a decision to go for two sessions just to please my wife. At first, it was torture to sit there. Inwardly, I scoffed at the whole thing. I kept thinking that I was the together one and that it was my wife who needed help. It took weeks for me to admit that I have a lot to work on, particularly my use of anger to control people. I was hardly acting like a disciple of Aaron!"

◆ EXAMPLE: "For years, I felt a lot of tension about food, including my own abuse of food and forcing my children to finish everything on their plates even if it caused a huge fight. One day, when I was fighting with one of my children about some food issue, I suddenly realized that I was thinking, If you love me, you'll love my food, and if you don't, it means you don't love me. It hit me that I was so anxious because I was equating food with love. I quickly realized that that was a childhood belief to be discarded. With a little work, I found healthier ways to give and receive love."

◆ EXAMPLE: "My parents have never accepted my return to religion, and often make disparaging remarks about the number of children we have and the fact that I study full-time. My initial response to their criticism was to attack back or be cold and shut them out of my life. But I knew that the more correct Torah response would be to act compassionately toward them. So the next time they said something, I focused on how scared they are of losing me, and how they probably connect love with total agreement. I stand up for my right to lead a Torah way of life, but my words come from love, whereas before, they came from fear and hostility."

An act of will: to make firm decisions and act on them

And I know that the king of Egypt will not give you leave to go except by a mighty hand.

(SHEMOTH 3:19)

With a strong hand has the Lord brought you out of Egypt.

(SHEMOTH 13:9)

God had to pull the Israelites out of Egypt forcefully. The same is true with us and our bad habits. Part of us wants to change, but then, like Pharoah, our hearts harden and we change our minds again whenever the pressure for change is off. We don't want to surrender control, however illusory it may be, and make God's will our will. We want to retain our sense of power, even if it is the power to destroy.

Thus, it is natural to experience resistance to new behavior, especially when it involves facing our deepest fears of failure or abandonment. That's when doing His will on pure faith brings the greatest rewards. To overcome our initial inertia, we must go against what seems most natural until new, positive habits become as fixed and natural as the old ones.

Every stressful event is an opportunity to lose control and feel more hopeless and isolated, or build trust by demonstrating to oneself that one is capable of acting in a consistently loving and self-disciplined manner.

◆ EXAMPLE: "To break my screaming habit, I decided that I would not yell at the children for one hour a day, from four until five o'clock, no matter what they did. I figured that if I started with one hour, then gradually I could hold out for longer. It was terribly difficult at first, but now I am much more in control. Each night, before going to sleep, I visualize each child as being as precious as a *sefer Torah* and deserving of the same respect. I imagine them misbehaving and see myself speaking in a low but assertive voice or walking away until I get control of myself. These visualizations help greatly."

♦ EXAMPLE: "Being a very critical person almost destroyed my marriage. The turning point came when I finally took to heart the words of my rabbi, which I had never listened to before. He said that many marriages could be saved if the husband would do one thing: if, as he entered his home, he would say one positive thing to each person he encountered, no matter how the place looked or what was going on. He said, 'What good is it if you express your love to God when praying, but never put theory into practice with your own family members? If you can express love to God, you have the ability to express it to the people around you!' Despite my reluctance, I knew I had to try. The first few times I walked into the house, I actually felt a pain in my chest from the effort to say something nice to each person. I felt phony and mechanical, and they were suspicious. I wanted to give up right then, but I forced myself to continue. Gradually, this insincere act became a natural habit, and the atmosphere improved greatly. I have a motto: If you can't think of something positive, don't think! If you can't say something positive, don't say anything. It works!"

♦ EXAMPLE: "When I expressed concern about allowing my children to go on a mountain-climbing expedition at camp, the head counselor told me that nothing builds a child's self-respect like facing his fears and then grabbing the ropes and pulling himself up the mountain anyway. I realized that it's the same with us. God creates difficulties and then challenges us to climb out of them. It's for our good, so that we can build self-confidence by facing our fears and going on despite them."

An act of will: accepting God's help

God brought us out of Egypt.

(SHEMOTH 12:12)

The Lord will fight for you.

(SHEMOTH 14:14)

There are two myths about addictions which must be avoided. One is that if a person learns enough about why he is addicted, the addiction will disappear on its own. So, many people spend years gathering more and more insights and information about their childhood traumas and present day frustrations. Meanwhile, they remain just as negative and abusive. The reason is because insight is useless unless combined with healthy actions.

> Anyone whose wisdom exceeds his [good] deeds, to what can he be compared? To a tree whose branches are numerous but whose roots are few, and the wind comes and uproots it and turns it upside down... (AVOTH 3:17)

The other myth is that overcoming addictions is simply a matter of sheer willpower. This attitude causes people to grimly control themselves through stern self-restraint. But this doesn't work for long either, because the person secretly fears that he can't hold out much longer and is going to lose control as soon as things get stressful. And it always happens. Unhealthy passions cannot be willed away. They fade away on their own as one builds a loving relationship with his *neshamah* and God.

As long as a person feels like he is fighting against himself, he ends up going back to his old habits for relief from the inner tension which is generated by his efforts to control himself. In fact, the more a person feels that he is depriving himself of what he secretly longs for, the more likely it is that he will repeat the negative behavior. That is why many compulsive eaters actually *gain* weight when they go on diets and why many hot-tempered people find themselves screaming more instead of less when they try to control their tempers. Grim self-deprivation reinforces addictive behavior.

True, a person needs to develop both insight and strength of will in order to change. But even more, he needs to feel that he is going *toward* health, not just *away* from illness. It is not enough to merely control negative impulses or understand why they exist. Growth must come from love. Only love for God, man and self can overcome the sense of inferiority, isolation and inadequacy which produces addictions in the first place.

An addict will always slide back into his old habits unless he focuses on his real goal: to develop unconditional love for God, himself and his fellowman. As he thinks and behaves in a more loving manner, his bad habits fade away naturally, without excessive force. In a loving atmosphere, he does not have the tension of being at war with himself, of feeling, "What I really want is to binge, hit or explode, but I'll see how long I can hold out." Instead, he experiences that what he really wants is health, that he wants to love and be loved. In this atmosphere, the desire to hurt cannot survive.

Remember, *addictions, like all other painful events in life, are God's way of creating a longing for a relationship with Him.* If we don't long for health, we won't create a loving relationship with God. We have to experience that He is with us, helping us overcome our loneliness, rage, depression, anxiety, bitterness and jealousy. That is why He gave us our particular problems in the first place. He wants us to form a relationship with Him.

Therefore, we must use every stressful event as an opportunity to program our minds with positive affirmations:

"I turn to God to help me control myself. With His help, I can bear the temporary discomfort of not giving in to my negative impulses."

"Every act of self-discipline increases self-respect."

"I am not a bad person for having harmful impulses. I only need to feel ashamed for giving in to them."

"I may be powerless over many aspects of my life, but I can always control my thoughts, speech and deeds."

"An insincere, forced gesture of love and joy is better than a sincere gesture of hate and despair."

Every stressful event is an opportunity to heal ourselves by acting differently than we have acted in the past. When painful memories arise, we can use that pain constructively, by reminding ourselves not to do or think anything which would make us, or anyone else, feel unlovable and incapable.

An act of will: to build love and trust

A person must "devote one's heart and mind to matters which stimulate love."   (LIKUTEI AMARIM, "Shaar Hayichud," p. 76)

A beautiful parable by the Hafetz Hayyim (*The Stories and Parables of the Hafetz Hayyim*, pp. 20-24) tells of a wealthy gem trader who took a long trip to another country to do business. After spending all his money, he was unexpectedly offered a fabulous collection of jewels for a ridiculously small price. But it meant giving up the money he had reserved for his return first-class ticket. He couldn't resist the deal, even though it meant traveling home in tremendous discomfort in the lowest class quarters. When an old friend spied him sleeping on a hard bench among the beggars, he was shocked and asked him if he had lost his money. After the jeweler told him the story, his friend asked him how he could bear being there in all that squalor and filth, to which the merchant replied that whenever he felt that his spirit was breaking, he would take out the fabulous jewels and, feasting his eyes on them, realize that, although he looked like a poor beggar, he was really a fabulous millionaire.

The Hafetz Hayyim states that we are all like that traveling merchant. When we feel like poor beggars, when our spirits are about to break, we need to take out the precious gems of Torah and mitzvoth and remember who we really are and where we are going.

Those of us who have been blessed with the awareness that we are on a spiritual journey will meet many disappointments along the way. How will we react to these situations? Will we reach for an addictive substance or mood, or will we devote ourselves to thoughts and actions which stimulate love for God and man? Hopefully, this book will help us remember our choices.

It is only human to falter and backslide in our quest to build love and trust. That is precisely when we need the fellowship of those who can teach us how to attain these goals. Spiritual support groups exist to provide training in developing unconditional love for others and to offer the opportunity to heal ourselves by helping others develop the traits which bring about emotional health. This is discussed in depth in the following chapter.

CHAPTER 5:
The Importance of a Spiritual Support Group

Two are better than one ... for should they fall, one can raise the other; but woe to him who is alone when he falls and there is no one to raise him.

(KOHELETH 4:9-10)

Spiritual growth is like climbing a mountain — except that this mountain has no top, only a succession of endless peaks and valleys. And because spiritual growth is about learning to love, we need the fellowship of others so that we can practice on them. This is especially true in the beginning, when our lack of trust can only be overcome in an environment of unconditional love.

When a person first attempts to change old habits, there may be a feeling of dread and pain each time he forces himself to use the spiritual exercises which are so new to him. While individual determination is the main factor, a support group keeps a person's momentum going and helps him through those inevitable times of inertia and despair.

Being with people who are diligently working to become honest, self-disciplined and loving encourages others to do the same. Also, once a person commits himself to going to a specific class at a specific time each week, he is far more likely to persist at it, if only from force of habit. This is just what is needed when he hits a plateau or a setback. In addition, once he discovers that he is not the only one with these problems, he feels normal and the problems seem more manageable. Finally, the good humor and love generated in a nurturing group help an individual see his problems as manageable and himself as capable of coping with them.

Hope and enthusiasm can be as contagious as gloom and hostility. A person cannot help but be influenced when he is in the presence of others who are talking excitedly about their spiritual growth. The resulting subtle development in his character is similar to what happens when a non-Observant Jew decides to follow a Torah way of life. Even if the initial spark is there, it is extremely difficult for him to nurture it properly in isolation. Only when he attaches himself to a community of Torah-observant Jews is he assured of receiving the positive input which will enable his growth to continue.

Basic rules for a spiritual support group

E.M.E.T.T. support groups offer the nurturing environment and spiritual disciplines which have helped many people to overcome their negative habits. The groups' basic rules are as follows:

(1) All attitudes expressed are in keeping with Torah ideals.

(2) No *lashon ha-ra* is allowed.

(3) The meeting follows a set structure which helps members use stressful events as opportunities to improve their *middoth* and experience God's love for us.

(4) Leaders are equal members of the group who share their own struggles to overcome their negative habit patterns. No one is in a position of inferiority or superiority. The leader's main task is simply to maintain group discipline and structure.

(5) The atmosphere is nurturing and noncondemnatory, so that members can feel free to share their deepest feelings without fear of being invalidated or shamed. Unless *halachah* is involved, no judgments are made about a person's experiences.

Changing attitude is not enough

Change in attitude means little unless it is accompanied by concrete changes in behavior. If a person has spent a lifetime thinking, "I'm unlovable and incapable," it will not be enough for him to keep repeating, "I'm worthwhile." He must also do things which make him feel self-respecting and know that it is all right to feel that way. Likewise, it is not enough for an anxious person to tell himself, "Calm down!" In fact, such an order may make him more nervous. Instead, he must challenge his feeling of danger with secure thoughts and combine this with calming physical actions, such as consciously relaxing the muscles in his neck and shoulders, or turn the anxiety-provoking situation into one which will provide an opportunity for growth.

Surprisingly, one does not have to be sincere in order to carry out these nurturing acts. In fact, we are told,

A man is influenced by his actions.

(SEFER HACHINUCH no. 16)

In other words, it is one's positive actions which produce a healthy change in attitude, even when one's thinking has not been positive in the first place.

A support group is one of the best places to begin practicing new behaviors because the members are supportive, patient and noncondemnatory. Members praise each other for their courage and self-discipline, knowing that a lasting healthy attitude will eventually be established if members continue to attend meetings and follow the spiritual disciplines which are taught.

Batya, for example, had grown up with the phrase "You can't do *anything* right" ringing in her ears. As an adult, she automatically assumed that people looked down on her and constantly replayed that old childhood message in her own mind: "You're incompetent and a failure." As a result, she was often angry or depressed.

At first, Batya had difficulty believing that the group members liked her. She also had to get used to the idea that she could choose to respond nondefensively to the things people said. To help her do so, group members pretended to be various people in her life. For example, one played the principal and said, "I want you to make up a new schedule for your students." Another played a child and said, "Mom, I don't like how this tastes." Another played her husband and said, "How come you didn't get my suit from the cleaners?" Although she initially felt threatened by their statements and wanted to counterattack, she practiced responding with such phrases as,

"Thank you for the information. I'll do the best I can."

"Do you want something different to eat?"

"I'm sorry. I'll do it tomorrow."

Little by little, Batya's insincere mask of neutrality and calm became a sincere one, and she found herself responding to people in a kinder tone of voice.

Putting Torah disciplines into practice is difficult, especially for those from nonnurturing backgrounds, which includes most people. In the beginning, one must make forced gestures, acting as if one is calm, confident, sane or loving. In time, these fragile hopes become firm convictions.

Learning to care

Like Batya, many people never learn how to relate to others in a mutually respectful, nondefensive manner. They were so used to being screamed at, ridiculed or ignored when they expressed their feelings that they either stopped trying altogether or alienated people with their excessive demands. As a result, they caused great damage in their relationships.

David, for example, came to group only at the insistence of his wife, who threatened to leave him if he did not develop some degree of concern for other people. Brought up in a wealthy home, his parents gave him everything money could buy — except love. While his parents were off pursuing their respective careers, David was taken care of by a succession of indifferent housekeepers. As a result, he never learned to connect to people. As an adult, he was completely preoccupied with his own needs and accomplishments while oblivious to others. He was emotionally paralyzed, except for his outburts of anger when he did not get his way.

When David first came to the group, he felt bored and showed his lack of interest by yawning frequently and fidgeting impatiently. The other members accepted him as he was, without condemning him for his air of superiority and disinterest.

Yet slowly, almost without realizing it, David began to feel concern for the other men in his group. He found himself waiting for the next session to discover how Aaron was progressing in his attempt to control his anger, or how Shlomo was getting along with a difficult boss, and how Chaim was coping with his wife's illness, etc. He saw people sharing and caring, and he began to do the same. His genuine interest in the members of his group slowly extended itself to include his family members as well.

Suri had the opposite problem. She alienated people with her overbearing attempts to control them. She was a "fixer," forever telling her friends and family members how they should think, eat, dress, spend their money and run their lives. She thought she was well-meaning, but others felt pressured by her and either avoided her, counterattacked, or fell silent in her presence. In group, the leader often had to firmly ask her to restrain her urge to tell everyone what to do and to make light of their difficulties. It took many sessions for her to realize that people improve spontaneously in a nonjudgmental atmosphere, without her pushing their growth. Little by little, she developed patience for the process of growth in others as well as herself. In group, she practiced saying the phrases she needed to use with her family members, such as:

> *"I don't want to tell you what to do. I have faith that you can work it out on your own."*
>
> *"If you want, we can work on this together and figure out some solution."*
>
> *"I love you and I'm happy with you as you are."*

Her family members delightedly noted that she was becoming less critical and overbearing.

Tova's parents had a stormy marriage and divorced when she was a baby. Her mother was a cold, unhappy woman who was always complaining bitterly about her lot in life. Tova became a compulsive approval-seeker, anxiously concerned about making others happy. But no matter how hard she tried, Tova felt like an unwanted burden and a reject who never belonged. When she married, she was certain that her husband felt the same way about her. And because he, too, was rather cold and critical, she was sure that she was right. She tried to be uncomplaining and happy, but inside she felt terribly alone and unloved. Because she didn't want to appear bitter and demanding like her mother, she never asked her husband for help, even when she felt overwhelmed or sick. Nor did she tell him directly how much she needed him to express his love and to have more pleasurable activities in her life. Instead, every once in a while, she would suddenly lose control and scream hysterically at her husband or children, accusing them of being selfish and not caring about her. Afterwards, she would feel terribly ashamed and depressed and would redouble her desperate efforts to please them.

Because Tova had never experienced a genuinely caring relationship, the group leader suggested that she work with a nurturing private therapist as well as come to the group. This proved to be a successful combination. In private therapy, she got the personal attention she craved, while the group provided the feeling of family and the sense of averageness which she also needed. In group, she practiced assertively asking for help and expressing her feelings by having members play the part of her husband and children:

> *"I would like you to come to the doctor with me tomorrow."*
>
> *"I want you to reassure me that you care about me."*
>
> *"I don't like being talked to that way. Let's make an agreement: you don't shame me and I won't shame you."*
>
> *"Maybe some women do not need a deep connection with their husbands. But I do. Maybe some people can take criticism. But I can't. That doesn't make me bad or immature. I need people around me who are loving and supportive. And I want us to learn how to be more caring toward each other."*

In the safety of a group, one can practice saying the things one has always feared to say, in order to break out of destructive patterns. This gives him courage to do the same outside of group. Furthermore, when other members have the opportunity to help those in distress, they build self-confidence and reinforce their own new-found insights.

Averageness: learning what is normal

One of the most destructive beliefs which many people harbor is the secret fear that they are abnormal. This leads them to feel that they must put on a performance for others and distance themselves from meaningful contact in order not to let anyone see how defective they really are. The isolation and fear then lead to even more abnormal behavior.

In order to reverse this pattern, it is essential for one to see oneself as an average human being. We cannot experience this as true unless we reveal our fears to others who let us know, "Oh, we all feel that way at times! Relax. We'll teach you the skills to help you deal with your fears."

To humbly accept oneself as imperfect, yet still strive continuously for moral perfection, is the goal of the philosophy of averageness.

An understanding of the concept of averageness is an essential step in the self-healing process, because it encourages us to be honest about who we are and accept ourselves as we are. We are neither complete saints nor hopeless sinners, neither the best nor the worst, neither completely crazy nor completely sane at all times. By striving to be within the normal range of humanity, we achieve inner balance. It is then that we will intuitively raise our standards in those areas where we have been lazy and lax, and lower our standards in those areas where we have tortured ourselves with impossibly high expectations.

For those who have spent a lifetime feeling exceptionally stupid, bad or wrong, it is an enormous relief to realize that they are not failures if they have only average abilities, for that is how, by definition, the majority of mankind is. Many people think that if they are not the most outstanding parents, workers or spouses, then they must be the worst, and they behave according to that negative self-judgment.

By accepting that we are still deserving of love and respect even though we are average, the inner tension produced by the fear of disapproval is reduced and we become more loving toward others and happier with our lives. Our energy is then freed for growth. In this atmosphere of acceptance, people strive for excellence naturally, but they do so in a healthy way, taking into consideration the realities and pressures of the particular moment, without the terrible inner tension and fear of failure which have, in the past, paralyzed us into inactivity or made us take on more than we could handle.

To think of ourselves as average is to be honest with ourselves. That is what we are! It is in striving to be different from the rest of humanity that we isolate ourselves with feelings of inferiority or superiority.

No book, lecture or private therapy session can make people aware of their averageness the way a group can, or provide the humor and relief which comes from this awareness. When an entire roomful of people raise their hands in reply to the query, "Who has ever felt the same as X?" Then X can only think, "Wow, others feel the same way I do. I'm not so bad (or crazy) after all! I'm not so alone!" The joy and relief are visible to all.

It is only when we respect ourselves with all of our imperfections that we are then freed to work on our spiritual and emotional development without self-torture or haughty contempt of others. Thus, it is this difficult-to-grasp concept of averageness which becomes the cornerstone for building self-acceptance and emotional health.

The power of self-revelation

One *derash* on the word Pesach, the holiday which celebrates our freedom from bondage, is that it is composed of two words: *peh*, meaning "mouth," and *sach*, meaning "to speak or discuss." In keeping with this theme, it is interesting to note that when *Bnei Yisrael* left Egypt, they passed by the city they had built which was called Pitom, which can mean a "closed mouth." The name of that city was then changed to *Pi ha' chiroth*, meaning "the mouth of freedom" (*Shemoth* 14:2). It was there, Rashi states, that they became "free men."

Bad habits are rooted in fear — fear of the unknown, fear of shame, punishment, failure and invalidation, fear of losing one's freedom and pleasures, fear of being controlled by others or discounted by them, fear of physical or emotional pain, fear of losing control or approval, fear of rejection and abandonment.

Supressed feelings don't die. They fester inside of us, causing damage to ourselves and our relationships. These same feelings fade when we talk about them openly and learn to trust that there are people who can listen to us with sympathy and understanding. Honesty creates trust. Trust makes it safe to care. When we talk about our shortcomings in a nonjudgmental group, and see that others care about us anyway, we feel less alone and our problems seem less overwhelming.

Perhaps this benefit was the reason for the Rambam's instructions for the penitent, in which he states that:

> It is highly praiseworthy in a penitent to make *public* confession, openly avow his transgressions and reveal to others his sins against his fellowmen. (HILCHOTH TESHUVAH 2:5)

Modern scientific research has "discovered" what our Sages may have had in mind long ago. Over fifty years of research on self-help groups has found that confession in group is one of the essential steps to recovery. It intensifies the person's resolve to change and helps him to forgive himself by seeing others forgive him.

The book of *Vayikra* discusses the importance of bringing public sacrifices and obtaining forgiveness. Everyone — from the High Priest to the common man — brought sin-offerings.

> There is no man so wholly righteous on earth that he will always do good and will never sin.
>
> (KOHELETH 7:20)

This verse seems to indicate that no one has it all together. Human perfection is an illusion and an impossibility.

To heal ourselves, we have to talk — not about impersonal matters like recipes, the weather and current events — but about who we are and what we feel, about our fears and doubts, and why we have difficulty being loving and self-disciplined. It is only by revealing ourselves to others that we can see ourselves more objectively. There is a powerful benefit to be gained from sharing worrisome thoughts and beliefs, because then we have the opportunity to examine them honestly, differentiating between those which are helpful to our growth and those which are not.

Change requires the courage to be emotionally honest. This can only happen in a safe environment, with people who know how to listen empathetically and without condemnations or demands. Unfortunately, this is rare. That is why most people learn early in life to lie about their feelings in order to win approval and avoid the shaming grimaces, patronizing advice, invalidations, put-downs or pat answers such as: "You're a bad person for feeling like that," "You're nothing but an ungrateful *kvetch*," or, "Don't take things so seriously."

It's safe to talk about the weather and recipes — nothing of our inner world is revealed, so we don't have to worry about being rejected or shamed. However, if we never reveal who we are, we can never experience being really cared about. And it is being cared about and helping others feel cared about that facilitates growth.

The power of acceptance

> You punished me, and I was afflicted, as an untrained calf
> [unaccustomed to the yoke]; turn me back, and I will be turned...
> Return me, and I will return...For after I returned, I regretted
> and...I was ashamed.
>
> (YIRMEYAHU 31:18-19)

Shame is an integral and necessary part of repentence. However, excessive shame about deeply ingrained habits can actually inhibit change. Sometimes a person must first experience his power to act differently, and only then will he be able to look back and feel ashamed without being paralyzed by self-hatred.

In other words, a person must first put forth the effort to change and see that change is possible. Only then will he have the confidence to face the truth, to take stock of the damage he has done and apologize to those he has hurt. It is only after he has become accustomed to the "yoke" of Torah disciplines that he can see how beneficial they are and can appreciate what a struggle it was to overcome his resistance to them.

The concept of change is exhilarating and also frightening, for although we want to improve, we also have an equally powerful urge to maintain our inner stability and identity by not changing! This means that we must take small steps which do not threaten our precarious sense of emotional well-being. After all, the survival skills which we adopted as children to protect ourselves from pain must be acknowledged and respected for the good that they did, even if they also caused much harm. We can't give them up until we have created a repertoire of new skills with which to face life's endless succession of challenging experiences.

The desire to progress quickly, while admirable, can actually block progress if we end up feeling discouraged by the enormity of the task and ashamed of our inability to do better faster. The initial stages of growth are like the initial stages of learning an instrument. A person who has taken two piano lessons and feels ashamed because he cannot play as well as his favorite concert pianist, will be too discouraged to continue. In order to avoid discouragement, a person must enjoy and appreciate his tiniest evidences of progress in the seemingly most insignificant events and not feel ashamed over the fact that he is not at a higher level. This is why the easily-understood phrases used in EMETT groups as well as the group humor and warmth are so effective and important.

Breaking out of the negative feedback loop

We have all experienced the effects of positive and negative feedback loops. For example, we know that if a child is weak in a certain area and we praise her for doing well and show genuine happiness with her as she is, she will usually improve. The more she improves, the more positively she feels about herself and we feel about her. The opposite also holds true. When we are anxious, unhappy and critical of the child, she usually persists even more in doing the very things which annoy us.

Or, take the case of the average hospital intern who feels insecure about his skills, yet knows that he must act calm and confident in order to perform his job effectively. The patients, in turn, usually respond to him according to the image he projects, which then builds his confidence in actuality. The reverse is true of someone who has just lost his job and feels helpless and worthless. He projects an image of despair, walking and talking like a reject and a failure, which causes prospective employers to shun him, thereby reinforcing his negative self-image.

Such feedback loops, in which behavior is reinforced by the outside world, which then leads the person to believe that what he thought of himself was really true, can get rolling without the person even realizing it. This is why it is so essential to avoid negative judgments of ourselves and others.

The most important opinion we ever form is the one we have about ourselves. It determines what we accomplish in life and how we relate to both God and man. Breaking negative self-images is one of the foremost purposes of the support group.

◆ EXAMPLE: "Whenever I was deprived of sleep, which was often because I have four small children, I felt so hostile and out-of-control. For a long time, I believed that the hysterical person who emerged when I was tired was the real me. That made me really anxious and even less able to cope, which also made the children nervous. So they became more demanding, which made me feel even more inadequate.

This vicious cycle kept getting worse and worse until I joined a support group. There I learned that all the other mothers got these symptoms when deprived of sleep. One woman told me to keep telling myself, 'I'm not crazy, I'm just sleep-deprived.' Another said she endorsed herself for whatever she managed to do under those difficult circumstances. These thoughts helped me stay in control. When I'm in control, I have self-esteem, which helps me stay calmer with the children and makes them happier, too!"

♦ EXAMPLE: "I am not a demonstrative person, and my wife was always accusing me of being cold and uncaring. I began to believe her and withdrew even more. When I talked about the problem in my group, one man said, 'You're not uncaring. It's just hard for you to express your feelings. If you were not caring, you wouldn't be here! We think you are a caring person.' That session created a change in my mind. I saw myself as an essentially caring person who lacked communication skills and was a little inhibited. I began to point out to my wife all the ways that I do show my love for her. That sparked a change in her image of me, and she became less hostile. As she became less hostile, I was able to be more demonstrative toward her."

Accepting ourselves

To experience what it feels like to be aware of our shortcomings yet, at the same time, to be accepting of ourselves, try the following exercise.

Take a picture of yourself from your early childhood and say the following:

"I love you just the way you are. I know you have faults. I know you are imperfect. But I love you anyway. You are a basically good person. I trust you and respect you. I am happy to have you around. I know you want to do the best you can in life. Your choices are determined by what you believe will protect you from pain and bring you the greatest comfort. You will make many mistakes in the future. That's okay. No one is perfect. You can trust me; I'll be here for you. I'll always love you and accept you no matter what. I want to be with you on this spiritual journey. I'll celebrate your successes and encourage you when things are rough. I don't want anything from you. I just want to be here for you."

This is the voice of the nurturing, Godly part of you. You need to hear it often. But this voice may not sound like the real you at first, since few people have ever experienced such unconditional love.

Acceptance does not mean smug complacency. It does not mean that we approve of or condone our negative traits or actions. It simply means that we accept who we are at this point in our lives and acknowledge that we are not on the spiritual level that we would like to be, without being contemptuous of ourselves in our entirety.

I'm not perfect. You're not perfect. And that's perfect. God did not create us perfect, so that we could experience being His partner in the creative process of self-refinement. We *need* to be imperfect in order to experience our ability to grow.

Members of EMETT groups are constantly amazed to discover that in changing deeply-ingrained habit patterns, acceptance precedes growth.

◆ EXAMPLE: "I was always terribly ashamed of my very intense emotional responses. I assumed that this meant I was not normal. The feeling of abnormalcy made me feel hopeless about getting any sense of control over my life. So, of course, I began to live up to that image of myself. But then, in group, I met other people with the same problem who had learned to be emotionally detached and objective. Once I realized how average I was, I calmed down because I didn't feel so exceptional anymore. I began to notice the times when I am not hysterical and when I do manage to get things fairly organized. I see myself as having a minor, God-given handicap, and that I'm not wrong or crazy for being like this. Now that I see myself as average, I have much better control over my reactions."

◆ EXAMPLE: "I was always ashamed of my desire for material things, like good jewelry and nice clothes. And my husband felt ashamed of his desire for a job with a lot of status. We both believed that these desires meant we were low-level and unspiritual. But then, in our respective support groups, we heard others expressing the same desires. Somehow, just talking about the *yetzer ha-ra* for status and material things, and knowing how common this struggle is, helped us to relax and not think we were such terrible people. Plus, bringing these secret desires into the open made them seem less overwhelmingly compelling for some reason. I saw that others could manage and that meant that I could, too. I thought I was protecting myself by lying to everyone. It's amazing how much better I feel when I am honest with people who can understand."

◆ EXAMPLE: "I have one child whose personality I disliked greatly. I felt terribly guilty for feeling this way, which led me to be even more cold and distant toward her. Somehow, expressing my anger in group made me less angry with her. That really surprised me. By accepting myself for what I am, I found it much easier to accept her for what she is. As I stopped trying to make her wrong for being who she is, our relationship improved greatly."

Being sane means being balanced

The Rambam characterizes a mentally healthy person as one who aims for the "happy medium" in each category of character traits. He states that human beings are characterized by numerous physical, emotional and intellectual dispositions, any of which can pull him to an extreme if he lets them get out of hand (*Hilchoth Deoth* 1:4). For example, it is normal to have a tendency to be either hot-tempered or dispassionate, aggressive or timid, meticulous about details or careless about them, stingy or generous, melancholic or light-hearted.

We needn't feel ashamed of these natural predispositions or try to uproot them completely, for that is impossible. But we do have an obligation to stay balanced by also strengthening the opposite tendency. Thus, the melancholy person can make a special effort to work on *simchah* (joy), the overly emotional person can work on detachment and objectivity, while the timid person can welcome opportunities to practice assertiveness.

However, we cannot balance these tendences until we first acknowledge that they exist. It is often necessary for other people to point them out to us, either privately or in a group.

◆ EXAMPLE: "I thought I was just being thrifty until my learning partner made me realize that I was actually very stingy. He kept asking if I ever gave my wife gifts or bought her something new for the holidays, and I kept saying 'no.' Once I stopped rationalizing my behavior as commendable thriftiness, I had to accept that I had a problem and that I needed to work on being more giving."

◆ EXAMPLE: "I didn't even realize that I was being self-destructive by constantly calling myself weak, stupid, klutzy, disorganized, etc. I thought I was being humorous, humble and honest. But the group members pointed out that I was continuing the same abusive criticism I heard as a child. Recognizing this made me realize that it was time to stop the self-torture."

◆ EXAMPLE: "I didn't think of myself as irresponsible. I thought I was just an easy-going person and that that's why I procrastinated so much and never bothered to keep the house in order. It was only in group, hearing others give examples of how they were trying to become more responsible that I realized that I was deceiving myself. The truth was that I was lazy and hurting a lot of people by being this way. That's when I realized that I had to stop making excuses for myself. After hearing them, I realized that I could get my act together if I really wanted to, and now I want to!"

◆ EXAMPLE: "Until I came to group, I didn't realize that I was being abusive to my children in my attempts to make them obedient. I hit them a lot. I also thought it would make them more self-reliant if I didn't respond when they asked for my help. I refused to help them dress when they were small or help them with their homework as they got older. I punished them a lot because I thought this was the proper way to educate them. It was only in my support group, after listening to other mothers' examples, that I realized how harsh I was being and how important it was to express more love toward them. At first, it was terribly difficult to change my ways. I had to force myself to remember to compliment them for their helpfulness and to take time to listen to what happened in school that day. It took a lot of effort, but we now have a much better relationship."

The self-discipline/self-esteem connection

A spiritual army is no different from a physical one. In both, discipline is necessary for survival. It is also necessary for self-respect. Strength of character develops when we "do the difficult" and go against old habit patterns.

◆ EXAMPLE: "I always thought that being able to take criticism was a sign of maturity. But when we consulted the rabbi who is the spiritual advisor of our support group, he said that the obligation of *pikuach nefesh* [self-preservation] means that we must do everything in our power to keep people from hurting us. Here I was, accepting abuse and thinking I was being holy, when I should have been speaking up or distancing myself! That gave me the courage to insist that certain people talk to me respectfully if they wanted to have a relationship with me. I think that what enabled me to reach this stage of being able to bear the pain of rejection was knowing that I had the backing of a group of women whose love and understanding I could count on even if other people rejected me."

◆ EXAMPLE: "When I discovered that my car had been stolen, I went to pieces. I thought I was going to lose my mind. I was so angry at the injustice of life and so jealous of people who didn't have my lousy luck. I felt I had been squashed down into nothing. When I talked about the event in my group, people were so sympathetic. Members called me every day to see how I was doing and to offer help. In my entire life, I had never had such an experience of people being there for me, caring about me, reaching out to me. Perhaps their love gave me the incentive to use the event as an opportunity to practice accepting God's will, which is what I'd been practicing in my support group for so many months. Every time I had to ask someone for a ride or take a bus or deal with all the other ramifications of not having a car, I saw the choice of either stewing in bitterness over what seemed like a stupid, senseless, unjust event or trusting in God's mercy and wisdom in giving me what I need for my growth. It was an incredible experience to see so clearly what my choices were and to consciously and deliberately choose God. As hard as this has been for me, I have grown not only from experiencing people's love for me but also from discovering that I could deal with a very difficult event in a positive way."

Any discipline, whether physical or spiritual, if motivated by love, gives us a sense of control over our lives, which, in turn, builds a genuine feeling of self-worth.

The resistance check-list

Most people experience a certain degree of resistance to joining a support group. They may feel uncomfortable listening to such an abundance of supportive, encouraging language as is used in a group. Or, they may want to retain unhealthy patterns because they think that is the only means they have to get attention, feel special or gain control. They will probably come up with the following reasons not to join a support group:

"My problems are too big to be talked about in group."

"I hate those cliche phrases. They're so childish. They can't possibly help me with my problems."

"It's immodest to expose one's problems in public."

"I can't change, so why go?"

"It's my spouse who has to change, not me!"

"If it's free, it can't be effective."

"I can't be helped by people who don't have professional degrees. I need expert help."

"If I go, people will think I'm disturbed, and then I won't be able to marry off my children."

"There are dishes in the sink and a million other things to do. I'll get behind in my housework if I go."

"Someday someone will discover a drug and it will make me feel better. I'll wait until the miracle pill comes along."

"My husband/wife/kids need me at home."

"I don't like the people there."

"I don't really have the time. The meeting is too far away. It's boring."

The excuses are endless. But the truth remains that joining a growth group can be one of the most important ways to signify one's commitment to change.

Celebrating our progress

The spiritual journey is often a lonely one. Our small acts of courage and self-discipline usually pass unnoticed, even by ourselves. After all, who knows that we spoke softly when we felt like screaming or apologized to someone despite the embarrassment it caused us? Who knows that our outward smile is hiding our inner battle against anger or grief? Who knows the effort it took to do a favor for someone when we didn't really want to, to get out of bed this morning despite a feeling of lethargy, or to hold on to our sense of worth after hearing a critical remark?

> The smallest victory that you win [over the *yetzer ha-ra*] regard as significant, so that it will be a step to a greater victory.
>
> (DUTIES OF THE HEART, vol .II, p. 23)

Each time our small steps are celebrated, we feel encouraged to take more. The memory of those encouraging faces helps pull us through the next difficult episode.

◆ EXAMPLE: "One night last week, I couldn't fall sleep. I'd heard so many examples in my group about sleep problems that I knew what to do. Instead of panicking myself by attaching danger to my nervous symptoms, I read *Tehillim* and calmed myself down with secure thoughts. Maybe most people will think nothing of this, but for a high-strung person like me, it was a victory to think calming thoughts and to go on the next day, bearing the discomfort of my fatigue without grumbling to everyone about how tired I was. It was important to be able to share this with people who understood what this meant to me."

◆ EXAMPLE: "In the past, when one of my kids would balk about helping me, I would automatically think 'This is a *chutzpadik* brat. He doesn't respect me or love me. And it's all my fault because I'm a failure as a mother.' And I'd often yell or give a whack. Then, yesterday, when I asked one for help and he didn't want to, I avoided all condemnations and thought, 'Hm...I just have to find a solution.' So I handed him the kitchen timer and told him to put it on for as long as he wanted to help me. I guess that giving him some sense of control worked wonders. He set the timer for five minutes but then gladly gave me twenty. It was such a victory for me not to get angry if I don't get what I want and to avoid condemning myself or my children. When I shared this with the group, I was really glowing. They knew what a victory this was for me."

◆ EXAMPLE: "For most of my life, I'd been a kind of emotional beggar, always seeking love from everyone and then getting angry when they didn't put enough in my cup. So, when a particular relative came on like a Mack truck, my initial response was to fume inwardly but to submit to her demands because I couldn't bear anyone not liking me. But last week, when she called to complain again about my religious views, I politely used the Broken Record technique and kept repeating, 'My way works for me just like your way works for you. I'm confident that I can handle things on my own.' Then I said I had to go and hung up with a cheery 'Goodbye.' My group knows from past examples that I usually squirm with shame and fear when I sense disapproval. I can't bear for anyone to think I am stingy, selfish, petty or unspiritual and I usually bend over backwards to change that view of me. And here I stood up for myself even though I knew it meant that she may try to punish me with hostile silence for a few months. I no longer try to control other people's opinions of me. For an easily intimidated person like myself, this is a big victory."

◆ EXAMPLE: "I wanted to withdraw in silence and say 'Just forget the whole thing,' when someone hurt my feelings. Instead, I took the bull by the horns, got myself out of the slump I was in and took charge of the situation. In a very low but firm voice, I told the person involved, 'I want you to know that you hurt me and not discount my feelings.' This was a victory which I was proud to share with my group, because since childhood, when people hurt me, I would just sulk, refuse to relate and often cut them out of my life completely."

◆ EXAMPLE: "A woman in group said that she thinks of her brain as being like a radio with many channels. She can choose any channel she wants. The next time I started to think about a certain depressing situation in my life which cannot be changed, I said to myself, 'Change channels!' And I did! What a victory for someone who used to entertain whatever negative thoughts happened to come into my mind."

Sharing such "small" acts of self-control in a caring group increases our desire to continue.

The group: love without demands, responsibility without coercion

> When demands begin, love departs.
>
> (STRIVE FOR TRUTH, vol.. I, p. 132)

The urge to use fear and hostility to distance ourselves from people begins to fade on its own when we experience that others truly care about us. A support group conveys the attitude that: We accept you as you are right now. We have no demands; we are happy to have you here as you are. We applaud you for having the courage to be honest about your problems. We hope you'll use healthy methods to grow. We are rooting for you, but the real work is yours alone.

A support group makes no demands of its members except that they follow the protective disciplines which prohibit them from hurting each other's feelings or from speaking *lashon ha-ra*. People come for the pleasure of experiencing that others care enough to listen and share. No one is forced to come or to sit there. No one is forced to progress any faster than he is capable of doing. This nonjudgmental atmosphere teaches people that it is safe to trust, safe to be honest and safe to choose new, healthy responses.

It is in learning to bond lovingly to others that we become emotionally healthy. A group is one way to fulfill that need. We learn to seek the Hand of God when a distressing event occurs by first learning to reach out to each other.

CHAPTER 6:
Understanding Mental Illness

Mitzrayim is a far worse place for some than for others. Some people are so trapped by their addictions that they have no inkling that their actions and thoughts are destructive or that they are hurting themselves or others.

It is important for us to understand what these people are going through for several reasons. First, it is important to understand the anguish and isolation of disturbed people in order to feel compassion for them when we must deal with them. Second, it is important to know when we can help them and when we may be endangering our own mental health by maintaining contact with them. Third, it reminds us to take our own mental health seriously, so that we can try to establish a healthy home environment and, thereby, minimize or prevent severe emotional problems from developing.

One-third of all Americans suffer from an acute mental illness at some point in their lives, according to *Archives of General Psychiatry*, November 1988. We see such people all around us — those who are chronically belligerent, critical, irresponsible, mean, irrational, anxiety-ridden, moody or depressed. Few are destructive or dysfunctional enough to be institutionalized, but they certainly are difficult and often abusive.

Emotionally disturbed people fall into two main categories: those who are aware of their problems and have the capacity to heal themselves, and those who are not even aware that they have a disturbance and, therefore, refuse to change. The first are often referred to as neurotics. These people know that something is wrong with their behavior and are unhappy about it. When they actively take responsibility for improving their behavior, then they can make progress.

Those with more severe disturbances are ofter referred to as psychotics or are said to have character disorders. These people have little or no control over their behavior. They lack self-awareness and may not even think anything is wrong with them, or be only dimly aware that their behavior is inappropriate or destructive. They take no responsibility for their actions, blaming everything they do on external factors or people.

The difference between a mild emotional disturbance and a severe one is like the difference between a limp due to a broken leg as opposed to one resulting from polio. With physiotherapy, the person with the broken leg can be expected to walk normally again. With polio, however, physiotherapy may produce some changes in functioning, but the severe structural damage means that full recovery is unlikely.

Knowledge is important, but can also be dangerous

The subject of mental illness is as vast and complex as that of physical illness. Yet the average person knows far less about his mind than he does about his body. On the one hand, people are quick to label others as crazy, and write them off as hopeless. On the other hand, people are just as quick to make light of a serious disturbance and expect a person to "snap out of it" on his own or after a few sessions with a rabbi or therapist.

Doctors are reluctant to publicize the symptoms of various forms of mental illness for the same reason that they were initially fearful of publicizing the Seven Warning Signs of Cancer, i.e., that the public would be unnecessarily frightened and either go running anxiously to their doctors for every minor complaint or avoid going for help at all for fear of the dreaded diagnosis.

A little knowledge can be a dangerous thing if it gives people the illusion that they can diagnose or treat problems by themselves. Thus, the reader should be forewarned that:

(1) People who do not have any serious mental disturbances might become unnecessarily frightened, thinking that they do.

(2) People who really are disturbed will try to hide it, feeling too afraid or ashamed to seek the help they need.

(3) People with disturbances may feel doomed, thinking that their condition is hopeless.

(4) People may jump to label others, calling them crazy, treating them cruelly or coldly turning their backs on them, instead of realizing that these tormented souls are in great need of compassion and understanding.

In writing his introduction to *Guide for the Perplexed*, the Rambam stated:

> When I have a difficult subject before me — when I find the road narrow, and can see no other way of teaching a well-established truth except by pleasing one intelligent man and displeasing ten thousand fools — I prefer to address myself to the one man, and to take no notice whatever of the condemnation of the multitude. I prefer to extricate that intelligent man from his embarrassment and show him the cause of his perplexity, so that he may...be at peace. (p.9)

The information in this chapter is meant for those "intelligent" people who will not misuse it.

These brief sketches are not meant to make psychiatrists out of the reader. If you suspect mental illness, consult an expert. And even then, get a second opinion, because just as with any case of physical illness, even the most respected experts can misdiagnose people.

Another pitfall to watch out for is the tendency of readers to over-identify with the descriptions of emotional disturbances. It has been noted that when medical students are studying a particular part of the anatomy, they become so highly aware of that part of their own bodies that they often begin to think that they have the illness they are reading about. Don't think you are mentally ill just because you have some of the behaviors described. Any normal person may display such symptoms in times of stress.

The difficulty in identifying who is disturbed

The Torah definition of mental health is a dynamic one. A person struggling to integrate the principles of the Torah into the most minute aspects of his life and manifesting an ever-increasing capacity to love unconditionally is mentally healthy. To be unhealthy means to be increasingly distant from God and man. One's direction can change from day to day, even moment to moment.

Thus, it is often difficult to define who is and who is not disturbed. Many disturbed people present a well-mannered and positive social image, while being abusive to close family members or toward themselves in secret.

Any behavior seen in a mentally disturbed person can be seen in the general population, only to a lesser degree. We all get depressed, angry and anxious at times. We all lose control and do things which we are later ashamed of. We all feel disoriented sometimes, as if our contact with reality is somewhat tenuous — especially after experiencing a great loss or having a series of unpredictable events occur.

Thus, it may be difficult to make a judgment, except in very extreme cases. For example, is that sloppy, unreliable family member merely immature and rather lazy or is she actually a hostile, passive-aggressive type? Is the person who lied to you a basically trustworthy individual who knows he lied and who feels badly about it, or is he a pathological liar who must never be trusted?

Ultimately, recognizing the difference between emotional health and illness involves three factors:

(1) F.I.D. — the frequency, intensity and duration of the destructive symptoms.

(2) The person's ability to form and maintain loving relationships on a steady basis.

(3) The degree to which the person behaves abnormally and feels compelled to continue acting that way by forces he does not acknowledge or attempt to control.

The medical model does not fit mental illness

The traditional medical model, in which a sick person goes to a doctor who takes control, gives medication, and cures the patient does not apply to emotional disturbances for a number of reasons.

(1) In the area of mental illness, all healing is, essentially, self-healing. Therapists and advisors do not cure anyone; they can only encourage the person to adopt healthier attitudes and behaviors.

(2) There is no magic pill to cure mental illness, just as there is no quick way to correct curvature of the spine. True, there are natural diets, vitamins and medications which may alleviate symptoms, but the ability to develop love for God, oneself and others requires self-disciplined action. Even when an emotional illness is due to a

chemical imbalance which can be corrected with medication, the person still has to unlearn the many negative attitudes and behaviors which he adopted during the period of time before the treatment began.

(3) Emotional illnesses are never limited to one person. In fact, the one showing the most difficulties may not be the most disturbed or the one who seeks help. For example, the spouse or child of a very violent or cold person may be seriously depressed for good reason, while the one who is causing the problem never seeks help. This is why therapy for the entire family is usually essential in order to get a complete picture.

Those friends or family members who apply the medical model to emotional illness often feel it is their duty to cure the disturbed person. Their unrealistic sense of responsibility for another person's health and happiness leads to a harmful condition called "codependency." Codependency keeps alive the false hope that outsiders can and should take responsibility for someone's illness by devising various tricks or techniques to get him well, such as by dragging him to therapy, displaying superhuman patience and forgiveness, or being tough and demanding. While these tactics may be effective at times, they do not cure. What cures people is their own diligent, disciplined efforts to follow the principles of Torah, particularly the "duties of the heart."

Major classifications of personality disorders

Although the behaviors listed below are quite variable, the reader will notice in all of them the underlying motif of fear and mistrust. Other common factors include: the inability to maintain emotionally intimate, loving relationships; lack of a healthy sense of humor; overwhelming feelings of shame or complete lack of them; and a combination of over-control of and lack of control of oneself and others. Their relationships are usually superficial. They are so wrapped up in themselves that they do not truly care about other people, except in so far as others can be useful to them.

Most people suffering from personality disorders had childhoods characterized by emotional and/or physical abandonment, abuse or neglect. However, some of the following behaviors can also result from chemical imbalances or senility.

Remember that all disturbed people have periods of normalcy. This can be very deceptive, because their co-dependents are then deluded into thinking that there is no real problem or that the problem is not serious.

Psychopathic behavior. Psychopaths (also called sociopaths) are characterized by their impulsivity and complete lack of shame and guilt over their immoral, criminal behavior. They feel no remorse for the damage they do to property and the pain they cause others. Psychopaths are extremely dishonest and pride themselves on their ability to dupe, lie, swindle and deceive without being caught. They can be so superficially charming that, afterward, their victims may find it difficult to believe that such cruelty and dishonesty could be carried out by people who pretended to be so nice and normal. Psychopaths become violent when they do not get their way, but shrug off their behavior as justified.

> ◆ EXAMPLE: "My daughter is married to a very violent man. He hasn't allowed us to contact her for over ten years. We don't even know our own grandchildren. Neighbors have told us that they know he beats her and the children. I can only assume that she's too scared and too scarred to leave or get help."
> ◆ EXAMPLE: "I have a very dishonest relative. When she gets caught in a lie, she gets angry at the one who exposed her, but doesn't feel at all bad about what she's done."

Although capable of behaving with charm in order to deceive others, psychopaths cannot sustain positive behavior for long. They show a characteristic pattern of instability in work and relationships. They often go from job to job, getting themselves fired by stealing supplies, alienating co-workers, being defiant toward bosses or not showing up on time. They get along for a while with family members and co-workers, then suddenly do something to ruin the relationship or get fired. They prefer criminal activities, unrealistic get-rich-quick schemes or sponging off of others to steady, hard work.

Paranoia. Paranoid people are characterized by their irrational mistrust and suspicions of others. They are humorless and stiff, always scanning the environment in a defensive, vigilant stance. An apt description is given in *Vayikra* 26:36: "The sound of a driven leaf shall chase them."

◆ EXAMPLE: "My mother automatically assumes that we are deliberately trying to hurt her whenever we don't cooperate instantly. She doesn't take into consideration that perhaps I was immersed in a book and didn't hear what she said or that my father simply forgot to get what she asked for or that maybe someone was busy and couldn't call. No way. She constantly explodes at everyone, accusing them of being disrespectful, selfish and uncaring. She's always divided family members into 'camps' and keeps demanding proof of their loyalty to her side while plotting against my father's side. Needless to say, everyone is very tense around her."

◆ EXAMPLE: "A paranoid neighbor is convinced that everyone in the neighborhood is plotting against him. He's constantly claiming that he has clues to prove that people talk behind his back and are bent on hurting him. He's nasty to everyone which, of course, makes them nasty back, which makes him think his anger is justified. If someone protests his innocence, he sees this as proof that the person must be guilty."

Paranoid people do not think that they are unreasonably hostile. They are certain that they are merely protecting themselves from all the untrustworthy liars around them. They talk a great deal about how often they've been gypped, conned, betrayed and manipulated.

Paranoia can also be a symptom of brain damage.

◆ EXAMPLE: "Since my mother got Alzheimer's Disease, she has become extremely paranoid. She is sure that her own children are trying to steal from her. If I merely look out the window, she thinks I am signaling to someone. She thinks that her illness is the result of poisoning by some family member or deliberate mistreatment by her doctor. If she does not find what she is looking for right away, she is sure that the object was deliberately hidden in order to aggravate her. The wonderful, loving woman who used to be my mother is gone."

Paranoid people are very secretive about personal matters. Those who try to help them are treated with hostility, since their help is intrepreted as an attempt to pry into their business. Thus, they are constantly angry.

Obsessive-compulsive behavior. Obsessive-compulsive people are not simply fussy and fastidious. They are self-defeating perfectionists, stingy with both money and affection, and are often inexpressive and robot-like.

A *compulsion* is a repetitive action that is inappropriate or even ridiculous, such as repeated washing, checking, touching or counting. They may repeatedly wipe the germs off doorknobs, reposition possessions in a specific order, or recheck the locks.

An *obsession* is a repetitive thought, such as constant worry about developing a physical or emotional illness, dying, or falling prey to other disasters.

> ◆ EXAMPLE: "I admit that I'm compulsive about cleanliness and germs to the point of absurdity. But I feel *driven* by an insatiable inner tyrant. If I don't get it right, some terrible catastrophe will happen. People think of me as very controlled and controlling. The truth is that I always feel that I am on the brink of losing control, which is why I can never relax about anything or really enjoy myself. I'm always nervous, always concentrating on what needs to be done, taxing myself to the extreme in order to keep from going under."

Lacking any real sense of self or self-determination, obsessive-compulsives do not ask themselves, "What would I like?" "What would please me?" "How can I develop my own unique talents?" Rather, they live according to externally imposed shoulds: "What should I be doing?" "What should I be like?" Joyless, anxiety-ridden and often heartless as well, their inner world is empty, save for an abundance of impersonal rules and regulations.

> ◆ EXAMPLE: "My obsessive-compulsive relative criminalizes the smallest mistake. He grimaces in horror over petty imperfections, such as discovering dust on the shelves or unshined shoes, yet he is oblivious to the effect this has on his own children. He'll reduce a child to nothing for putting the juice in the wrong place in the refrigerator. Order is more important than people's feelings."

Stilted, rigid and punitive, obsessive-compulsives feel they must plan everything ahead of time, thus minimizing any possibility of loss of control. Pleasure is viewed as sinful. In religious matters, they are so preoccupied with the physical details that they miss the spirit of the Law concerning genuine joy and love. To keep themselves feeling clean and right, they project their innermost forbidden desires onto various "enemy" groups who are then classified as immoral and evil, while they remain the good and the holy.

Since they believe that there is only one right way to think or behave, they lack flexibility and tolerance and cannot bear compromise or choices. Their personal relationships are marked by constant clashes and power struggles, since they have a strong need to control people's thinking and behavior.

Manic-depressive behavior. These people fluctuate in mood between ecstatic elation and suicidal depression. In the manic phase, they may be filled with enormous excitement, energy and optimism, and are capable of creative, intelligent and dynamic action. In this phase, they may accomplish a great deal, though they tend to be careless and ignore details as they rush around madly to get things done, barely stopping to eat and sleep.

> ◆ EXAMPLE: "I have a relative whose manic phases involve religion. In her manic phase, she wants to take care of the whole world. She barely sleeps, talks a mile a minute, and runs herself ragged doing things for people, like taking food to Jewish patients in hospitals and taking distressed families into her tiny apartment for weeks on end. This would be really admirable if it were not for the fact that she is a nervous wreck and completely neglects her own children. She is so frantic and worn out from not sleeping that she screams at them angrily when they need her attention. Eventually, she falls apart and goes into her depressive phase and thinks she is a complete failure, the most wicked thing that ever existed. She isolates herself and refuses to get out of bed. Medication has helped to stabilize her somewhat, but she lives in fear of another attack."

Autistic behavior. Infantile autism, in which a baby cannot make contact with the outside world, is due to an actual disturbance in the brain. But autistic behavior in adults is the result of never having learned how to form or sustain loving relationships. These people may sometimes appear to make contact with others, but their connection is superficial and shallow, and they quickly lose interest when their needs have been satisfied. They rarely show true concern about anyone else.

Those who suffer from emotional autism cannot connect to others in any meaningful way. A short, superficial interchange consisting of a few sentences may seem like a long conversation. A critical remark may be interpreted as having made contact. They are often withdrawn and self-absorbed, oblivious to what is going on around them. Distant loners, they usually have no friends and find excuses to avoid being with people and to keep visitors out of their homes. They feel threatened when others try to make meaningful contact.

◆ EXAMPLE: "I feel like I have to break through thick walls to get his attention. I knock, but it's like no one is home. He gets impatient and angry when anyone tries to make contact. Even when he does respond, he is totally devoid of sympathy and understanding. Every once in a while there is a spark of concern for someone, but it is quickly extinguished. When he does come out of his isolation booth for a few minutes, it's usually only to criticize someone. My life has become so isolated that I feel like I'm turning into a stone wall too!"

Schizoid behavior. Schizophrenia is based, to a large degree, on the presence of specific abnormalities in the brain. These people may appear to be daydreaming or in a kind of trance. They may sit in one place for hours, oblivious to everything around them. When they talk, it may be a "word salad" about bizarre matters or in sentences which skip randomly from one topic to another. Their thought processes are separated from their emotions.

They perceive reality in a distorted fashion, often accompanied by delusions and hallucinations. They laugh inappropriately, such as when speaking about dangerous or abusive situations and exhibit other bizarre behaviors.

Passive-aggressive behavior. Passive-aggressive people express anger indirectly by complaining, shifting blame, making excuses and procrastinating. They are escape artists, avoiding responsibilities by feigning illness, claiming lack of information or simply forgetting.

◆ EXAMPLE: "It isn't so much what this person does, but rather what he doesn't do which causes everyone so much aggravation. He never cleans up after himself. He needs to be pushed out the door to get any place. He is always late. And he conveniently forgets — forgets to pay bills, forgets about appointments and promises he has made, forgets where he put things, etc. Whenever anyone asks him to help, he acts totally helpless or makes lame excuses about not feeling well or not knowing how to do it."

◆ EXAMPLE: "I have a passive-aggressive teenager who seems compelled to do the very opposite of whatever those around her want. For example, in the mornings she'll dawdle in the bathroom while others are waiting anxiously to get in. She always has some excuse as to why she can't help me and why her room is a mess. She leaves her dirty clothing on the floor by her bed or the tub. She leaves various, unfinished projects all over the place. When I demand an explanation of her behavior, she simply stares at the wall behind me blankly, as if I had just spoken Swahili. I have no idea what to do!''

Typically, passive-aggressive types promise to take care of something, such as fixing a broken item or getting a job, and then undermine their own intentions with complaints, excuses or other forms of obstructionism. Their behavior is a covert expression of hostility toward the person who begs them day after day to behave more responsibly and reliably. They see themselves as nice people, victims of circumstance, who really are trying their best, and who, despite all their efforts, are unlucky and are always being picked on unfairly by people who make demands and are hostile for no reason.

Overly-dependent behavior. Excessively dependent people are characterized by indecision, a feeling of helplessness and an insatiable need for approval. They underestimate their strengths and overestimate their weaknesses. Their constant demands for attention and approval are so annoying that they end up provoking what they fear most, i.e., rejection and abandonment.

◆ EXAMPLE: "I know I am overly dependent. I'm constantly asking my husband if he really loves me, and then I don't believe him when he says he does. I want him to make me feel secure,and though he does his best, it's never enough and I end up getting angry at him. I just can't be satisfied."

◆ EXAMPLE: "My husband is a very dependent type. He is forever accusing me of not giving him enough time or attention or not respecting him enough. But I've found that no matter how much I give, it never is enough for him. He has this kind of emotional thermometer out all the time, measuring how much people are giving to him. If he doesn't get what he thinks is a reasonable amount, he goes off sulking in resentment."

While the goal of overly-dependent people is to make sure that they will be taken care of, their lack of trust in others makes them supersensitive to rejection, and they tend to overreact when they detect the merest hint of disapproval. Thus, they sabotage their very efforts to get what they want most by reacting angrily to the normal disappointments and conflicts inherent in relationships.

◆ EXAMPLE: "My mother-in-law is forever complaining to me that she never gets enough attention, so that she lives in a state of chronic dissatisfaction and resentment."

Dependent types may visit doctors and therapists, yet refuse to do the things which would make them healthy, because deep down they feel they must maintain their illnesses in order to get others to take care of them. In contrast to psychopaths, dependent people turn their hostility against themselves with suicide attempts, eating disorders, substance abuse, etc.

Narcissistic behavior. While all disturbed people are self-centered, narcissistic personalities feel an even more exaggerated sense of self-importance and demand that others treat them with special consideration. They view themselves as very desirable and talented, entitled to favors and exceptional treatment from everyone around them (mates, children, doctors, clerks, etc.). They think they should be the center of everyone else's universe, the king or queen in the family or place of work. No matter how badly they behave, they feel entitled to unconditional acceptance. If they do go to therapy, they overestimate their progress ("I'm a completely different person!") and underestimate the severity of their disturbance. Narcissistic people don't care that other people have their own problems and pains. They want what they want when they want it, or they feel slighted and fly into a temper.

Borderline personality disorder: While BPD seems like a kind of "catch-all" category, it deserves special attention. It is a common yet contradictory, elusive and inconsistent disorder with a wide variety of symptoms. There is a strong hereditary predisposition to BPD.

BPD is characterized by lack of any stable sense of self, self-mutilation ("If I hurt myself, I'll feel real and alive and gain control over my inner chaos and confusion"), intense fears of abandonment along with fears of intimacy, impulsivity, loneliness, identity confusion (gender, goals, values, etc.), wild mood swings, stormy relationships, food disorders, a sense of being "untogether" or nonexistent, relentless search for stimulation to avoid inner numbness and isolation, suicidal impulses at a young age, hypersensitivity to rejection, craving for ecstatic experiences, unpredictable outbursts of intense rage, magical thinking, unrealistic belief in perfection combined with self-loathing over lack of perfection and a sense of not deserving success, frantic attempts to get others to rescue them combined with resistance to all attempts to help them control their destructive tendencies.

Undisciplined borderlines are unstable and intensely emotional, overreacting to almost every stress. They have an incessant craving for reassurance, yet never feel secure or trust that anyone can really love them.

While BPD cannot be "cured," it can be well managed with a disciplined lifestyle. With proper training, these people can be very successful and productive.

Why don't they just stop acting so crazy?

Emotionally disturbed people resist change because they believe their behavior is essential for their survival. In fact, they think their behavior is:

(1) *Normal*. The kind of parenting a person received in his early life is what seems normal to him. People parent others as they were parented. Thus, abnormal behavior can seem normal while healthy behavior can feel uncomfortable and wrong. To a disturbed person, an atmosphere of chaos, tension and fear may seem completely normal, though painful. They actually feel uncomfortable and anxious when things are going well.

(2) *Necessary*. Even if they acknowledge that their behavior is harmful, disturbed people believe that they must act the way they do in order to gain attention, pleasure and power, or protect themselves from the pain of rejection, abandonment, failure, or punishment. They are convinced that terrible things will happen if they change. For example, paranoids are sure that they'll be stabbed in the back if they act nice or if they trust someone. Dependent types are sure that if they do stand up for themselves, they'll be abandoned. Fastidious compulsive types fear unknown catastrophies if things are not "just so."

(3) *Good, right and holy*. For example, compulsives believe goodness means absolute cleanliness at all times or completing a

detail-perfect piece of work. Dependent types may think that they are being saintly when they passively accept abuse or fail to act when action is required. Disturbed people hold on to these views tenaciously. Otherwise they would have to take a deep and painful look at what they are really like.

Sabotaging relationships

There is no really sane response to insane behavior. In fact, sane people may feel that they have to act slightly insane in order to protect themselves from the destructive behavior which is always present in disturbed people.

Because they lack trust, people with emotional handicaps avoid true closeness and provoke rejection with their irritating and abusive acts. Thus, they prevent the establishment of the one thing they need most: sustained, loving relationships with others and the development of self-respect which comes from self-discipline.

Eventually, even their most patient family members and friends get fed up or develop their own signs of disturbance. After all, how can someone succeed in relating to a paranoid person when all he has to do is look out the window to arouse that person's suspicions? How can someone relate successfully to a passive-aggressive person who can never be relied on to act responsibly, or to a depressed person who resists all attempts to engage in meaningful activities? And so, healthy people usually withdraw, either emotionally or physically, as well. Feeling abandoned, the disturbed person then thinks he has all the more reason to continue acting in a destructive manner.

Now that you know

Just recognizing that you or a certain troublesome family member may fall into one of the above listed categories can bring a certain measure of relief and a change in attitude, helping you to realize that:

(1) *You are not helpless.* If you, or anyone you know, is out of control much of the time, get professional help and use the spiritual exercises mentioned in this book to heal yourself. You now realise that you are not alone.

(2) *You can make your expectations more realistic.* No one expects a person with a broken leg to be able to dance well, but many

expect emotionally disturbed people to think and behave normally. People are always asking, "How can I get through to X and make her see how harmful her actions are?" "What's the magic key which will enable me to communicate with this repressive tyrant?" The sad fact is that you cannot relate normally to abnormal people. Your efforts will usually be sabotaged and your best intentions maligned and regarded with suspicion. Trying to get through to someone in an emotional coma is as rewarding as trying to get through to someone in a physical coma. People don't make progress unless they develop a will for health.

> ◆ EXAMPLE: "All these years I was sure that there was something wrong with me! What a relief to realize that it's not my fault that he acts the way he does. He's the one with the problem, and now I'm determined not to make it mine. It's about time I stopped bashing my head against a stone wall trying to reach someone who can't be gotten through to. I can accept my limitations without feeling like a failure. I can be self-protective without feeling that I am selfish or uncaring."

(3) *You don't have to feel ashamed.* Hopefully, the information presented here will remove the burden of inappropriate shame you might feel concerning aspects of your life over which you have no control. These are behaviors which you probably adopted early in life in an effort to protect yourself from pain and to gain some sense of power and love.

> ◆ EXAMPLE: "I used to feel so ashamed of the fact that I am high strung. Now I see that I'll just have to be patient with myself as I learn the disciplines necessary to achieve mental health."

(4) *You don't have to feel guilty.* You don't have to feel guilty for not being able to cure the disturbed people around you or make them happy.

> ◆ EXAMPLE: "I always believed that, with the right communication techniques, I could have a good relationship with just about any person. I believed that if I would just be loving enough, people would act loving back to me, and that if they didn't, it was my fault. But I no longer think that it's my fault if people are explosive or

cold and critical. A lot of people have serious problems that have nothing to do with me."

Mothers are especially prone to feeling excessively responsible for other people's happiness and unnecessarily guilt-ridden because outsiders often blame mothers for any emotional disturbance in family members. However, mental illness cannot always be blamed on poor mothering. It can also result from birth trauma, chemical imbalances, neurological defects, traumatic life experiences or poor fathering. Mothers tend to take the blame for their children's emotional problems which resulted from fathers who were coldly indifferent, critical or cruel. Being aware of this will, hopefully, reduce or eliminate the shame and guilt which many mothers feel.

(5) *You can better advise others.* Rabbis, counselors, friends and relatives are often approached by people seeking guidance regarding jobs, living conditions, family size, etc. Advice-givers should realize that people with a strong foundation of mental health can handle quite a bit of stress. But those with real emotional handicaps cannot. Under the stress of poverty, a new baby, illness or other difficulties, they are more likely to crumble and become violent or depressed. Thus, advice which would be appropriate for an emotionally healthy person is inappropriate for one who is not.

A typical example concerns marriage. All too often, disturbed children are married off by their parents with the attitude that "everything will work out afterwards." Although this is sometimes true, marriage will exacerbate problems in disturbed people. When children come along, often in quick succession, the already weakened foundation may collapse.

(6) *You can feel compassion instead of anger.* When readers realize how deep and complex an emotional illness can be, they will be more compassionate of, and patient with, those who are disturbed.

An atmosphere of unconditional love within a framework of Torah values combined with meaningful work are the essentials of good mental health. Unfortunately, such an atmosphere is very difficult to find. Many books on psychiatry never even mention the words God or love. One must search carefully to find those people with a true Torah outlook who model the *middoth* which can help others break through the barriers of shame, fear and despair.

Do not be discouraged

If you see yourself in any of the above descriptions, do not panic. First, realize that everyone has moments when they display some of these symptoms for brief periods of time. Second, the fact that you care enough to read a book of this nature means that you do want to change. Third, even if someone has a strong familial tendency toward various disturbances, that does not mean he is necessarily doomed to insanity. Having a predisposition to heart disease or diabetes is quite different from having a heart ailment or being severely diabetic. However, having a tendency toward an illness requires that one be more aware and self-disciplined than one who does not have the same tendencies.

A woman with BPD described her emotional handicap as similar to having an enormous boulder sitting in her living room. She couldn't possibly move it, but she could walk around it and function adequately despite its presence. She didn't deny her handicap or the pain it caused, but she was proud of being able to accomplish a great deal despite her fears.

If you see someone close to you in the above descriptions, you now have a better idea of what you can do for him and what you can't. You can encourage him to get help, but you cannot get him to do anything he does not want to do. After you show this person that you understand and care and are willing to help him in any way that is healthy, you must do specific spiritual exercises to bolster yourself and keep you from getting sucked into the other person's negativity.

> No one really enjoys anything unless he has first longed for it.
> The essence of pleasure and enjoyment is gratification of longing.
>
> (STRIVE FOR TRUTH! vol. I, p. 72)

It is not necessary or helpful to curse the darkness of one's childhood. It is more constructive to view that time as one's personal *Mitzrayim*, decreed by God to be the way it was in order for you to yearn for and appreciate health. The greater the darkness and the harder the struggle, the greater will be the joy in discovering what it means to lead a life dedicated to maintaining physical, emotional and spiritual health.

CHAPTER 7:
Overcoming Condemnaholism

> *Hillel told the proselyte, "What is hateful to you, do not do to your fellowman. That is the entire Torah. The rest is commentary."*
>
> (SHABBATH 31a)

No doubt, one of the most hateful things we can do to others is to hurt them with criticism. Criticism is a destructive weapon — the verbal equivalent of a loaded gun, because not accepting ourselves or another carries a death wish, i.e., "Die. Be something different from who you are." Sadly, this psychological gun is fired often in the course of human interactions. Only a tremendous effort can rid oneself of the inclination to use this weapon carelessly.

People who suffer from an uncontrolled urge to criticize themselves and others might be termed "condemnaholics." This addiction is characterized by the constant shaming of oneself with self-deprecatory thoughts and remarks, and the shaming of others, as well, with grimaces, stares, sarcasm, teasing, and sometimes explosive rages and physical violence.

Condemnaholics grew up in families where criticism was the means by which members formed attachments to each other, and they continue this pattern of "negative bonding" into adulthood. They actually think that this is the way to have a relationship with another human being and the only way to achieve the perfection which they feel they must reach in order to be loved and respected! This is why they do not even see that there is anything wrong with what they do.

The tendency to make oneself feel good by making others feel bad is often seen in the lust for honor:

There are two main branches of desire, desire for wealth and desire for honor, each as evil as the other and each bringing about many evil consequences... The desire for honor is even greater than the desire for wealth, for it is possible for a person to overcome his inclination for wealth and other pleasures and still be pressed by the desire for honor, being unable to tolerate being, and seeing himself beneath his friends... In fine, the desire for honor pulls at a person's heart more than any of the other longings and desires in the world.

(THE PATH OF THE JUST, pp. 167-71)

Condemnaholism: the craving to shame

While it is a mitzvah to rebuke others with love (*Vayikra* 19:17) and to constantly monitor whether or not our thoughts and actions are in keeping with the values of Torah, it is destructive to do so to the point of self-loathing and hatred.

Many people do not realize that they are filled with hatred because they delude themselves into thinking that their condemnations are merely truthful observations of reality. Condemnaholics believe they are simply noting aloud that they, their family members, and everyone else they come into contact with are lacking in proper *middoth*, and that it is their right and duty to express their displeasure over this fact. However, condemnaholics do not simply report facts; their reporting is combined with a feeling of superiority or inferiority which poisons hearts and minds and prevents loving relationships.

Below is a questionnaire to help identify whether or not you are a condemnaholic:

(1) Were you criticized a great deal by your parents? _____

(2) Do you criticize yourself throughout the day, finding fault with yourself for every little thing and constantly criticizing your spouse, children and parents ? _____

(3) When you go out, do you find yourself judging everyone to see whether you are inferior or superior to them according to what they wear, how much they have accomplished, etc.? _____

(4) Do you fly off the handle easily, blaming everyone around you for what went wrong? _____

(5) Do you feel contempt for entire groups of people, (e.g., women or people from other cultural backgrounds)? _____

(6) Do you get depressed easily, eating yourself up over every mistake and imperfection in yourself? _____

If you answered yes to any of the above, you have a predisposition to condemnaholism. But don't condemn yourself for being a condemnaholic! You became a condemnaholic early in life in order to distance yourself from people who hurt you. Experience taught you to fear emotional closeness. Like most children, you thought that hostility was your best protection against the pain of rejection. But you are an adult now. You no longer need to protect yourself with hatred and fear. Be proud that you have the courage to recognize that you have a problem, because awareness is the first step in gaining control. Your honesty means you can change!

Why do people become condemnaholics?

People become condemnaholics for numerous reasons, most of them unconscious. For example:

(1) *Self-protection.* Whether they are one-up or one-down, judgments maintain distance, thereby preventing the emotional closeness which might bring painful rejection. Anger provides an illusion of having a protective shield around oneself.

(2) *As a misguided expression of love.* People think, Criticizing is my way of showing how much I care about making people better so that I can then love them.

(3) *To feel superior to others.* Condemnations provide an illusion of superiority. A perverse pleasure is derived from looking for other people's flaws and thinking of oneself as cleaner, more intelligent, more spiritual, etc., by comparison.

(4) *To divert attention.* Focusing on other people's flaws diverts attention away from one's own.

(5) *To punish and gain control.* Critical people think they have a duty to punish those who do not live up to their standards. They feel powerful when they see others frightened into submission by their harsh criticism.

(6) *As a motivator to improve.* Many people believe, Criticism is the only way to get others to improve or to keep them in line.

(7) *To bring about closeness.* People think that love equals sameness. They hope, If I criticize her enough to make her become

like me, then we'll be close and loving. Or, When he reaches the standards I want him to reach, I will be able to show respect and feel love for him.

(8) *To display one's intelligence.* Many people think it is a sign of intelligence to be critical.

People shame themselves for similar reasons:

(1) *To feel holy.* Critical people think, The fact that I notice my every flaw and failure means that I am superior to and more spiritual than those clods who aren't even aware of their shortcomings. In this way, I'll win God's approval.

(2) *To permit themselves to be destructive.* They think, Since I'm so bad, I might as well just go ahead and do all the bad things I want. After all, what else can I expect from myself?

(3) *To prevent themselves from being destructive.* They think, The only way to keep myself in line is to criticize myself constantly. If I stop, I'll do terrible things.

(4) *As a magical measure.* Shamers hope, If I dwell on my faults long enough, they'll disappear and I'll become what I've always hoped to be — perfect! Although constant self-criticism is a form of self-abuse, they are certain that, If I just criticize myself enough, I'll eventually stop feeling that I am so evil. Growth through self-torture!

(5) *As a substitute for action.* Condemnations give people the illusion that they are doing something positive about their deficiencies, even if they are only feeling guilty about them.

(6) *As punishment for real or imagined sins.* People who feel defective think they must continue to torture themselves with criticism in order to atone for their imperfections.

None of these reasons works to bring about positive results. In fact, people actually do more of whatever they criticize themselves for or what others criticize them for! Excessive criticism intensifies bad habits because it makes people feel that they can never be any different. If people think they are no good, they continue to act that way. Even if they see that criticism does sometimes get people to improve in a specific area, what they do not realize is that the shamed one's hatred toward the criticizer or the self-loathing which is aroused by constant harping, will inevitably be expressed in some other equally obnoxious and destructive habit.

Condemnaholics can never be satisfied. No matter how much they accomplish or how much others try to please them, they remain unhappy with God, people and themselves. As time goes on, they get even angrier and more depressed when they see that their hostility fails to bring them the control, pleasure or approval they seek. Thus, condemnaholics are often grim and anxious. They may delude themselves into thinking that they are loving, but their joylessness betrays their true hostility. This is why rebuke or constructive criticism from a loving person is appreciated, while the same words from a condemnaholic spark so much hostility.

Judgments: good and bad

> The entire Torah is dependent on the correction of our *middoth.*
>
> (THE WAYS OF THE RIGHTEOUS, p. 15)

This statement implies that we must always be alert to our shortcomings. The word for prayer, *l'hitpallel*, comes from the root *pallel*, "to judge." The more spiritually sensitive we are, the quicker we experience shame over our most minor failing. We also need to make judgments since we, the Jewish people, are responsible for each other and have an obligation to try to help others recognize and overcome their shortcomings. In addition, we also have to protect ourselves from the truly evil people in our midst, we must have the discernment to judge whom to associate with and whom to avoid.

We also need to discern when our judgments are necessary and helpful, and when they are harmful and destructive.

To hate yourself or others is to hate God

> At the root of the precept in regard to blaspheming the Divine name lies the reason that by this evil utterance a man becomes emptied, bereft of every goodness; all the radiance of his spirit [*hod nafsho*] turns to destruction, and he can be reckoned like the animals. For with that very thing by which the Eternal Lord (be He blessed) set him apart for good...and by which he became man — i.e., speech, by which he is differentiated from the special of beasts — with that he sets himself apart for evil; he removes himself completely from every boundary of sense, and he becomes as a loathsome, degenerate crawling creature, and even worse. Therefore the Torah adjured us about this: because the

good, benevolent God desires our good; and every single utterance brings a deprivation of that goodness, goes against His wish...   (SEFER HACHINUCH, precept 70, pp.273-275)

To speak disrespectfully about ourselves, therefore, is to show disrespect for God, for our own Divinity and to lose our ability to respect the holiness in others.

♦ EXAMPLE: "When my husband was a child, his father would lock him up for an entire day in a dark basement closet for misbehaving. That abuse seemed to have killed his ability to connect lovingly to people. He must have felt such overpowering shame and hatred down there that he never got over it, because he takes out his anger on me and the children all the time. He is hypercritical and sees nothing wrong with the harsh punishments he imposes for the most trivial mistake."

The quality of our relationship with God is reflected in our relationships with others. To love Him is to love His creations and to treat them with concern and consideration. A person who feels distant from God becomes lonely and bitter, convinced that he is the unlucky victim of a cruel and unjust God. He views the people around him as manipulative and untrustworthy. This attitude then justifies his retaliatory actions against both God and man.

In addition, such a person's sense of worth is insecure, because it is dependent on external signs of success, such as a spotless kitchen, expensive possessions or a public position of importance. Whenever these external signs are threatened or absent, the person feels like a nothing and he falls into depression or lashes out at those who are not giving him the respect, approval or obedience he thinks he needs in order to be happy. Those close to such a person can easily get dragged into a vicious cycle. The condemnaholic's hostility makes them feel like hurting him back. Hostility generates more hostility, causing all concerned to lose their sense of *hod nafsho* and love of God and their fellowman as well.

Follow the Rambam to avoid excessive shame over your sins

It takes work to overcome a tendency toward hypercriticalness. One of the most important ongoing exercises a person can practice is to constantly forgive. Not to forgive others is an indication of cruelty (*Bava Kama* 92a). Not to forgive oneself is cruelty to our Self.

When we do something wrong, we should feel the degree of shame which is appropriate to the event and then follow the Rambam's formula for successful *teshuvah* (*Hilchoth Teshuvah* 2:2). As applied to condemnaholism, this would mean:

(1) Stop the abusive criticism.

(2) Remove the desire to repeat the behavior from our hearts.

(3) Prove the sincerity of our *teshuvah* by refusing to condemn when the opportunity to do so arises again.

Since relationships always involve some disappointment and pain, we have endless opportunities to avoid condemning ourselves and the people around us. Each time we refrain from doing so and instead find a caring response, we are simultaneously healing the wounds which others have caused us and which we have caused ourselves.

Nothing is to be gained by continually castigating ourselves or others. Even David HaMelech, who said "My sin is before me always" (*Tehillim* 51:5), asked God to help him hear "gladness and joy" (Ibid. 51:10). If we are not experiencing much "gladness and joy" in our lives, then we are experiencing excessive shame.

Shame: to use it or not

Rav Yisrael Salanter states that one should discipline children in a way which raises their self-esteem — for example, by saying, "Is this the way a child of the King should act?" (*HaMeoroth HaGedolim*, p. 256). The same is true for adults. It is far better if the impetus to behave correctly comes from a person's desire to maintain his sense of human dignity, in a manner fitting for a *ben Melech* (child of the King), rather than from self-hatred or as a result of someone's caustic comments.

Rebuke is powerful emotional medicine because it awakens shame. It should not be used except for deliberate sins or acts of cruelty or negligence. If we feel rebuke is necessary, then, like a surgeon, we should (1) prepare the "patient" by reassuring him that we care, (2) think clearly and objectively about how best to effectively perform the "surgery," and (3) provide after-care — making sure that our relationship with the "patient" has improved because we had the courage to be honest.

The Rambam states that a person must be merciful and compassionate, yet be able to express "anger, revenge and wrath in proportion to [another's] guilt, but not from personal motives or angry passion" (*Guide for the Perplexed*, p. 54).

♦ EXAMPLE: "I was trying to sleep and I asked my teenager to turn down his music. He did a little, but not enough. I was so violently angry at him for being so inconsiderate that I was actually shaking. Then I thought to myself that I don't have to use my sledgehammer to pound him with hatred. I have to figure out a diplomatic way to help him be more considerate. I guess I have this old programming from childhood that if I want respect from someone, I have to run him over with a Sherman tank."

He who shames the face of another in public has no portion in the World to Come.   (BAVA METZIA 59a)

Rebuke is only effective if the one being rebuked knows that the rebuker loves him. Otherwise, it does far more damage than good, causing the one being rebuked to hate the other.

We are also told not to rebuke if we are sure that we will not be listened to (*Beitzah* 30a). There are many people with little or no capacity to feel shame. This includes those who do not even realize anything is wrong with them, and "foolish scoffers" who are impervious to moral rebuke. Of them King Solomon writes with much exasperation:

He who corrects a scorner gets himself shame, and he who reproves a wicked man acquires his defects. Do not reprove a scorner lest he hate you; reprove a wise man and he will love you.

(MISHLEI 9:7-8)

Since insensitive people become even more resistant when shamed, and sensitive types tend to be shattered by it, we must find a loving approach to shortcomings.

How do we stop?

Many people admit that they are overly critical of their children or spouses, but say "I just can't stop." Furthermore, when they try to give up their criticalness, they feel alone, disoriented, vulnerable and powerless. There is a terrifying fear that, "If I stop being critical, I'll *never* get the love, control and respect I want from people! I'll be all alone!"

Condemnaholism feels so natural and effective that it seems impossible to overcome. But it can be done. The following suggestions will help one discipline one's mind and one's mouth:

(1) *Ask Hashem for His help.* The weaning process is painful in overcoming any addiction. The initial steps are taken in darkness, and often without hope. That is why it is important to remember that,

> If a man consecrates himself in a small measure down below, he is sanctified much more from above.
>
> (YOMA 39a)

> If the Almighty did not help him, he could not overcome his evil inclination. (KIDDUSHIN 30b)

You will soon find new, healthy substitutes for your destructive addiction. Soon, love will replace hostility as your primary method of forming attachments; forgiveness and detachment will replace resentment as your means of protecting yourself from abusive people.

(2) *Be fiercely protective of your Godly essence.* Tell family members, "For the sake of our *shalom bayith*, we are creating a shame-free environment in this house. From now on, no one shames anyone, except for a deliberate transgression of Torah law. And in that case, we condemn the deed, not the doer. That means telling the person, "I care about you, but what you just did is really wrong." If appropriate, tell a criticizer, "Please check the *hechsher* [rabbinic supervision] on what you just said." Here are some House Rules:

(a) I respect myself.
(b) I respect others.
(c) I encourage others to respect me.

When you stop being a faultfinder, you do not turn into a doormat or a passive pushover. On the contrary! You become more protective of your human dignity. God did not command us to love and respect only perfect saints. He commanded us to love each other unconditionally, as we are right now. But that does not mean that we must accept abuse without fighting back. There is no mitzvah to suffer unnecessarily. That is foolishness!

(3) *Go to the opposite extreme to overcome a bad habit* (Rambam, *Hilchoth Deoth* 2:2). Be extreme about avoiding the "woodpecker habit" of pecking at yourself and others all the time. Instead, flood yourself and those around you with endorsements in equal proportion to all your previous condemnations. From morning till night mention the good in yourself, in others and in the world, and express your gratefulness to God out loud.

Don't worry about this leading to arrogance or apathy. The opposite will happen. The paradox of acceptance is that the more you accept yourself and others for what you and they are at this moment, the more likely you are to strive for improvement.

> ◆ EXAMPLE: "I tell my children that God made shoulders so that we could pat ourselves on them when we need an endorsement! When they misbehave, I tell them that I am endorsing myself for my self-control and that I expect them to do the same. When I'm going through a difficult time, I pat myself on my own shoulder to remind myself that I'm doing a pretty good job considering the circumstances. That helps me stay calm and in control."

(4) *Program your mind positively.* Look for moments when you are engaged in the opposite of your usual bad habits. For example, even the most passive, undecisive person sometimes acts in an assertive and decisive manner, and even the meanest person is sometimes nice. At these times, tell yourself or the other person, "See, this is proof that I (or you) can change!" This tactic can also be extremely helpful in getting a family member to see himself in a more positive light.

(5) *Record the positive.* It's not enough to think positively. Take action. Hang small sheets of paper on your refrigerator, one for each member of the family. It takes only five seconds to write one good thing they have done. Read your lists at the Sabbath table, or at the end of each day if you are having unusual difficulties with a child. When they feel cared about, they will be much more cooperative and sensitive to your needs, which saves you time in the long run.

(6) *Do something for the one with whom you are angry.* Give her a hug, a gift or make time to talk.

◆ EXAMPLE: "My children are like me, hot-tempered and impulsive. To help them speak to me more respectfully when they were upset about something, I would say very calmly, 'Hold my hand, look in my eyes, and just tell me what you want.' Then, if I wanted something, I would look them in the eyes and tell them what I wanted. They were much more cooperative. Before long, I also got them used to looking each other in the eyes when they wanted to say something. This decreased the amount of yelling considerably over the last year."

(7) *Be patient.* One does not overcome curvature of the spine in a day or a lifetime. It takes constant, steady pressure to keep one's back and one's psyche straight. If you've been screaming and condemning for many years, it's a giant step forward just to notice the amount of shaming you are doing. Endorse yourself for this awareness. The more aware you become, the sooner you will begin to change.

Some of our greatest Sages admitted that they had to work hard to control their tempers. For example, in his later years, the Rambam recalled with pride an incident in which he controlled himself when he was treated with utmost disrespect. He stated, "I testify that I did not feel insulted, nor did I feel any anger toward this man. On the contrary, I felt great joy because I understood that at last, with the help of God, I had attained a proper level of patience and humility; even though I am not at all placid by nature but tend to be hot-tempered. All my life it had been my goal to achieve this level. I felt no anger: only surprise that the young man could have forgotten himself so far that he behaved like an animal" (*Pathways to Peace of Mind*, p. 43).

(8) *When you notice a shortcoming, do not dwell on it.* Instead, ask yourself, "What steps can I take *right now* to help?" If there is absolutely nothing you can do at this moment, refuse to waste time dwelling on what cannot be changed. Rabbi Yisrael Salanter said, "According to the Torah, we should only think about other people when we want to help them in some way" (*Chayei HaMussar*, vol. 1, p. 107). If you can't think something positive, don't think about that subject!

(9) *Forgive yourself and forgive others.* Do not torture yourself with shame and guilt over your own or others' mistakes of the past. Instead, learn from the past. The way to heal your childhood wounds is

for you to treat yourself and others differently from how you were treated as a child. If you came from a nonnurturing home, you probably don't realize that criticism is wrong. Abuse feels natural to you. But you do not have to continue that pattern. Your parents were scared, alone, insecure and lacking skills. Forgive. Blame gets you nowhere.

You cannot forgive or accept yourself until you forgive and accept others. Blame diverts your attention from the work that needs to be done today. To help you let go, ask forgiveness from the people you have hurt, and let those who have hurt you know that you realize that they were doing the best they could with the limited tools they possessed. Do this mentally if the person is no longer alive. If the person cannot hear you, you can write a letter and not send it. Such actions will free you from the past and start the healing process in the present.

Forgiveness is good for both your mental and physical health. Researchers have found that the immune system is weakened and the heart muscles adversely affected by the cortisol, norepinephrine and epinephrine which are released into the bloodstream when you are angry. So, even if you don't really feel like forgiving the other person, do it for yourself; the peace of mind it brings also strengthens your immune system.

◆ EXAMPLE: "We loaned money to a man who finds one excuse after another not to pay us back. Since then, my husband lost his job and we are in financial straits. But this man still gives excuses. Last Friday, I was so furious after my phone conversation with him that I had fantasies about different violent ways of dealing with him. Then it came time to light the Shabbath candles. It suddenly occurred to me that the best response in this situation is to forgive and just pray for him, because he is not emotionally well. As I lit the candles, a feeling of total serenity came over me."

◆ EXAMPLE: "I used to be so resentful of my parents because my condemnaholic upbringing led to a lot of destructive behavior. But then I began to realize that my childhood was Divinely ordained. That meant that God wanted it to be that way. If He created the situation, He also gave me the inner strength to free myself from my abusive mentality. I cannot erase my past completely, but I can forgive my parents and have compassion for them. They were young and inexperienced and had many problems of their own. They loved me to the extent that they were capable of loving at that time. I can heal myself with compassion for everyone I come in contact with."

Every instance of *nichum*, consolation, has the connotation of 'reconsidering' or reversing one's mind.

(BERESHITH 6:6, Rashi)

(10) *Use love as your impetus for growth.* Everything you do, from taking a bath to looking for a job, can be done out of shame or out of respect for your Divine Self. The latter reason is the healthiest. Stop punishing yourself and those around you. Instead, celebrate whatever small gains you make in overcoming your judgmentalness, even if they feel like ant steps.

Be proud of your victories every time you restrain your urge to give in to *lashon ha-ra*, grimacing or criticizing. It is a pity that others do not notice these extraordinary feats of self-discipline. But Someone sees. And there is immediate reward in terms of increased joy and love in your life. Success does not mean perfection; it means putting forth effort.

(11) *Get a study partner who is also working on the same problem.* Listening to and helping each other will be inspiring and encouraging. Study material which will encourage you to stay on this path. Especially recommended are *Peace of Mind* by Rabbi Eliyahu Teherani, *Gateway to Happiness* by Rabbi Zelig Pliskin, *The Ways of the Righteous*, and the other books mentioned in the bibliography at the end of this book.

(12) *Practice your nonshaming attitude when you walk down the street.* Instead of feeling superior or inferior, silently say to each person "You, too, have infinite value. You, too, were created in His image." According to the Torah, this is true of all men, not just those who agree with your particular way of life.

(13) *Give the benefit of the doubt whenever there is a doubt as to the person's intentions.* Have the humility to admit that you don't know why someone has hurt you. Who are you to judge? Do you know what that person has been through? Do you know what pains and pressures he is under? Do you really know what is in another's heart or head at any moment?

When people aggravate you, as they are bound to do, repeat over and over to yourself, thousands of times if necessary, "For the sake of *my* spiritual health, I assume that this person is doing the best he can with the limited tools he has at the moment." You can tell yourself, "S/he acts this way because s/he is lacking in awareness, self-control or sensitivity or too immersed in pain to respond properly." Giving the benefit of the doubt does not mean being passive:

♦ EXAMPLE: "My oldest daughter is going through a big depression following the break up of her engagement. At first, she sat around moping and wouldn't help with the chores. But after a while, I couldn't take her gloomy face any more. Instead of condemning her in my mind and yelling at her to pull herself together, which is what I would have done in the past, I gave her the benefit of the doubt. That calmed me down so that I could feel love. I told her, 'I want you to know that I'm in a lot of pain, too, about what happened.' The lines of communication opened and I was able to ask her to fold the laundry and do the shopping afterwards. She's in a lot of pain, but it will not help if I let her indulge herself endlessly."

(14) *Replay the scene mentally and give a positive conclusion this time.* When you lose control, you condemn and scream or stew in hostility. But afterwards, it is important for you to close your eyes for a minute or so and replay the scene, except this time imagine a positive ending. Imagine the person aggravating you, but this time imagine yourself responding in a civilized, constructive manner. This replay will put a positive "program" into your "biocomputer" (i.e., your brain). Then, the next time you are confronted with an overtired child, incompetent clerk, defiant teenager, or critical relative, you can reach into your memory banks and pull out a mental imprint of yourself responding in a constructive manner.

(15) *Focus on what you hope to accomplish with your condemnations.* When angry, fill in the blank, "I must continue to criticize this person because it is the *only* way I can _____." Now, do some reality testing. Ask yourself, "Am I succeeding? Is my anger useful?" Whatever you hope to achieve with anger, can be achieved better with love.

♦ EXAMPLE: "It is so awful to see my daughter-in-law crushing my grandchildren's spirits with her constant criticism and slaps, and to know that I cannot say anything to her because she will lash out at me or forbid me to visit. So I don't say anything in order to visit and give them some warmth. Whenever I want to lash out, I think of my grandchildren. I hope that if they have me as an island of love and sanity, perhaps they will not be completely crushed."

◆ EXAMPLE: "I was really berating myself for not having prepared a lecture as thoroughly as I should have. I couldn't sleep and was very grouchy. Then I gave myself a stern order to drop it because this self-torture was getting me nowhere. If my goal was to motivate myself to do better next time, the important thing was to make a firm decision to prepare earlier and more thoroughly in the future."

◆ EXAMPLE: "I was furious with my surgeon for misleading me by minimizing the aftereffects of my operation. But he's so impervious to feelings that he wouldn't have been fazed by my anger. I thought of my goal, which was to save other patients from having to go through what I went through. When I wrote to him and the director of the hospital, I mentioned practical ways to change the situation, instead of just venting my rage."

(16) *Avoid, ignore or work around those who cannot be reached.* One of the sad facts of life is that the people who hurt us the most are the very ones who usually cannot be talked to! If you have no choice but to live or work with such a person, save your sanity by refusing to react in kind.

(17) *Don't call names.* If you find yourself yelling angrily, make an effort not to also lapse into name-calling (e.g., "selfish brat," "inconsiderate slob," "creep," etc.). Make a firm decision never to condemn yourself or anyone else in entirety and to use constructive criticism only on those aspects of yourself or others which can be corrected.

Blanket condemnations are lies. Unless a person is a publicly acknowledged evildoer, our condemnations are lies because we are seeing one aspect of the person, not his totality. No one is *completely* selfish, incompetent, insensitive, uncaring or stupid. To overcome the tendency to generalize negatively, focus on something positive about the person, situation or yourself. True, she may not be the best housekeeper, but does she have a good heart? True, that child has trouble concentrating, but doesn't he often offer to help you? True, you are high-strung, but are you also very responsible? True, things are terrible between you right now, but haven't you also had wonderful times together?

◆ EXAMPLE: "I wish I were the perfect mother who never screams or hits. But I'm not. My calming thought is that if I were perfect, my children would not have the opportunity to see a mother who is really working on herself to control her negative impulses and who can apologize and be honest about her own weaknesses. I'm working hard to overcome the effects of my own childhood. Each time I treat my children differently than I was treated, I feel that I am healing those childhood wounds."

(18) *Don't wish evil on anyone.*

Hate and revenge…are very difficult for man's spiteful heart to escape, for in view of his being extremely sensitive to insult, and suffering great anguish because of it, revenge, being the only thing which will put him at rest, is sweeter than honey to him. Therefore, if it is within his power to abandon the urging of his nature and to overlook the offense so as not to hate the one who ignited hatred within him, nor to take revenge against him when the opportunity to do so presents itself, nor to hold a grudge against him, but to forget the whole affair and remove it from his heart as if it had never occurred — if he can do this, he is strong and courageous. Such conduct is easy only for the ministering angels among whom the aforementioned traits do not exist… But the King has decreed (in perfectly lucid language, requiring no interpretation) (*Vayikra* 19:17, 18), "Do not hate your brother in your heart… Do not take revenge and do not bear a grudge against the children of your nation." (THE PATH OF THE JUST, p. 141)

It is no easy thing to "abandon the urging of…nature" and do the exact opposite of what our hearts tell us to do. It's easy for the ministering angels, but not for us. Yet that which we achieve with difficulty is far more precious to us. This is why the creation of a truly loving spirit takes so much effort and courage.

Condemnaholism is a sneaky addiction

If you are a condemnaholic, then like an alcoholic, you cannot afford to drink even a tiny drop from the bottle of condemnations, because that "innocent" little bit of fault-finding will start you on the downward spiral into bitter depressions, angry explosions and other addictive behaviors. And you can never finish the "bottle" of condemnations. It refills itself indefinitely.

True, some people can handle "social drinking." They can say, "Oh, I'm such a *klutz*," or "Oy, I'm such a stupid idiot," and not really take these remarks to heart. But condemnaholics cannot afford to think of themselves as stupid or failures even for a second, because they believe their condemnations are true.

Whenever a condemnaholic gets hurt or makes a mistake, he is tempted to get out his "hammer" and smash himself or some other person. He can prepare himself in advance for such moments of weakness by deciding to use them as opportunities to practice healthy spiritual exercises, such as forgiveness, compassion and rebuking without crushing.

It is difficult to fight condemnaholism because shaming thoughts sneak up on us when we are least aware. We may just happen to see a family member doing something and find ourselves thinking, What an idiot. Or, we'll be in the kitchen doing the dishes and angrily think, My lazy, selfish brats aren't helping, or I'm not as smart or as organized as my neighbor. Or, we'll be in *shul*, a place of holiness, and think how obnoxious this one is for praying so loudly, or how extravagant that one is for wasting money on fancy clothing or a big *simchah*.

Not only do such thoughts seem true, they seem so harmless. After all, they're only thoughts. How harmful can a thought be? Very harmful! First we condemn, then we think we have the right and the duty to crush ourselves or others by our actions.

Neutral noticing: the "oh...response"

The Ba'al Shem Tov said that the way to practice "That which is hateful to you, do not do to your friend," is by "noticing his faults and imperfections, whether in his social conduct or in his spiritual behavior, but considering them not to be concrete or substantial. Let your love for him be so great until it covers his flaw, and do not permit it to move from intellectual awareness to a negative emotional feeling" (*Ahavath Yisrael*, Kehot Publication Society, p. 27).

How do we keep our awareness in our minds without affecting our hearts? Obviously, we cannot ignore the tactless remarks, lost keys, or unwashed dishes, etc. However, we can learn to notice them without assigning condemnations or making catastrophic conclusions. Usually when we notice a fault, we add a condemnation afterwards. For example, "I stained my suit. I'm such a failure." Or, "He isn't communicating with me. He's a jerk." We will continue to have likes and dislikes, but we do not have to crush ourselves or the other person with shame in order to motivate change. We notice, then quickly jump to, "What is the best solution to this problem?"

The "Oh...response" is a constructive reaction to such a situation because it allows us to take note of the fault without the poison of the added condemnation. Since our noticing has for so long been inseparable from our condemnations, this is a difficult exercise to do. With practice, it will be easier.

The first step to "neutral noticing" is to practice on objects in your environment. For example, note that "The table is hard." "The grass is green." "I am nearsighted." "She has brown hair." The next step is to transfer the same neutral tone to an assessment of people's shortcomings and determine whether this is something you can fix or must ignore.

> *"Oh...this visitor is really overbearing. I'll just have to bear the discomfort until the visit ends."*
>
> *"Oh...this child is quite sloppy. Let me check my 401 Ways to Get Your Kids to Work Around the House and use those suggestions."*
>
> *"Oh...there I go trying to play God again and thinking that I can handle everything perfectly and make everyone happy. I'd better come back to reality."*
>
> *"Oh...I forgot that appointment. I feel so bad. Next time I'll put a big red circle on my calendar."*
>
> *"In the past, she has proven to be quite irresponsible. I'll have to do the job myself, hire someone else, or ignore it. Those are my only choices."*

◆ EXAMPLE: "Our financial situation is really bad. Every time my children would ask for something that we could not afford, I would condemn myself for being such a failure as a provider, and then get angry at them for asking for things they should know we can't give them. Every time I looked at some broken piece of furniture or something else we don't have the money to fix, I'd sink into bitterness and hostility. But I've worked on my attitude. Now, when I get a bill or see something I cannot afford to fix, or the children ask for something I cannot give them, I focus on solutions and practice gratefulness and forgiveness. As a result, I feel a lot calmer."

We can train ourselves to take a deep breath when we need to calm down. With practice, each breath will remind us that we have to stay calm and loving in order to have a positive influence on anyone else.

◆ EXAMPLE: "I have a learning-disabled child in the sixth grade. I was ashamed of his being a slow learner and was very impatient with him. I was forever making some shaming grimace or remark whenever he forgot some basic math concept which I'd been repeating for the past four years, or when he forgot how to spell a word that most first graders know. Now, I neutrally notice that he's forgotten and simply repeat the information again. I take a deep breath each time I feel myself getting all emotional because I know that my emotionalism won't help things. He needs me to be patient and accepting of him."

The wicked are under the control of their heart.
(BERESHITH RABBAH 34:10)

With the neutral "Oh...response," we can begin the process of getting our hearts under the control of our heads.

In time, after a great deal of practice, we really will be able to notice people's imperfections without the automatic condemnations. The best motto for a condemnaholic is: I will fix what I can without shaming, and ignore whatever I am powerless to change. This includes those thoughts or words which make us or others feel bad, inferior or unloved.

Combine a positive muscular act with trust to make it real

We see from the Torah that it was not enough for the Israelites to express an intellectual belief in God. They also had to perform certain positive physical acts of faith: e.g., to sacrifice a lamb while still in

Egypt, circumcize themselves, depart Egypt with few provisions and jump into the Red Sea while it was still raging.

The same holds true for each person. Attitudinal change is not enough to alter a condemnaholic mentality. We have to constantly demonstrate our dedication to a more caring way of life by making caring gestures, even if they are totally forced or insincere at the moment. That includes giving encouragement and praise, hugging a child, rebuking without name-calling, offering to help someone, calling a friend, etc.

People often say, "When I feel loving, then I will act loving." "When I feel more confident, then I will act more assertive with people." "When I am sure that he didn't do it on purpose, then I'll give him the benefit of the doubt." But this is not how change takes place. In order to change, we first have to perform some act of lovingkindness, courage, forgiveness or assertiveness — and do it in the midst of our darkness, anxiety, fear or anger. Only then can we experience the joy of having broken through our limitations, and know that we can sustain a different attitude. An insincere gesture of love is better than a sincere gesture of hatred. Forced gestures eventually awaken a sincere feeling of love.

Learn to accept your limitations with humility

Rabbi Matis Weinberg once gave a lecture called "Crying Over Nothing," in which he stated that Adam's greatest sin was in thinking that he was lacking in something, and that he needed the fruit of the forbidden tree to become more than who he was. "To think you need to be other than who you are is to lose your whole world," concluded Rabbi Weinberg.

We, too, have difficulty accepting that we are less than perfect. The dissatisfaction we feel about our own and other people's imperfections can be an impetus for our growth, rather than a cause for chronic shame or despair. Our need to change should not keep us from loving each other as we are right now.

Whatever our status, talents and predispositions, each of us is given exactly what we need in order to accomplish our personal mission in life. We only need to use whatever talents God gave us to the best of our ability, given the pressures and pains of the present and the conditioning of our past.

The most powerful tool

The beginning of the downfall of the Jewish people (their exile in Egypt) is often seen as starting with the hatred between Yosef and his brothers. We are told that the *Beith HaMikdash* was destroyed also because of *sinath chinam*, "baseless hatred" (*Yoma* 9b). The *tikkun* for it can only come by practicing *ahavath chinam* (baseless, seemingly irrational love for Him and for our fellowman). That means loving people just for the sake of loving, especially when it is most difficult, i.e., when you feel the most hurt and disappointed in people, your family members in particular.

A wonderful example of this recently took place in the Meah Shearim neighborhood of Jerusalem. An elderly man was rushing for a bus, his *tzitzith* flying and his face red with exertion. He had just managed to reach the back door and bang once, when the driver pulled away. As he watched the departing bus, he called out after the driver, "I bless you. I bless you." He didn't condemn! He could have been very angry. Instead, he forgave and he blessed! As he waited for the next bus, he was at peace with himself instead of fuming with hostility. He used the opportunity to demonstrate Torah ethics.

With every loss, God offers us a gift — the opportunity to heal our own wounds by practicing our spiritual exercises, especially by remaining loving when it seems most absurd and irrational to do so. When we say "I bless you" often enough, either silently or out loud to God and man, we gain greater objectivity and have greater control over ourselves. It is extremely helpful to visualize ourselves doing this ahead of time so that we will be prepared for the real thing!

When we look for the guiding Hand of God in the minor incidents in our lives, and use those incidents to improve our *middoth*, we will be blessed by being able to feel His Hand during our more difficult trials.

To think that our silent condemnations of ourselves and others do not harm anyone is like thinking that we can drill little holes at our end of the boat and not endanger all the other passengers. It is just the opposite: our thoughts and our words affect the entire Jewish nation.

As you break the condemnaholic cycle, you will make two incredible discoveries. First, when you are less critical of others , you experience them as being less critical of you! And when you are less critical of yourself, you experience yourself as more forgiving and accepting of others!

CHAPTER 8:
Depression

Atzvuth [sadness] is on the side of *kelipah* [evil, impurity] while *simchah* [joy] is on the side of *kedushah* [holiness] (*Zohar* II:281, *Derech Emeth*).

There is *simchah* and there is *atzvuth*: the one is life, the other death; the one is goodness, the other evil; the one is *Gan Eden* [heaven], the other *Gehinnom* [hell] (*Zohar* II:255a).

We are required to serve God with joy (*Tehillim* 100:2). The Divine Presence rests only on one who rejoices in a mitzvah (*Shabbath* 30b). But joy is a difficult state to achieve, more so for some people than for others, some because of their nature and others because of their circumstances.

We all have bouts of dysphoria, those inevitable periods of lowered feelings, either because of some disappointment or simply as a part of the natural cycle of mood changes. This is different from the grief we experience over major losses and the longing to bring back what was lost. There is also spiritual melancholia, which stems from our sense of isolation in this world and our soul's longing to be united with God. These normal responses must be distinguished from severe depression, in which a person becomes a virtual prisoner of his pain, unable even to experience hope or joy.

In talking about the saintly Rabbi Aryeh Levin *z"l*, his biographer said:

> There was a thread of melancholy in him, that he acquired perhaps from the ocean of troubles and anguish of the great many people to whom he went, which he absorbed and bore with them. But he never allowed anyone to talk to him about it. His face always smiled and even beamed, so as to cause no one any pain.
>
> (A TZADDIK IN OUR OUR TIME, p. 26)

As we see, this "thread of melancholia" did not prevent this incredible man from devoting time to the study of Torah and prayer or from working indefatigably for the welfare of the Jewish people from dawn to dusk, and from sharing both their joys and their sorrows.

Shelomo HaMelech also struggled with despair, writing "So I hated life, for I was depressed by all that goes on under the sun, because everything is futile and a vexation of the spirit" (*Koheleth* 2:17). Yet he recognized that he had to go through that darkness in order to reach the conclusion that "The sum of the matter, when all is considered: Fear God and keep His commandments, for that is man's whole duty" (Ibid. 12:13). In this statement, he provided the ultimate solution for all those who suffer from depression.

However, when one is enveloped in that terrible, lonely darkness of depression, it is hard to believe that anything will ever make it go away. Gripped by a heavy lethargy, with functioning difficult, if not impossible, life seems too painful to bear. One may feel, "I want to die. I feel dead already. No matter how much I try to cheer myself up, I feel hopeless. I simply have no will to go on." Overcoming this "deadness in life" is very difficult.

Serious depression is a frightening experience because one feels that one has lost control over one's life, one's mind and one's muscles. Even the fact that one has had numerous depressive episodes and recovered each time may not provide hope, for there is always the nagging fear that, "Next time, I'll get stuck in that black hole and won't come out of it."

No one should think that depressed people enjoy being depressed. Although there may be secondary payoffs in terms of attention or excuses to avoid certain people or obligations, depression is torture. The emotional isolation is terrifying. Trying to function in that state is like trying to walk on a broken leg. Just brushing one's teeth or reading a sentence in a book seems like too great a chore to manage. And it only makes things worse to condemn oneself for being depressed, or hear people say, "You're just feeling sorry for yourself. You could snap out of it easily if you really wanted to."

As awful as depression is, many people simply do not have the emotional or spiritual skills to deal with crushing situations, such as the loss of all meaningful work or the loss of a loved one. Many are afraid of what will happen if they stop being depressed, for very complex reasons. If depression is the one thing which has brought some measure of attention, freedom, identity and control or comforting numbness in the face of an oppressive situation, it is frightening to face the world without this protection.

◆ EXAMPLE: "I always felt like a lost soul. My father was very distant and my mother had numerous nervous breakdowns. They were so immersed in their own pain that they didn't seem to see me or hear me. I did the same thing to myself, ignoring my needs as if I didn't really matter. Then I married an autistic type who was just as love-starved as I had been, except that he protected himself by not connecting to people, whereas I felt insatiably needy and would do anything for a few crumbs of attention. When I couldn't even get that, I got so depressed that for years I just wanted to die. My husband's coldness and criticism made me feel like I was crazy. He would hit me and the children whenever he was nervous and then withdraw into his shell again. I stayed alive only for the sake of the children. Finally, I accepted the painful truth that my husband was very sick and could not give me the love I needed. I would have to nourish myself somehow. My first act of health was to do embroidery work in the rich, deep colors that I love. Then I went to night school, which gave me a whole new feeling of self-respect. Despite my inner sense of isolation, I am developing a feeling of self-worth and making contact with people. I had to fight for years to make God a part of my life and to feel that I had value. But because I fought for it on my own and created it myself, it's now a deep part of me."

Endogenous depression: a learned activity which can be unlearned

Depression is often divided into two major categories: (a) exogenous depression which is a response to external traumas such as loss of a loved one, loss of a job, extreme poverty, oppression, etc. and (b) endogenous, or inwardly caused depression which arises not from any immediate trauma, but is based on earlier losses which convinced the person that he is powerless, inadequate and unlovable.

Often, the source of endogenous depression can be traced to the lack of a nurturing mother figure. If the mother died or was absent for long periods of time or was emotionally cold and unavailable because of mental or physical illness, there is a higher risk of chronic depression and suicidal impulses in adulthood. Having never experienced a loving attachment to anyone, these love-starved children often feel distant from God and their fellowman as adults. Just as they felt powerless to win their parents' love no matter how much they cried or how hard they tried to be good, these people now feel powerless and unlovable as adults. The feelings of isolation, helplessness and inferiority are reinforced by their tendency to be harshly critical of themselves, to choose unrewarding careers and nonnurturing marital partners.

People who suffer from endogenous depression often have no more problems than other people. But they interpret their losses in a way which creates tremendous emotional pain. They do not realize that staying depressed requires repeating certain depressing thoughts and self-defeating behaviors over and over again. These thoughts and behaviors do not feel conscious or deliberate. They are so much a part of the person's very being that they seem normal and unavoidable.

It is essential to become aware of the three main components of endogenous depression which encourage feelings of self-loathing, inertia, isolation and helplessness

(1) *Auditory component.* One believes the inner voice which seems to provide protection and power. That voice says, "No one could love you, so don't get close to people." "Stay depressed so people will see that you just cannot handle any more right now. If you stop being depressed, you'll have to take on more obligations and then you'll really collapse." "Stay depressed to punish yourself for all the terrible things you've done." "Because you're such so untogether, you must be taken care of by people who will make sure that you won't make any more disastrous mistakes." "Depression is the only way to avoid being a threat to people who would be very angry with you if you became independent and successful." "It's the only way to get your spouse to pay attention to you. It's the only way to get people to take you seriously."

(2) *Visual component.* One must constantly see oneself as helpless and hopeless, and as inevitably ending up isolated, forgotten by everyone, friendless, perhaps in a mental institution, etc., in order to remain depressed.

(3) *Behavioral component.* One's body language must fit the mental state: long and drawn face, hunched shoulders, slow, lethargic movements, etc., in order to maintain the depression.

One must wage a veritable war in order to overcome the creeping paralysis of the muscles and the paralyzing negativity of the mind. Changing such thoughts and behaviors is like chipping away at a rock. Only by consciously choosing healthy thoughts and actions will one eventually feel powerful, enthusiastic and loving. That takes time and courage.

Don't condemn yourself for being depressed. Instead, be willing to go down into the mine of depression in order to bring back the jewels of greater awareness. The next step is to aggressively satisfy the unfulfilled needs which are keeping you in that state.

Recognizing the gift of depression

It may seem strange to think of the predisposition toward depression as a gift. But like all handicaps, this one is meant to impel people to become aware of aspects of themselves which they would not otherwise be aware of, both their weaknesses and their creative talents. Those with a strong desire to overcome depression have become self-disciplined and assertive, whereas before they were weak-willed and easily intimidated. They have turned to God and devoted themselves to dance, music, writing, art or community projects not only for the creative pleasure which these activities provide, but in order to escape the pain of their depression.

◆ EXAMPLE: "My supersensitive nine-year-old would sometimes say that life was so painful that he didn't want to go on living. I told him that for people with such strong feelings it takes a lot of courage to go on living, because people like us do suffer more from life's many blows. When I see that the very intensity of his feelings frightens him, I tell him that feelings are nothing to be afraid of, but to share them with someone who can understand. We also focus on ways to bring more happiness into his life, like finding creative outlets and doing *chesed* for others. One evening when he was feeling low, I had to go out. When I came back, I saw that he had cleaned up the kitchen without being asked. His face was beaming. He said 'I found a solution! When I do a *chesed*, I feel good!' What a wonderful solution! That's just what he'll need to keep his spirits up all his life. I also organized a choir in his school, which is the high point of his week."

◆ EXAMPLE: "A few years ago I was very depressed, barely able to drag myself through the day. With my first therapist, I got even more depressed. By continually complaining about all the negative aspects of my life, I was only reinforcing my negativity. But by getting so much attention and sympathy for being depressed, I was even more afraid to let go of it. Thankfully, I had the courage to find a new therapist. She focused on health. Her therapy consisted of two parts: insight and action. For insight, I listed all the negative messages I had absorbed as a child which made me feel so inadequate, unlovable and insecure. For action, she made me get involved in various positive activities, including keeping a gratefulness notebook, exercising and group therapy. I hated having to work so hard, but I knew I was on the right path because I was beginning to feel normal for the first time in my life. I was taking charge of my life. I got a job teaching learning-disabled children. At first, all I could handle was fifteen minutes a day. Two years later, I was made coordinator for our entire community. I now work on it about ten hours a day. When I begin to feel down, I remind myself that I can't afford the luxury of wallowing in pain. I know where that will lead me!"

◆ EXAMPLE: "The angrier I got about my husband's lack of attention, the more distant he got. I was angry that he didn't care about my depressing thoughts and feelings. Then a friend told me that no man wants to hear a never-ending list of complaints, and that perhaps my excessive emotionality was driving him to be excessively distant. She suggested I that if I lightened up and was more positive, perhaps that would give him space to come near me without feeling like he was going to be swamped with emotional demands. I was angry because I thought a husband should be a best friend who listened to everything I had to say. But when I pretended to be happy, I found that he became more attentive and happy with me. At first, that made me even angrier, because I thought, What kind of a marriage is this if I have to hide my feelings! But the amazing thing is that I did become more positive as I got busy doing constructive things with my life."

◆ EXAMPLE: "I used to be very negative and was depressed a lot of the time, always complaining how no one respected me. Then, one day my twelve-year-old was talking about how much he hated himself. That's when I realized that my negativity is highly contagious. Even if I had to fake it, I had to become more positive for the sake of my children. My love for them, not myself, made me put forth the effort to stop being so critical. One of the most important lessons I learned is that if I look down on myself, others will, too. If I respect myself, then others are more likely to treat me with respect."

Recognizing the difference between mourning and depression

No man dies with even half his heart's desires fulfilled.

(MIDRASH RABBAH KOHELETH 1:13)

It is said that after being informed of Yosef's death, his father, Yaakov, was in a state of mourning for twenty-two years, during which time the Divine Presence departed from him. Only when he was told that Yosef was still alive did his spirit revive and he visibly came back to life (*Bereshith* 45:27).

We all have our "Yosefs," the relationships and activities which make us feel alive and worthwhile. When we lose them, life may simply not seem worth living. Whatever has been lost, whether it be a dream, a loved one or a job, the sadness cannot be forced away. Mourning is the time when we learn how to live with the pain of our losses and the seeming unfairness of life. Each of us, by strengthening our faith in God, must struggle in our own way with our own limited skills to accept what we can never have . This is a skill which we must all learn the hard way, and at glacial speed.

It is important not to confuse mourning with depression. Legitimate grief must not be stifled. What we do want to avoid is paralyzing self-pity. The major difference is that the mourner is responding appropriately to an actual loss, but gradually experiences a renewal of his enthusiasm for living and loving. In contrast, self-pity leads to bitterness and dysfunction. Mourning turns into depression when the person becomes so filled with shame and guilt that he loses his will to live and love.

> ◆ EXAMPLE: "When my husband's business failed, he went into a deep depression. He kept repeating over and over that he's a failure and a burden on me. He was so ashamed that he wouldn't even talk to his old friends or listen to advice about new lines of work. This bitter, self-hating, critical man is not the man I married. It gets me depressed to see him like this! I'm mourning the loss of a husband and a standard of living, but I have hope, whereas he is sunk in apathy."

The symptoms of depression

Most experts agree that in order for a person to be accurately labeled as depressed, he must have four of the following symptoms, persisting for at least two weeks:

(1) *anhedonia*: an inability to experience pleasure.

(2) *recurrent thoughts of death or suicide.*

(3) *change in appetite*: noticeable weight gain or loss.

(4) *feelings of worthlessness*: that one is bad, crazy, incompetent, inferior, unworthy and unlovable.

(5) *inability to concentrate or make decisions.*

(6) *changes in sleep patterns*: often awakening at 3 or 4 A.M. and being unable to go back to sleep.

(7) *numerous physical complaints with no detectable cause.*

(8) *a feeling of death-in-life*: life feels dreary, drab, empty. The will to live is diminished or absent.

(9) *feeling totally alone, incapable of making contact.*

(10) *feeling of impending disaster or collapse.*

Depression as a way of life

People who suffer from endogenous depression often express the following attitudes:

(1) "I am totally alone. I can't care about or trust anyone." Often their isolation is self-inflicted, for they distance people with criticism and impossible demands, which leave others feeling drained and inadequate.

(2) "The cure will come from some external source." They think that some external person or event (e.g., a new relationship, new doctor, new pill, etc.) will miraculously and instantly give them a sense of love, worth and purpose. They are sure everything will change, "When I get married," "When I get rich," "When my parents/children/mate/boss treat me better," "When I find the right medication." With exogenous depression, a fulfilling job or a loving relationship can change things dramatically. But if the person has a deeply-imbedded feeling of failure, the change will not last, at least not until the belief changes.

(3) "I cannot take care of myself." Because chronically depressed people feel helpless, they tend to underfunction and want to be

dependent on someone who will care for them and take control of their lives. Many are afraid to grow up, because to them that means becoming like their parents, whom they reject; or they are afraid of having to work hard, which they fear will bring only more failure and possible physical or mental collapse.

On the other hand, depressed people often swing to the opposite extreme and become overdoers as well, believing that unless they are doing seventeen things at once, and all of them perfectly, and keeping everyone in the environment happy, that they are failures, which then pushes them into depression.

(4) "I am hopeless." They make efforts to improve, then give up too soon, thus reinforcing their belief that, "Nothing works. I'm hopeless." Convinced that they are hopeless, they have little motivation to struggle for health.

(5) "I can't control myself." Convinced that their impulses are uncontrollable, they are certain that, "I'm so disturbed that I can't possibly avoid screaming, sulking, overeating, withdrawing." Thus, although depressed people say that they want health, they often sabotage all their own efforts to engage in healthy activities or relationships.

In other words, depression is an indirect way of giving people certain messages, many of them contradictory: "I want you to love me, but keep your distance." "Lay off! I can't take any more! Take charge of my life. Take care of me. But don't take control of my life." "Let me be in control even though I'm not in control."

The cry of the healthy child is, "See me as I am. Love me for what I am. Make me feel important and valued." Although that need may not have been satisfied in childhood, as adults we discover that we can do it for ourselves. This requires that we consciously and deliberately wean ourselves away from thoughts which make us feel like hopeless, lonely failures.

Seeking nourishment for the neshamah

Depression is the *neshamah's* cry for the activities and relationships which will provide the nourishment it desperately needs. Just as we have basic physical needs, such as for food and shelter, we also have "meta needs," which are deeper cravings for emotional, intellectual and spiritual fulfillment. One must identify what it is that the *neshamah* craves, and then actively seek fulfillment in that area. For example:

Closeness to God. The deepest need of the *neshamah* is for closeness to God through the study of Torah, prayer, and performance of *mitzvoth*. Ultimately, it is this attachment alone which enables us to overcome despair and loneliness. Depression is often the catalyst which pushes us to make God a part of our lives.

Challenging goals. The human psyche is growth-oriented. We all know how wonderful it feels to accomplish something worthwhile or to have something exciting to look forward to. Suddenly we are full of life. We need less sleep, are more tolerant of minor irritations and are less sensitive to pain. Yet without worthwhile goals, we lose enthusiasm and interest in life. We are more irritable, self-preoccupied and less self-disciplined. Life feels empty and meaningless without a goal. People can bear the most intolerable conditions if they feel there is meaning and purpose to their pain.

♦ EXAMPLE: "I was always angry that I had to work so hard to stay sane, when other people didn't have to put up the same fight. It didn't seem fair that my inner world was so full of chaos and turmoil while no one else had these ups and downs all the time! I kept wondering, 'Why can't I just be calm and confident? Why do I have to struggle all the time? I'm not a fighter! I need someone to take over and take care of me. I need someone to make me feel secure and loved.' I was bitter because no one showed up to take care of me. Finally I realized that I had to take care of myself."

Even if one's goal is purely spiritual in nature, there must be a physical correlate to make it meaningful. For example, if someone wants to draw closer to God, he can learn a certain amount of Torah each day or do a specific *chesed* for others or strengthen a particular *middah* each week.

♦ EXAMPLE: "After weeks of being sick, I became very depressed. I needed a goal, so I decided to use my time to overcome my condemnaholism. I used every opportunity not to react angrily or condemn the people who were taking care of me or visiting. I constantly gave people the benefit of the doubt and responded politely each time I felt like snapping angrily. It was a tremendous struggle to overcome the depression which gripped me, but I felt that my *neshamah*, as well as my body, was being healed by my efforts to be more loving."

◆ EXAMPLE: "As I got older, I began to suffer from depression and a variety of physical problems. I went to numerous doctors and tried all kinds of medication, but I still felt that I was going steadily downhill. It was like my spirit had died. I had nothing to live for. Then my daughter was involved in a car accident and she and two of her children were hospitalized for three months. Suddenly, I had something to live for. Between going to the hospital and taking care of her other children, I was so busy that I didn't have time to be depressed. It took a near-tragedy to make me wake up, but now I realize how important it is to take the initiative and find meaningful activities for myself."

Creative expression. Many people have strong creative drives which must be expressed through writing, teaching, dancing, music, art, hobbies and craft work, etc. If their creative urge has no positive outlet, their energy then festers inside them or turns outward in destructive behavior. No amount of philosophizing can make these people feel better if the creative drive remains unsatisfied. Intense inner restlessness is a sign that one is not doing what he was put on this earth to do. When one's passions are suppressed, one's whole being feels depressed.

A famous Israeli sculptress, Mazal Boussidan, began her career in a hospital. Critically ill with myasthenia gravis (a neuromuscular disease), connected to machines which helped her to breathe, swallow and maintain her heartbeat, her situation seemed hopeless. Her hands were tightly locked in a claw-like position. Her son, Yaakov, trying to find some way to give strength to her almost useless limbs and hope to her mind, began to teach her how to work with clay.

Mrs. Boussidan proved to have tremendous talent and determination. Within nine months, she returned home from the hospital filled with a passion for life and art. Her works are praised by artists around the world. At age seventy-five, she had her first one-woman exhibition. She is so full of energy that she often rises in the middle of the night to sculpt.

◆ EXAMPLE: "I saw my naturally happy and exuberant son become more withdrawn and depressed as he got older and the school day got longer. He is not an academically-oriented child. He craves adventure, physical activities and working with tools. His principal suggested that I transfer him to a school with less academic pressure and more practical life skills. His entire outlook changed. He became so much happier."

◆ EXAMPLE: "When I was very depressed, I called a friend who is a writer. She suggested that I put my feelings on paper. When I told her that I had no talent and had never written before, she said it didn't matter; I should just put my feelings down and call her back in an hour. For her sake more than mine, I took out a piece of paper and started. I couldn't stop! As I wrote, I realized that none of my meta-needs were being met. No wonder I was depressed! I was not nourishing myself. By writing, I discovered my own inner source of guidance and strength that I hadn't known before."

Love. Isolation and depression go hand in hand. Thus, those in unhappy marriages or those who are homebound or socially isolated, especially young mothers, the sick and the aged, often suffer from depression.

◆ EXAMPLE: "My whole life, I was always measuring myself against everybody, feeling either one-up or one-down. In my support group, I learned that whether I'm feeling superior or inferior, I'm creating distance and isolating myself. To become a truly loving person, I must avoid both of these."

◆ EXAMPLE: "My husband is a very caring person. But when he was learning from early in the morning until late at night, we almost never had a chance to talk. We were like strangers to each other. I had no social life because living in a fourth floor walk-up apartment made it hard for my friends with young children to visit and hard for me to get out with my own small ones. I also had no intellectual stimulation, which is so important to me. The more I told myself that I should make peace with my life and that it was wrong to be unhappy, the unhappier I got. When I found myself thinking about death all the time, I knew that I had to take charge of my life and be assertive about making changes. We moved to a ground floor apartment so that people could visit and I could get out more easily. My husband and I scheduled times to talk. And I make sure to go out to *shiurim.*"

◆ EXAMPLE: "After my wife died, I didn't want people's pity, so I pretended that I was doing well. But the truth was that I felt numb and dead inside. Now that I am about to marry a wonderful woman, I feel alive again. Without her love, my life felt so empty. I thought strength meant not needing anyone. Now I know that true strength means recognizing our need to love and be loved, and not being ashamed of that need."

Not everyone has a strong need for emotional intimacy. Those who do can be surrounded with friends or family members and still feel lonely if their need for a deeper level of communication remains unmet.

Having a critical person in one's environment can also make it difficult to feel self-respecting, because it means one is living with another person's death wish for oneself.

◆ EXAMPLE: "My wife is a very self-contained person with almost no need for emotional closeness. Her coldness is terribly painful. I push myself to stay active, but the pain is still there when I open the door to our home."

◆ EXAMPLE: "It's not just talk that I need when I'm down. I need to communicate with another deeply feeling, spiritually sensitive and intellectually aware type. That's the only thing that satisfies my strong need for closeness."

◆ EXAMPLE: "I used to feel so ashamed of having a problem with depression until I learned to think of these periods as being like attacks of sinusitis. It's as useless to condemn myself for my emotional problems as it is to condemn myself for my physical ones. I learned to focus on healing techniques. I now know that the thoughts I think when I'm depressed are so destructive that I must be tough and refuse to listen to them. If I gave my inner critic free reign, it would condemn me night and day for not having everything neat and organized, for not serving fancier food, for not being popular, for not always being in control, for not always knowing what to do, and a million other things. The more I shut that inner critic up, the better I feel about myself!"

Self-esteem. To be deeply, consciously aware of our infinite worth is a Torah obligation (*Alei Shur*, p. 168). In Hebrew, the word for honor is *kavod*, from *kaved* ("heaviness"). Depression always involves a feeling of having lost one's sense of personhood, of mattering to the world. Depressed people often feel, "I don't matter; I have no use."

The belief that one is superfluous or useless is one of the most devastating of all attitudes. Unemployed or chronically ill people often feel that they have lost their importance. Many elderly people feel that as their bodily faculties deteriorate, their value as human beings decreases proportionately.

◆ EXAMPLE: "I was the rabbi of a thriving congregation in America. Then I retired and moved to Israel. It was wonderful at first, but after a while I found myself at a terrible loss. No one turned to me for help. I felt useless and superfluous. Once I had been a very important person; now I was just another old man. What saved me was a part-time teaching job and volunteer work. My *neshamah* needs to teach and serve. Now that I'm involved in *chesed*, I feel a lot better."

◆ EXAMPLE: "After I lost my baby, I could only think that God must hate me for giving me such a terrible punishment and so much pain. When a rabbi visited me, I told him how I felt. He said that the concept of punishment is meant to bring us closer to God, to make us feel cleansed. If it doesn't do this, he said, then it's not the right attitude for me at this time. He suggested that I ask God to help me understand how I could grow from this experience. I didn't feel like praying, but I did. Little by little, I began to feel God as a loving presence in my life. My spirits revived slowly and, for the first time, I had a desire to go back into the world."

◆ EXAMPLE: "I went to an EMETT class for a whole year, all the time thinking secretly that I was hopeless and would never make any progress. But a friend kept dragging me to meetings, saying that if I just sat there, it would eventually sink in. I was determined to prove that she was wrong. I had a strong will to fail, but no will for health. I didn't want to think of myself as lazy; I wanted to believe I was deeply disturbed. Nevertheless, I said the stock EMETT phrases mechanically at first and began to believe in the concept of working for health. Somehow, those phrases became integrated into my life and I actually did become more self-disciplined and much happier."

Pleasure. God meant for life to be pleasurable (*Yerushalmi Kiddushin* 4:12). Since the inability to experience pleasure is the primary symptom of depression, it is essential to find pleasurable activities which will restore your desire to live. This is a very individual search which no one else can dictate for you. One person may find it healing to work in a garden, while another needs to dance, write or do volunteer work. If you cannot think of anything which would give you pleasure, think back to your high school days and remember what gave you pleasure back then. Or, ask yourself, "If I were told that I had only a short time to live, what would I do to make myself happy? Where would I want to go? Who would I want to be with and who would I avoid?" These answers will give you a clue as to what you need to do. When you begin to satisfy your innermost needs, life will become pleasurable again. If poverty, illness or other oppressive conditions prevent you from doing any of the things which used to give you pleasure, the fight against depression will be a difficult one indeed.

Control and security. Any loss of control, including loss of control over one's behavior, health, finances or relationships can provoke a depressive episode.

◆ EXAMPLE: "Whenever I felt the least bit depressed, I would give in to my worst impulses. I'd overeat and sulk and snap at everyone. To me, being depressed gave me the right to lose control. But losing control made me lose respect for myself, which made me even more depressed. One day my best friend told me, 'I love you, but you're addicted to *kvetching.* I won't talk to you again until you have something positive to say about your life.' I was furious at first, but I knew she was right. I started to keep a list, writing down every minor act of self-control, like not giving in to my urge to criticize people, just so I would have something positive to say to her. It was like going to war with my negative self. That was the beginning of my long road to self-respect. I still keep a happiness notebook to remind me to appreciate God and the good in my life, because the tendency to whine and complain never goes away completely. When I joined a support group, I found that what helped more than anything was being able to help other people to get out of their depressions. Giving them encouragement gave me encouragement and a sense of power!"

◆ EXAMPLE: "A friend helped me out of my depression by telling me to make one small change in my thinking to gain a sense of control. She told me that when I blame others by saying 'It (meaning my spouse, my job or the weather, etc.) makes me depressed,' I feel like a victim. Instead, I should say 'I'm depressing myself by drawing negative conclusions about this situation.' This new way of thinking forces me to see that I have choices as to how to think. As a result, I don't get stuck in those gloomy moods for such a long time. And I've become more disciplined in other areas of my life as well. Being in control of my thoughts makes me feel more secure."

Freedom. Feelings of powerlessness, dependency and hopelessness are fundamental causes of depression. Under the rule of oppressive tyrants, when people are deprived of the freedom to make their own decisions and express their individuality, large sectors of the population suffer from depression. Likewise, in a repressive home, where there is no freedom to express one's individual talents or opinions, family members often become depressed. The depression is often manifest as a kind of "robotization," in which people go through life mechanically, without feeling.

Illness can also cause both the sick person and the caretaker to suffer from depression, since freedom of movement is greatly restricted.

Extreme poverty is terribly oppressive and often terribly humiliating as well. For this reason, Rashi says, "A poor man is considered as one dead" (*Bereshith* 29:11). While some people do not seem to be adversely affected by poverty, and even reach great spiritual heights in the midst of great deprivation, most people feel diminished and stifled and lose hope, ambition and initiative.

> ◆ EXAMPLE: "I don't feel really alive because my day is focused on sheer survival. We have no money for a babysitter, so I can't go to a *shiur* or buy the art supplies I need to practice my skills. I spend my life just trying to make it through the day, worrying about where I can get the cheapest food and shoes, how to keep warm in the winter and how I'll survive without proper medical care or decent food. I know people who are proud that they manage so well under the same circumstances. But I hate the tension and the humiliation of poverty. There's nothing to look forward to except more bills."

When poverty, illness or other oppressive conditions deprive one of one's most pleasurable outlets, depression is often the result. It is the person's way of numbing himself to the pain of having his deepest longings remain unfulfilled. While we must allow ourselves to grieve without guilt for the real losses in our lives, we must strengthen our faith in God in order to go on without bitterness.

The chemical connection

Depression can have a physiological origin. For example, hormonal imbalances are one of the major causes of postpartum depression. In addition, people are far more prone to depression if their parents have the same predisposition. One research study has shown familial patterns of too much cortisol and too little thyroxin and serotonin in the bloodstream. These imbalances increase the brain's sensitivity to stimuli, leading to depression, anxiety or extremely aggressive behavior (*The New England Journal of Medicine*, vol. 311, #4).

A person can *lower* his cortisol level and *raise* his serotonin level by forcing himself to engage in healthy activities. Even some minor positive act such as smiling or straightening his shoulders can bring some small measure of self-mastery, even if these gestures are insincere at first. Of course, a phony smile will not help a person who needs to express his grief over a very real loss, or help someone who should be making actual changes in his life, such as finding a new job or getting professional help. However, in ordinary daily situations, a smile may remind him that he does have a choice as to how to respond and must patiently function with the discomfort until the setback passes. The more control he has over his thoughts, the more likely he is to gain some control over his chemical cycle and may be able to prevent a major depressive episode (*Recovery from Depression*, pp. 10-30).

The gender connection

The Jewish ideal of the *Esheth Chayil* (the woman of valor) is a strong, dynamic, wise, competent woman ruling over her empire with compassion and courage, so that her appreciative husband is free to fulfill his duties. Unfortunately, women often see themselves as needy, dependent, weak, powerless and inferior, all of which are major components of depression.

Women are more prone to depression than men, if they: (1) feel that they are inferior to and of less value than men, (2) feel that they have little control over their lives and have no choice but to passively submit to other people's abuse, (3) are financially and emotionally dependent on people who do not love or value them, and (4) think they must please everyone and have continuous approval from others in order to feel worthwhile.

Women also tend to blame themselves if a relationship is going poorly. They're the ones who tend to be most concerned about getting people's love and keeping it. They're the ones who think they're abnormal if they are abused or unloved by their mates. They also worry more about their security and fear rejection and abandonment if they fail to win others' approval. They often exhaust themselves trying to please others, yet have deep, unacknowledged resentment toward those whose needs they cannot satisfy, whether it be a husband, child or parent. They are more likely to suppress their anger in order not to arouse the disapproval of those on whom they are dependent.

Also, mothers of young children are more likely to suffer from low self-esteem if they feel that they are not coping perfectly with the myriad demands of a home and family. Many young mothers feel that they must suppress their own dreams and interests lest others think of them as selfish. The resulting loss of a sense of self often leads to depression.

However, depression is not exclusively a women's problem. Many men suffer from depression, especially if they do not have fulfilling work. However, many men hide their depression, even from themselves, by acting angry rather than showing any hint of vulnerability or fear. If a man is not succeeding in his work or studies and feels like a failure, he may attempt to protect his masculinity and build himself up by tearing others down and blaming them for his problems. Also, men with dependent personalities use depression as an excuse to avoid responsibilities and to force others to take care of them, thereby remaining at an infantile stage of developoment.

Depressed people, depressed thinking

Depression which is due to external losses or chemical imbalances is easier to deal with than depression which is caused by a deeply-ingrained sense of helplessness and failure. Dr. Martin Seligman (*Journal of Abnormal Psychology*, vol. 87, no. 1, pp. 49-74) found that people suffering from endogenous depression have a kind of mental filter which reinforces their feelings of hopelessness, powerlessness and failure by blocking out any good in themselves or the world. They do this by:

Discounting the good. For example, a depressed mother will discount all the hours she devotes to her children by saying, "I could be doing so much more. I should be happy and in control all the time." If someone says that she seems to be functioning quite well, she will say, "I may seem normal, but I'm not. Sometimes I lose control and scream. I feel as though I'm barely hanging on even though it doesn't seem that way."

Expecting rejection. Depressed people expect to be rejected. Furthermore, they perceive people as rejecting even when this is not true. Perhaps people who are not depressed pick up on depressed people's defensive body language and attitudes and decide that these people are unfriendly and unpleasant. Consequently, they avoid them, thereby reinforcing the depressed people's conception that they are unlovable. Thus a negative feedback loop is created, in which depression and rejection reinforce each other.

Drawing negative conclusions. Depressed people assign negative symbolic meanings to ordinary events. Spilled juice, a minor slip-up or an inappropriate remark is taken to mean, "See, that proves I'm abnormal, incompetent and unlovable." They also interpret their depression as a sign that they are crazy and are incapable of ever functioning normally.

Depressed people also use a temperamental language which reinforces their feeling of victimization and helplessness. Thus, they are likely to keep repeating phrases such as, "She's driving me crazy." "He's killing me." "I'm a basket case." "I can't do anything right." "There's nothing to look forward to."

Dr. Seligman also noted that the meaning people give events determines whether or not they get depressed about them. Whenever they make a mistake, depressed people draw erroneous conclusions, believing that their failures are:

(1) *Stable over time.* "It's not just today that was lousy. I *always* mess things up and I'll keep messing everything up in the future. Things are bound to get worse."

(2) *Global.* "I burned the chicken. But it's not only my cooking that's no good. I mess *everything* up!"

(3) *Internally caused.* "I failed because I'm a failure. I am basically defective, stupid, bad and crazy."

People who aren't depressed explain their mistakes and failures differently:

(1) *Unstable over time.* "I goofed on that project, but I'm sure the next one will work out." "What I said was stupid, but I'm not stupid." "I was rejected at that place, but I'll go some place where people can understand and appreciate me."

(2) *Specific.* "I can't handle a large classroom, but I'm good on a one-to-one basis." "I'm lousy at math, but great in art." "I'm not the most creative cook, but I have a good heart and care very much about people."

(3) *External.* "So, I failed. I'll prepare better and do well the next time." "I lost control, but that's not typical of me. It's probably because I'm nervous about my in-laws coming to visit. I can stay calm next time by avoiding all judgments and all unrealistic expectations and demands."

To discover if you have erroneous beliefs which are keeping depression alive, write down as many endings as possible to the following sentences, even if they may seem silly: (1) "I *must* get depressed, because it is the only way I can get _____." (2) "If I stop being depressed, I'll lose my _____." Now, go back and figure out how you can get your messages across directly and get your needs satisfied in a way which makes you feel powerful and lovable.

Because one's attitude has such a tremendous impact on one's feelings, it is important for depression-prone people to get in touch with all the beliefs which make them feel powerless and hopeless. This is very painstaking work which often is best done with a therapist.

Perfectionism: setting oneself up for failure

Depressed people are often anxiety-ridden perfectionists who have despaired of ever getting the love and respect they want because they have failed to meet their own impossible standards. The perfectionist thinks, "I must be the best." "If I can't do it perfectly, I won't do it at all." "I must get very upset about my mistakes because this is the only way to avoid making any more." "I must not act, because if I take action, I will fail." "If I don't try, then my efforts won't be criticized."

To get less than a top grade — whether on a meal, a project or a relationship — is, to them, to have failed completely. If being imperfect — which is what we all are — means being a failure, then it seems *safer* not to do anything or connect to anybody and risk more failure.

Perfectionists are always giving themselves (and those around them) a death message, i.e., "Be something different than who you are." Perfectionists also put themselves into doublebinds, believing, for example, "I must be sweet, passive and subservient, yet strong, competitive and aggressive."

To discover if you fall into this category, ask yourself, "As a child, in order to be deserving of my parents' love, I had to be _____." "In order to be deserving of love and respect now I must be_____." The healthy reply is, " I deserve love and respect because I am me."

To think that one must be other than what one is creates the atmosphere in which depression, anxiety and anger flourish. The Torah obligates us to love ourselves and others as we and they are. It requires that we struggle to love and fear God and strive for moral perfection throughout our lives — not that we achieve it today. Our task is not to be perfect *tzaddikim*, which is a category reserved for a miniscule number of people, but only to be "intermediate types" (*beinonim*), i.e., people who involve themselves in the struggle for self-improvement (*Likutei Amarim*, ch. 27).

Getting in touch with your inner nurturer

A tendency toward depression may be with you for the rest of your life, like a tendency toward heart disease or diabetes. This is not to be pessimistic or despairing, only realistic. By facing this reality, you can accept that you face an uphill battle and avoid the false expectation of completely eliminating this tendency. Also, you don't feel like a total failure when those inevitable setbacks occur. You simply focus on developing the skills needed to keep you in contact your *neshamah*.

Numerous skills will minimize the intensity and duration of depressive episodes. Your major spiritual work is to remain loving and devote yourself to meaningful goals no matter how badly you feel. You must work on this just as you would any job, day in and day out. The two major keys to overcoming depression are: (a) making God an integral part of your every waking moment and, (b) exercising your power to choose healthy thoughts and actions.

As you gain insight into the three components (i.e., auditory, visual and behavioral) which maintain depression, you can use the same analytical process to figure out what you can do to put youself in a state of joy, love and enthusiasm. For example, think about the last time you felt strong, hopeful and happy. Make that scene as real as possible in your mind. What were you thinking? How was your body responding? Let all those positive feelings fill you. Notice how you have the ability to duplicate those positive feelings right now.

As you develop skill in using your mind and muscles to produce positive or negative emotional states, you soon realize that you are not a helpless victim. If nothing else, you always have a choice of attitude.

You can break the cycle of self-hatred and self-abuse by getting in touch with that ignored "inner nurturer," that voice of the *neshamah* which has been struggling to be heard. Listen. It will tell you that "You are loved. Be kind to yourself. Forgive yourself. Forgive others." If you listen often enough to that voice, you will eventually establish a whole new way of thinking and behaving.

By repeating the following affirmations throughout the day, you will break the patterns which have made you feel abnormal, hopeless and victimized:

To build trust in God: "I trust that God is with me in this darkness. He will help me out of it. The inner strengths which He has given me will pull me through."

To build trust in oneself: "I am average, not abnormal." "I always have choices, even if only in attitude. I can focus on the good or the bad in myself and my life." "I will do the difficult! I will stretch myself to my limits in order to build self-respect. I will function with this discomfort." "I can bear this situation with courage and love."

To overcome bitterness: "I am grateful for all that God has given me, instead of angry for what He hasn't." "Each depression is useful because it shows me where I need to work, especially what myths I need to eliminate from my mind."

To strengthen stability: "Even if I don't always feel like being disciplined, I will stick resolutely to my schedule of healthy activities, getting up and going to sleep at decent hours and eating properly at set times." (This is especially important for those with a tendency toward manic-depressive cycles and those who feel a great deal of inner turmoil and chaos.)

To build confidence: "I will make firm decisions and stick to them." "I endorse myself for my efforts to be productive. I don't have to do anything outstanding to be deserving of love and respect. I only have to work on my *middoth*. I refuse to torture myself with comparisons to more "together" people. A lot of people would have given up, but I'm doing a pretty good job considering the pain I'm in."

To overcome fear of failure: "I do not have to be perfect to be deserving of love and respect. I only have to do the best I can. Effort is up to me; success is up to God."

To overcome fear of rejection: "Rejection and criticism are distressing, not dangerous. I am loved and capable. God loves me. My value is determined by God, not man." "I accept myself as I am and will be more accepting of others." "Those who know how to love will love me as I am, without my having to perform, please or prove myself. Those who do not know how to love will never love me no matter what I do."

To show gratefulness to God: "Having learned the strategies necessary to overcome depression, I will give this gift to others and help them learn to manage this handicap. (Joining a support group is one of the best ways to prove to oneself how common the problem is and to help others with it.)

To overcome fear of setbacks: "I refuse to indulge in fear of possible future setbacks. I have better things to do with my time. If I do have a setback, I will emerge with greater strength. Setbacks are temporary. They are merely uncomfortable, not dangerous. Comfort is a want, not a need."

To overcome shame: "I will condemn myself only for deliberate transgressions. I will then repent and forgive myself quickly. I don't need to hit myself with a sledgehammer to remind myself to improve. I will not shame myself for my personality or Divinely-determined tendencies or events."

Note: You do not have to believe these affirmations when you say them! During times of severe distress, these may seem like silly lies.

However, you will find that by saying them over and over, they will eventually penetrate your consciousness and have an uplifting and calming effect. Belief is the last to come and the most difficult to achieve.

Physical exercise

The body, mind and spirit are one. There is no such thing as a physical illness that doesn't affect the mind or an emotional illness that doesn't get translated into physical pain of some sort. Thus, physical exercise provides a sense of control which builds self-esteem and overcomes the defeatist mentality to which a depressed person is enslaved. Unfortunately, depressed people tend to be resistant to anything which requires mental or physical effort. The quickest way to overcome this initial opposition is for the person to sign up for a regular exercise class and force himself to go. After about six to eight weeks, the pleasure of healthy movement will overcome the resistance.

Although you may feel awkward, phony and mechanical at first, it is ultimately your muscles which will teach your brain that you are trustworthy, that you can keep to a schedule, can ignore the defeatist babble of your brain, can be self-disciplined and can function with discomfort.

Establish a regular schedule and keep to it religiously, despite the inner voice which whines, "But I don't feel good. But I don't feel like going. But it's cold out and I don't have any energy." These fixed daily routines build a sense of stability and self-respect. Also, by exercising you are saying that you want to take control of your life and will fight to do so. That is the most powerful message you can give your brain.

Research has shown that strenuous physical activity produces changes in body chemistry and helps to restore emotional stability. The release of norepinephrine during exercise lifts the spirits and reduces the intensity and frequency of depression (*Journal of the American Medical Association*, vol. 252, no. 4).

The Torah path to mental health is to give when we feel deprived, to strengthen others' faith when our own faith is weak, to control our harmful impulses when we feel most like giving in to them, and to stretch ourselves to our limits when we feel most despairing. Every act of self-discipline builds self-respect.

Medication

Numerous medications exist to combat depression. People with manic-depressive cycles, for example, find blessed relief from mood swings when they take lithium. There is a type of depression found among the elderly which responds well to medication. Some find that short-term medication breaks the cycle of depression and allows them to experience what it is like to feel stable and healthy. Others get no relief from medication and become even more depressed as a result.

Pills have their shortcomings. They cannot magically overcome a lifetime of negative mental conditioning which has filled a person with bitterness, resentment and lethargy, or made him think that he is crazy, incompetent or worthless. Attitudinal change does not come without concurrent change in behavior. Pills can do neither by themselves.

Medication does not teach a person how to love, act considerately or think rationally. And pills won't give a person the courage to take those first difficult steps back to mental and physical health. Pills may help a person feel good enough to get into the water, but they can't make him expend the effort to swim vigorously every day on schedule. These are efforts which raise self-confidence and give a person a feeling of control over his life, thereby reducing the depression.

Furthermore, medications have side effects which may be as distressing as the depression itself. Common side effects are: loss of appetite, insomnia, blurred vision, fatigue, dry mouth, nausea, constipation, urine retention, sweating, weight gain, tremors, rashes, fuzzy thinking, loss of libido, increased anxiety and agitation, palpitations, feelings of unreality, reduced concentration, memory loss and headaches. Long term use may cause serious damage to the central nervous system.

Nevertheless, short-term medication may be worth a try if it gives a person hope and helps him get started on the road to self-control.

There are also helpful natural remedies, including vitamins and a healthier diet. A nutritionist can be consulted about the connection between poor diet (especially a high sugar and caffeine intake) and depression, and recommend natural products which raise the level of serotonin in the bloodstream (which is commonly low in depressed people). Women who suffer from monthly mood swings can ask their doctors about taking gamma linoleic acid (GLA). When the amount of this substance is very low, as it is before the menstrual period in a high percentage of women, many uncomfortable symptoms result, including lowered feelings, anxiety and loss of control over aggressive impulses.

For family members of depressed people

People often ask how they can get a depressed person to become less self-centered, morose, lethargic or erratic. Depressed people need both love and discipline. Family members can encourage the depressed person to express his fears and reassure him of their love for and faith in him, but they should realize that only a self-loving person can experience that others love him. And a person cannot become self-loving unless he engages in confidence-building activities. Also, allowing the depressed person to complain endlessly about how awful everything is, intensifes the depression.

Relatives often mistakenly think that it is their job to make the depressed person better, and that it is their fault if they do not succeed. Such people, called codependents, end up feeling furious or depressed themselves if they take responsibility for anothers' depression and feel guilty when the peson does not improve, no matter how much they try to please and perform.

♦ EXAMPLE: "My daughter was always blaming me for her problems. When she would begin her mother-bashing, I'd squirm in shame and guilt and either distance myself or attack back. Finally, I simply told her, 'I did the best I could. When you were born, I was young and inexperienced and had to work full time. You'll never accept yourself until you accept me.' That broke the ice. Now, when she starts blaming me, I refuse to squirm like a worm on the end of a fishing rod. I tell her to tell me what she is doing now to heal herself and heal our relationship. That gets her to take responsibility for her own moods and *middoth*."

♦ EXAMPLE: "My mother-in-law blames me for her depressions. She visited after I gave birth to my seventh child and, after she went back home, complained to everyone in the family that I didn't take her out to eat or pay enough attention to her. In our codependent state, I would have squirmed with shame and guilt, and my husband would have been furious with me for not doing more for her. Now, however, we stay compassionately distant and refuse to squirm. We feel sad for her. She is very lonely and very needy, but I cannot let her destroy our lives."

Codependent thinking furthers the addictive illusion that recovery is tied to some external source and that unhappiness is the best way to get attention. The recovery process is actually thwarted when others allow the person to dwell on the negative, thereby encouraging him to stay the way he is, or bend over backwards to please the depressed person.

It is important to realize that no one can build another person's self-respect or give another person *emunah* and *bitachon*. No one can make another person move his muscles to do something constructive or restrain his harmful impulses. If the person feels like a failure and refuses to do the work necessary to develop a strong will and overcome his isolation, inertia, self-pity and despair, neither logic nor love can motivate him. In fact, the depressed person usually will resent another person's efforts to get him going again.

Occasionally, it is helpful to get tough and insist that the person do things which will give him back a sense of control and self-respect. For example, the sister of a depressed man hired him to work in her business, but drew up a list of conditions that he had to honor, such as that he had to come on time every morning, put in a full day's work, and successfully complete a certain quota each week. He knew that she meant it. Her "tough love" worked. His self-discipline increased and his self-respect was restored.

One husband humorously told his wife that if she didn't get out of the house and go to one exercise class and one *shiur* a week, he was going to use that time to take up skydiving! She got out and started to feel better.

♦ EXAMPLE: "My husband has been very depressed for months. At first, when he kept telling me what a failure he was, I'd argue and tell him how wonderful he was. But it didn't help. The more I tried to please him, the more demanding and critical he got. No matter what I did, he'd complain. He was dragging me right down along with him. At first, I thought I was selfish for thinking about myself and going on with my life, but I saw that I was crippling him by catering to him. When I became bitter and depressed by his behavior, he felt good because he felt he had power over me. That only rewarded him for his depression. As I became more independent and happier, he got angrier and more tyrannical at first, but I persisted in doing the things which made me feel happy and fulfilled. He finally got upset enough to seek help."

It is important for the family members of depressed people to pursue meaningful goals and make their own lives pleasurable. Often, when disturbed people see that they cannot control others by staying depressed, they decide it is more worthwhile to get well.

CHAPTER 9:
Generalized Anxiety Disorder (GAD)

Behold, God is my salvation. I will trust and not fear.

(YESHAYAHU 12:2)

...he who trusts in God...is afraid of no one. What is trust? It is tranquility of soul...; it is reliance on the one in whom he trusts, that the latter will do what is right and proper... The essence of his trustfulness is his sure confidence that the person in whom he trusts will fulfill what he promised...and even in matters wherein he made no promise nor gave a pledge, has it in mind to benefit the one who trusted him — and all this out of pure benevolence and kindness. (CHOVOTH HALEVAVOTH, vol. I, pp. 285, 295)

In times of danger, it is normal to experience waves of anxiety, a terrible sense of dread, hyperventilation, stomach distress and suffocating sensations. However, some people have this feeling nearly all of the time. They have a condition known as GAD, (Generalized Anxiety Disorder), or what doctors call "free-floating anxiety," i.e., a pervasive fear about falling apart or going crazy which is connected to nothing specific, but to everything and everyone in general.

A feeling of existential anxiety is an inevitable part of the human condition, something we all live with to some degree, given the precariousness of human existence — the tragedies, natural disasters, illnesses, financial upheavals and the continual world crises. So it is no wonder that the word "trust," *emunah*, comes from *l'hitamen*, "to practice," and *oman*, meaning "a highly developed skill." True *emunah* requires repeating over and over the mental and physical disciplines which build trust in God and oneself.

Whoever listens to Me will dwell secure and will be tranquil without fear of evil. (MISHLEI 1:33)

192

We would all like to "dwell secure." Why is this a more difficult goal for some than for others? The answer often lies in the person's early parent-child relationship. When parents are consistently loving and provide the fair discipline which makes a child feel secure, he internalizes this as a feeling of trust in himself and trust in the world at large. The protective arms of loving parents provide the child with his initial experience of trust, which is later manifest as a secure sense of God's ongoing presence and protection.

However, some people are, by nature and temperament, more highly sensitive and insecure. Others have difficulty internalizing the concept of a loving God because they never received a foundation of trust and security from their parents. Whenever they feel frightened or overwhelmed and turn to God to get that feeling of "dwelling secure," the same feelings of fear and mistrust which they experienced throughout childhood are reawakened. Because they have no actual experience of being able to rely on people, they assume that their lack of trust is normal and appropriate, even in relation to God, the supreme Parent. This leads them to feel isolated and threatened by the most minor upsets. And it is that feeling of danger, coupled with the feeling of vulnerability and loneliness, which is the essence of GAD.

Normal vs. abnormal anxiety

What distinguishes normal anxiety from the more severe and sometimes disabling Generalized Anxiety Disorder (GAD) is that those with GAD hold three deeply-ingrained beliefs which cast a pall of gloom over their lives:

(1) "I am basically inferior and, therefore, am certain to be punished and abandoned by the people I turn to for support or love. No one is really there for me."

(2) "Terrible things are certain to happen to me which will cause me to collapse physically and emotionally. Then people will see how incompetent I really am."

(3) "My anxiety keeps me on guard, protecting me from danger and motivating me to behave correctly. To lose anxiety would be to lose protection, motivation and self-respect, and to turn into a carefree do-nothing and a heartless clod who is unprepared for the disasters which are imminent."

Normal anxiety is protective and motivating. It gets us to try our best, avoid sinning, take care of ourselves and others, go to a doctor if we suspect that something may be wrong and be suspicious of those who may be untrustworthy. But it is crippling to be in constant anxiety about "What will others think?" or to think that terrible things are about to happen.

It is normal to experience anxiety during periods of unusual stress, to wonder if we can take the pressure and what might happen if we cannot hold up. These moments of anxiety and doubt usually pass, and we eventually get back to ourselves — perhaps after reorienting ourselves with prayer, a good night's sleep, a decent meal, a talk with a caring friend, or discovering that we do have the inner resources to cope with the situation.

However, people with GAD never really get back to themselves. They feel as if they are always on the brink, living on the razor's edge, about to fall into some terrifying, dark abyss. There is no stable, secure, inner self to get back to, and no inner strengths to trust. In fact, such people might be most anxious when everything is going well, because their expectation that something terrible will happen keeps them tense. And when the disaster they worried about does happen, it is almost a relief from the ongoing tension of waiting for it to come. This justifies future anxiety as a way of preparing themselves, and they think, I knew something terrible was going to happen. I was right to be so anxious.

Childhood roots of GAD

A high-strung nervous system is an innate characteristic. Soon after birth, high-strung babies can already be observed in the hospital nursery, hypersensitive to noise and more reactive to other discomforts than the other infants.

The tendency toward anxiety can also be created or be exacerbated by traumatic childhood experiences, such as war, divorce, chronic criticism or the loss of a parent or sibling through death. These events convince the child that he must keep himself in a state of preparedness since disasters are inevitable. An abusive environment prevents the child from experiencing that there is a secure, consistent source of love and stability in the world. Or, the parents may have been very loving people, but suffered from GAD themselves. Their own anxieties and insecurities created a chaotic home atmosphere. More often, the parents were unable to form close emotional bonds with the child. No matter what the child did, he could not win the parents' consistent love and approval. In their presence he felt discounted, invisible, unsafe, inadequate, not good enough to make them happy. The anxiety about not measuring up, of not being good enough, of being inadequate to handle life, continues into adulthood.

Parents who are driven by a desperate need for public approval and status communicate unspoken messages to their children, such as: "It's disastrous to fail. It's your responsibility to make us proud and happy. If you cannot satisfy our needs, we cannot love you." The child's attempts to live up to their impossible expectations put him under continual, severe stress, for he can never accomplish enough to win lasting love.

In such an atmosphere, his anxiety serves as a safeguard, reminding him to hide his true feelings, to maintain a phony external image to please others and to lie to avoid being disapproved of. Anxiety reminds him to motivate himself to try his hardest to win his parents' love by getting the highest marks, having the tidiest room and accomplishing the most.

Such a child comes to believe that anxiety is the only thing which keeps him in line. He also learns an inferior type of love, the kind which is meted out according to how others look and what they accomplish. He does not realize that love which is given for external looks, material possessions, scholastic achievement or neatness is not real love because it is transitory and conditional. This child only knows of conditional love — the kind that makes him afraid to trust, be honest or accept himself for who he is.

A love-starved child assumes that he is unloved because there is something very wrong with him. He is a failure. His need for approval, combined with his conviction that he is undeserving of it, create constant inner turmoil. He is always nervous and on edge, waiting for the next rejection.

On the other hand, feelings of powerlessness and unworthiness can also result from parents who are overprotective or overindulgent, for they then deprive their children of the opportunity to face confidence-building experiences. If children never have to face hardships and persevere despite them, they don't know that they have inner strengths and resources to cope. They fear that they will fail or collapse under pressure. This causes them to panic over minor stresses.

[Note: This section is not meant to make children angry at their parents, or blame them for their present problems. Blame blocks growth. Each person is responsible for his actions and *middoth*, no matter what his childhood was like.]

Other sources of GAD

Other circumstances can contribute to GAD:

A highly emotional nature. Deeply feeling people are often frightened by the very intensity of their emotions and their tendency to react strongly even to minor events. They often feel inferior to colder, more dispassionate types.

Emotional isolation. We learn to trust others by revealing our deepest feelings and experiencing that we are understood and validated. When traumas occur and children have no one to honestly explain the situation to them or listen to their feelings about it, the lack of honest communication implies that it is shameful even to talk about one's feelings.

> ◆ EXAMPLE: "After my mother died, no one wanted to talk about it. I hid my feelings because I feared I would be ridiculed or told to be quiet. But I was scared. Poof! My mother was gone. Poof! I or anyone I loved could disappear just like that. I was always waiting for the next blow. I also believed that I was somehow to blame for what happened."

Unless there is an understanding adult who takes the time to form a secure relationship and convince them that they are not to blame, such children will always feel anxious, utterly alone and secretly ashamed of being terribly bad.

Unfortunately, many adults assume that children will forget traumatic events in time if these events are not talked about. The exact opposite happens. Hidden feelings fester.

> ◆ EXAMPLE: "My father died of cancer when I was six. Everyone said, 'Don't cry. Be a man.' My mother worked full-time and was depressed and irritable. She had no patience for us. She never

talked about her own feelings, so I grew up thinking that it was wrong to do so. I harbored the secret belief that I had caused my father's death by being bad. I also thought that I, too, would die young, like my father. I am now very emotionally inhibited and nervous."

A highly developed imagination. Anxiety is largely a function of the imagination. It takes a vivid imagination to imagine all the possible catastrophes which might occur, in order to maintain a high level of anxiety.

Gender. GAD afflicts more women than men for the same reason that they suffer more from depression, i.e., they experience themselves as powerless and inferior. Being more dependent on others for emotional and financial support provokes anxiety because it implies having less control over one's life. Boys are socialized to act independent and confident, even if they don't feel it inside. What begins as external bluff often becomes an internal reality. Girls are not encouraged to feel resourceful and strong.

In addition, women who suffer from wide fluctuations of their hormonal levels often interpret this to mean that they are emotionally unstable. Women who feel out-of-control during certain times of the month think that this is the "real me," and come to doubt their sanity in general.

Stress overload. Normal people can suffer from GAD as a result of a cluster of losses, one after another, such as divorce, job loss, marital problems, financial losses, illness, etc. Stress overload can cause confident people to suddenly lose trust in their ability to cope. Overcrowded living conditions is another major source of stress overload.

Motherhood. Motherhood is a high-stress job. What with the noise level, the constant demands and the need to always be on the alert for danger and make so many spur-of-the-moment decisions, even the most emotionally stable woman may sometimes find herself fearing for her sanity, especially when she is ill or deprived of sleep. If she has a critical husband, the anxiety is often severe. Anxiety is especially strong with the first child, before a mother has built self-confidence. Also, mothers who have unrealistic expectations of being in control and loving at all times fret constantly and feel like failures when they cannot live up to that glorified image.

A critical atmosphere. Chronic criticism makes the recipient feel unlovable and incompetent. Trying to function well in a chronically critical atmosphere is like trying to function while being hit. One never knows when the next blow will come and lives in a constant state of anticipatory anxiety, especially if the attacker is a Jekyll-Hyde type — alternately nice and nasty. Unpredictability creates anxiety. One can no more get used to being criticized than one can get used to being physically assaulted.

> ◆ EXAMPLE: "I was so criticized as a child that I still tend to overreact whenever anyone disapproves of me. I also married a very nervous person who thinks that being nervous gives him an excuse to snap at everyone. I am always tense, not knowing if he will be nervous that day or not. However, it helped to give up trying to control his opinion of me. I learned that no matter what I do, I can't please him or most of my relatives. Someone is always going to tell me that I have too many children or too few, that my food and clothing are too fancy or not fancy enough, that I'm too strict about religious matters or my children's discipline or not strict enough. To stay calm, I have to endorse myself for doing my best and not get hysterical about disapproval."

Heredity. Researchers have found that people can inherit a hypersensitive nervous system. When under stress, the brains of such people do not receive or transmit messages effectively because the brain's screening mechanism allows too much extraneous stimuli (e.g, noise, thoughts, feelings) to enter. Thus, they reach a state of "sensory overload" sooner than normal people, becoming irritable and upset. They misinterpret the excess of stimuli as a threatening situation: their hearts race, their digestion slows and their adrenalin flows. They may feel overwhelmed and may suffer stomach distress. These people may suddenly "space-out" or become aggressive in an attempt to control or minimize the onslaught of stimuli. Lack of sleep is particularly stressful for GAD sufferers, since they need more relief than others from the stress of their overstimulated nervous systems (*Superimmunity*, pp. 233-243).

Relationship wreckers

In relationships, anxiety-ridden people provoke the results which they feared most, i.e., isolation and rejection. Their excessive demands for control and hysterical reactions to ordinary events alienate others.

◆ EXAMPLE: "I love my parents a lot, but they are so anxiety-ridden that I end up not telling them anything about my life. How can I have a close relationship with them when there are so many things I can't talk to them about?"

Having become used to rejection and betrayal in childhood, anxiety-ridden people often pick mates with whom they have little in common, so that there is no possibility of forming a close emotional bond. Those who lost parents early in life, for example, often pick mates whom they don't really like so that if they lose that person, they won't be as devastated as they were as children.

One of the most common neurotic patterns is for an anxiety-ridden person to pick a mate who is emotionally cold and even tyrannical, because these people seem outwardly strong and protective. Then they feel abused by these critical types who were supposed to make them feel safe and secure. Or, they marry loving people, but sabotage the relationship with impossible demands for attention and affection and respond angrily when they don't get it. They never trust that others really care and they keep expecting rejection.

◆ EXAMPLE: "It was only after my divorce that I realized how much I hurt my wife by being so overcontrolling. Because I was so insecure, I tried to have total control over her life. I didn't even want her to talk on the phone for any length of time or have close friendships with anyone. I exploded if she disagreed, and kept accusing her of not showing me enough respect. She tried her hardest to please me, but I was always criticizing her. No amount of control was enough to make me feel secure. I kept wanting more and more."

◆ EXAMPLE: "My wife is so desperate for contact and approval that she talks nonstop. I love her very much, but I sometimes leave the house just to have some space for myself. I don't want to hurt her, but her need to talk all the time and her demands for constant attention are driving me away."

◆ EXAMPLE: "I always felt ashamed of myself because, as a man with a very deeply feeling nature, I felt different from other men. When I met my wife, I thought she was just what I needed because she seemed so strong and self-assured. But it turned out that what I thought was strength was really coldness and inflexibility, toughness and an unaffectionate nature."

Unless the person suffering from GAD has training in disciplining his mind, it is of little use to tell him, "It's nothing but nerves." This only increases his sense of alienation by making him think that no one understands or validates his feelings.

Phobias, obsessions and compulsions

Anxiety is a survival tool, a way for people to get others to pay attention to them and a way to make themselves feel safe. The obsessive-compulsive rituals which many anxiety-ridden people develop is their attempt to create some sense of order and gain some sense of control over their inner chaos.

◆ EXAMPLE: "Since my inner world is in such turmoil, at least I can keep the kitchen counters spotless, the closets in perfect order and the germs off the doorknobs."

◆ EXAMPLE: "People tell me that I'm a hypochondriac. But I believe that if I am alert to every tiny ache and pain, I will discover a health problem early on, and thus have some control over the situation."

◆ EXAMPLE: "I'm agoraphobic. I remain housebound, thinking I'll be safer if I never go to public places. When I have an anxiety attack, I feel like I'm hanging by my fingertips from the wing of a plane in flight. The feeling of impending doom is real and frightening."

How to reduce your anxiety level

People who lead lonely, insular lives suffer from more anxiety, which leads them to be even lonelier and more insular. They can spend thousands of dollars on an endless succession of therapists and medications in the mistaken belief that something "out there" will cure them of this affliction. But anxiety can only be overcome by engaging in healthy activities and by developing faith in God and loving relationships with others. A person cannot change his nervous system, but he can decrease his anxiety level with the following mental and physical disciplines. These disciplines lessen the feeling of danger and build trust in God and oneself:

Build a strong connection with God. As a child, you felt separate and alone. You depended on others to make you feel good. But as an adult, the more you rely on others to make you feel secure, the more unsafe you will feel, since the sense of isolation can only be overcome by experiencing God's presence in every aspect of your life. Even if the words seem insincere at first, tell yourself constantly that God is with you, and that all that He does is out of pure benevolence and kindness, even though it may not seem that way at the time. Repeat the words thousands of times. Faith requires that you engage in the struggle to believe. Practice on the small disappointments first, like stained clothing and traffic jams. The reward for this work is that eventually, often after many years, true faith is developed.

Each time you are tense, use the tension as a reminder to turn to God and give up trying to control whatever you cannot control. Give over to God all those aspects of your life which are not in your control, including all your fears and physical aches and pains, your worries about the future and your obsessive reflections on the past and other people's approval or disapproval of you. Concentrate on the only things a human being can control, i.e., your thoughts and actions.

Whenever you feel tense, repeat the words from the prayer *Adon Olam*, "Into His Hand I surrender my spirit, when I sleep and when I wake. The Lord is with me, I shall not fear." By using anxiety as an internal cue to to reconnect to God, the anxiety will bring you closer to Him! Then you'll calm down.

Accept yourself. True, life would be easier if you were not so high-strung. But that applies to anyone with any handicap. A handicap simply means you have to work harder to build faith and confidence. That's all it means. Honor yourself as a unique individual. Then you can honor others.

Don't draw catastrophic conclusions from ordinary events. For GAD sufferers, it does not take much to set the inner sirens of anxiety wailing. The most minor discomfort or disappointment becomes the launching pad for major catastrophic conclusions: "Does that tired child have leukemia, God forbid?" "Does the headache signify a brain tumor?" "Does that critical remark mean the end of a relationship or a job?" "Does this moment of confusion or indecision mean I'm losing my mind or perhaps becoming senile?" Keep making molehills out of the mountains. This mental work must be done throughout the day.

Don't take your nervous symptoms seriously. This is one of the major keys to overcoming anxiety. We are told, "Answer not a fool according to his folly, lest thou also become like him" (*Mishlei* 26:4). This principle can be applied to obsessive thoughts and nervous symptoms as well. Don't draw catastrophic conclusions from normal nervous sensations and allow yourself to become unduly frightened by the chest pains, air hunger, faintness, stomach distress, insomnia, dizziness, heart palpitations, nausea, fatigue, headaches, etc. which are merely harmless responses of an oversensitive nervous system and an overactive imagination. Fear increases the frequency, intensity and duration of the symtpoms, which makes you even more anxious.

When others tell you to ignore your symptoms, you want to shout, "But my feeling of danger is real!" Instead, discipline yourself not to speculate endlessly about whether or not your symptoms presage imminent mental or physical collapse. Assume they do not, unless a doctor tells you otherwise. To feel crazy does not mean to be crazy. Do not dignify the nervous symptoms by paying attention to them. Like stray cats which whine to be fed, they will leave you alone if you don't feed them. Notice how they fade away when you get busy and ignore them. If not, then try another doctor, especially a holistic health specialist who can prescribe a proper diet and exercises.

Apply the "humor test" if you wonder whether or not you are crazy. One of the foremost signs of a severe emotional disturbance is the lack of a sense of humor. If you are anxious, but also have a sense of humor and can often enjoy life, you are within the normal range. A person with no sense of humor or one who laughs inappropriately about extremely distressing events or at the expense of others' feelings may have a serious disturbance.

Choose anxiety-reducing thoughts. To stay anxious, you must keep rehashing frightening thoughts over and over again, killing any positive feelings or plans with endless doubts and fears. Weaning yourself away from these anxiety-provoking thoughts is like weaning oneself away from sugar or any other bad habit. It's agonizingly painful at first, almost like a death experience. And you never know how much you've gained until you've gotten away from your addiction.

It takes a strong will to deliberately choose anxiety-reducing thoughts and firmly reject all others. "I cannot afford the luxury of dwelling on fearful thoughts. If I don't eat *traif*, why think it?" As a child, you felt vulnerable and defenseless. But you can develop adult skills which build trust in God and yourself.

Motivate yourself from love, not fear. Stop believing that, "I must constantly worry in order to motivate myself to do well and show people how responsible and caring I am. If I stop being anxious, I will become heartless and irresponsible." (If you care enough to read a book of this sort, this is highly unlikely.) You can motivate yourself far more successfully out of love. Happy people accomplish a lot more and are far more caring of others than unhappy people. Worry only about God's approval, not the approval of man.

> ◆ EXAMPLE: "I constantly remind myself to do things from love, not fear. For example, I can clean my house out of terror of disapproval because my relatives are coming, or I can clean it for my own self-respect. Cleaning out of fear puts me in a state of panic, so that I scream at the children and get exhausted. The second way makes me feel happy and grateful that I have a home to clean and the strength to do it."

Ask yourself, How can I show people that I care about them and their problems and that I am striving to do my best, without keeping myself in a state of anxiety?

"Say little and do much" (Avoth 1:15). Talking about your fears all the time gives them more power and reality. Doing so is also boring and alienates others. Put a new tape in your mental cassette player. Talk about the positive things in your life and your hopeful plans for the future.

Confront the anxiety objectively. Just as depressed people have to avoid getting depressed about feeling depressed, anxiety-ridden people must avoid becoming tense about their tension. Instead of fighting the anxiety, note what is going on in your mind and body like an objective observer by practicing the following steps:

(1) Ask yourself what specific discomfort or disaster you are afraid of. Losing control? Rejection? Death? Confront the fear. Ask yourself, Is there realistic danger right this second? If not, go on to the following:

(2) Measure the intensity of the anxiety on a scale from zero to ten. Be honest. How bad is it? Anxiety-ridden people often exaggerate, which is nothing more than "fancy lying."

(3) Stay in the present when you feel panicky. Do not think about what may happen in the future when you are anxious. Focus on the moment. You might not be able to solve the major problems in your life right now, but you can think, What positive action can I do right this second which will increase my trust in God and myself, and bring me some pleasure? Do something — anything — which gives you an immediate sense of control, such as breathing calmly, reading *Tehillim*, calling a friend, or going for a walk.

(4) Endorse yourself for functioning in spite of the discomfort, even if that means endorsing yourself for simply sitting still, breathing calmly or doing some insignificant act. Give yourself credit for coping at this moment.

(5) Watch how the feelings rise, peak and fade on their own while you keep your thoughts and actions positive.

(6) Expect to feel anxious again. Don't judge yourself for being anxious. Don't get tense about being tense.

Do not view disapproval as disastrous. You may feel irrationally endangered when you are criticized or cannot get through to someone. In childhood, disapproval was experienced as disastrous because you were dependent on adults for survival and your sense of self-worth. But as an adult, you can maintain your self-esteem even if others are disapproving by reminding yourself, My worth is determined by God, not man.

Don't try to get through to everyone. Most people do not connect to others at a very deep level. Make your encounters with them as polite as possible, but don't get upset if you cannot get the understanding you would like. This is especially true if you are a supersensitive Intuitive-Feeling Type (See *Appreciating People*).

Avoid anticipatory anxiety. Another neurotic pattern to avoid is trying to control the future by being anxious about it. Anticipatory anxiety has a magical quality, i.e., "If I worry enough about possible calamities, I can keep them from happening." But it doesn't work. Such worries will not keep them from happening, nor will they prepare you to cope with them. The only preparation is to build your self-confidence and your trust in God right now. Yehudis Karbal, director of EMETT in North America, has a helpful saying: "If you can't anticipate joyfully, don't anticipate!"

Find a pleasurable activity and make a discipline out of it. This might be in the area of music, writing, study, exercise, crafts or dance.

Build self-sufficiency and self-respect by forcing yourself to do things which are difficult. Be anxious and do them anyway. Command your muscles to move as though you were an army sergeant. Don't allow self-doubt, indecision and nervousness to lead you to retreat from the very activities which would build your self-confidence. Nothing will reverse this pattern until you do the very things you fear doing. Positive thinking is meaningless unless combined with some constructive actions which change your self-image. This might include asking your boss for a raise, learning a new skill, getting a job, going back to school, taking up a hobby or insisting that the people around you refrain from criticizing you. Such acts build self-respect.

You can put up signs in prominent places in your home saying: Every act of self-discipline increases self-respect.

Practice relaxation techniques. Controlled breathing is a powerful relaxant. Whenever you feel anxious, let it be a cue for you to drop your shoulders and focus on your breathing. Breathe out twice as slowly as you breathe in. For example, breathe in for a count of two and out to the count of four for three minutes. Keep saying, "For every breath, praise God" (*Bereshith Rabbah* 14:9). Calm breathing will also help you to determine whether or not your feeling of being endangered is realistic or not. If you were really in danger, you would not be able to breathe in this relaxed manner.

Your muscles will eventually teach your brain that you do have the courage and resources to cope. Also, when you keep breathing calmly or moving purposefully, your muscles will teach your brain that there is no real danger. If you still feel nervous after using these techniques, reassure yourself that your feeling of danger is just a feeling, not a fact.

Give to others. Your own healing will be enhanced when you help others overcome their anxiety. Ironically, when you help strengthen others' *emunah* and *bitachon*, then even if yours is weak, it will be strengthened. When you teach others how to liberate themselves from the prison of fear, you will be liberated. When you forgive others for their imperfections, you will become more self-accepting. Do *chesed* in direct proportion to the amount of your anxiety. The more you love others, the more loved you will feel. Only love overcomes fear.

◆ EXAMPLE: "Whenever I would talk to my mother, I'd be full of anxiety, knowing that at some point, I would feel rejected again as I had been as a child. I finally realized that my anxiety was a way of blocking my grief at never having been accepted for who I am. The only way to relieve the grief and anxiety was to have love in my heart, both for her and myself.

Avoid temperamental lingo. You don't realize it, but the mere use of words like "crazy," "miserable," "catastrophic" and "awful" have an anxiety-provoking effect on your nervous system. Don't pepper your conversation with phrases like, "I can't take it," "I can't go on," "I'm a basket case," "I'm going to have a nervous breakdown." You are not a doctor or a prophet. These phrases get your adrenalin pumping and make you nervous by weakening your trust in yourself and reinforcing your self-image as a person who is unstable, unreliable and powerless. Temperamental lingo is really just "fancy lying."

Don't take trivialities seriously. A triviality is any event which is not dangerous, illegal or involves a major life change. If the event does not fall into one of these categories, it is a triviality which can be handled calmly or ignored. Lighten up! You may have an initial response of fear even though there is no danger, because the child in you still responds as you did when you felt defenseless and ashamed of yourself. But you are an adult now. You are on a healing journey, and every event can heal you if you respond differently from how you did as a child.

Trivialities include nervous symptoms, minor accidents and mistakes, and almost anything connected to sleep, money, traveling, food and clothing. Be honest. If there is no danger, no violation of *halachah*, and no major life change, it's a triviality, even if it doesn't feel like one at the time the tickets get lost or the juice spills!

Join a spiritual support group. It is essential for GAD sufferers to have contact with understanding people. This helps make up for early childhood deprivation, and also shows how common their problem is. Those who are successfully recovering from GAD are often the most helpful and insightful.

Also, hidden fears fester and grow with time. When you expose your fears to others in a safe group setting, they lose their intensity and power over you. A support group may be the only place where you can talk openly and honestly about your innermost feelings. You will find out that you are not alone. You will also learn not to take your nervous symptoms so seriously, because you will see that so many others have them and manage to cope.

Bless stressful events as opportunities to connect to God by working on a particular middah and trusting that it is ultimately for your good. The more you see the Hand of God in everyday events, the more you will feel His Presence with you at all times.

Put forth maximum effort, but don't try to control the success of those efforts. Success is in God's hands. Your determination and effort are what count.

Drop your condemnations. Every self-condemnation reduces your level of trust in yourself. You are not bad, crazy or wrong for having this handicap, or for not being a great success, or for being an insecure person. Don't be anxious about the fact that you are sometimes anxious. Trying to grow from self-contempt is like trying to swim with shoes on. You won't get far and you won't enjoy it much.

Drop your comparisons. No doubt you have relatives, friends and neighbors who are calmer, neater, richer, healthier and more together. The less you compare yourself to others, the better you will feel. You are a unique individual and deserving of respect even if you are high-strung and insecure. When you are happy with who you are, you will be happier with life and people in general.

Make your own decisions whenever possible. Don't agonize over whether they were right or wrong (as long as *halachah* is not involved.) When you run to others to ask what gift to buy or what meal to serve, this lowers your self-confidence. Have the courage to take risks and decide for yourself. Endorse yourself each time you do so, even for the most minor choices. In time, your self-confidence will grow.

Eat healthy foods. You need proper nourishment for your body as well as your spirit. Poor diet can affect the nerves. For example, coffee consumption can increase anxiety. Lack of folic acid, iron and calcium can lead to apathy and exhaustion, shortness of breath, mental clouding, headaches and anxiety. Calcium has been called "nature's tranquilizer." See a qualified nutritionist to discuss your diet.

Numerous drugs can be responsible for anxiety, including antispasmodics for ulcers, anti-inflammatory agents for arthritis, sleeping pills and antidepressants. On the other hand, there are many natural remedies which can lower anxiety.

Heal the inner split between
the real me (bad) and the public image (good)

Because GAD sufferers feel that they are essentially unlovable and inferior, they fear rejection and are often devastated by disapproval, whether real or imagined. In an attempt to keep others from finding out what they really are, they develop a phony external image to present to the public. Then they live in fear of others discovering the ugly truth about them. They think:

> *"I am always particular about my personal appearance, clothing and furnishings. I hope this will keep people from seeing how messed-up I am on the inside."*

> *"I appear very religious on the outside so that people won't know how materialistic and bad I am on the inside."*

> *"To the world, I always try to present a smiling face and act like I have everything under control. But at home, I'm always screaming and feeling like I'm going to have a nervous breakdown any minute."*

> *"In public, I'm the community do-gooder, always giving to everyone. I don't want anyone to find out that I'm on the go so much because I don't really want to be with my own children. I resent their demands and want my independence."*

> *"I act very passive and accommodating on the surface, but really I'm very lazy. I always say that everything will turn out all right so that I don't have to get involved."*

The need to maintain a phony public image means you can never relax and be open and honest with others. The fear of disapproval keeps you from having true emotional intimacy. In addition, this self-imposed isolation makes you even more untrusting of others and more anxious. The harder you work to keep up a false image, the more you reinforce the fear that you would certainly be rejected if anyone knew what you were really like. Without positive feedback, you become convinced that you really are bad, lazy, stupid and selfish. Hence the cycle of self-loathing and anxiety is perpetuated.

To break this cycle, you must share your feelings with others who can love you unconditionally, as you are. When you see that others accept you, you will accept your imperfections as part of the Divine plan for your growth. As you become more self-accepting, you will accept others. As you feel less alone, you will feel more loving toward God and man.

You are an adult now. Love of God, yourself and others will erase fear and self-hatred. Acceptance of yourself and others creates the environment in which growth can take place.

Guidelines for choosing a therapist

Emotional problems arise from lack of love for God, oneself and others. Love cures. Unfortunately, many books on psychiatry and psychology never mention the word. Therefore, if you do seek therapy, make sure you:

Find a therapist with whom you feel a close rapport. Do not continue to see a person who is cold and aloof. You need to experience being cared about and being able to trust.

Find a therapist who gives you homework which forces you to change negative habits. Talk is not enough. You need to change your behavior to gain a sense of self-confidence. The most important question a therapist can ask is, "What changes do you want to make and how do you plan to make them?"

Feel understood. After three or four sessions, you should be able to assess whether or not your therapist has a grasp of you and your problems and whether you are gaining tools to cope with them. Don't be afraid to switch.

Make progress. The therapist should be helping you identify and then discard the negative beliefs which you adopted early in life and which continue to make you feel helpless and inadequate. Cognitive therapy and Neurolinguistic Programming are particularly helpful since they help people think rationally and change behavior.

Be realistic. Therapists don't fix people. They cannot choose your thoughts or move your muscles for you. They can only guide you and encourage you in your struggle for health.

Distinguish between healthy
concern vs. unhealthy anxiety

There is an enormous difference between healthy concern and unhealthy anxiety. Healthy concern moves you to look for constructive solutions, whereas unhealthy anxiety leads to destructive thoughts and actions.

Healthy Concern: "I'm so worried about our financial situation. We must consult a financial counselor to help me make up a strict budget and look into job training."

Unhealthy Anxiety: "Oy, I'm so worried about our financial situation. But there is nothing we can do. We're stuck. Trapped. I'm going to collapse under the strain. I eat myself up with jealousy when I think of my brother, who is making so much money."

Healthy Concern: "Oy, Pesach is just a month away. I'll do a little each day. Even if I only do one shelf in the morning and one in the evening, that's still progress. I can trust myself to get it all done on time. I'll get some good Torah cassettes to listen to while I clean."

Unhealthy Anxiety: "Oy, Pesach is just a month away and already I'm feeling paralyzed. I hate it, hate it, hate it! I can't cope. I'm going to have a nervous breakdown. I'm so helpless and incompetent! Everyone else manages, but not me!"

Healthy Concern: "I'm really concerned about my son. Our relationship has deteriorated. He's so defiant and often withdrawn. He's doing poorly in school. I'd better see a professional. In the meantime, I'm going to keep a notebook of the good things he does to remind myself that he's not so bad after all. I'm going to spend more time with him each night, just talking to him. I'm also going to start a *chavrutha* with a friend and we'll encourage each other to be more creative and positive with our children. I trust that God gave me this child as a gift, and that I can handle him. I trust that he will grow up to be a caring, productive person."

Unhealthy Anxiety: "Oy, this kid is going to be the death of me! I can't stand him. I should never have been a mother in the first place. I don't know how to handle kids. I'm driving them crazy and they're driving me crazy. I just can't stop screaming and hitting. I'm such a failure."

Healthy concern means changing what can be changed and being tolerant and ignoring what is beyond our control — such as the past and the future and other people's behavior. Anxiety substitutes crippling fear for positive action.

Getting free: learning coping strategies

A woman, whom we'll call Tova, suffered from an undercurrent of anxiety all her life, and it was getting worse. Feelings of panic would hit her more and more often, like when she was shopping or washing dishes. They were especially severe during transition periods, such as going to sleep, at sunset, leaving the house, planning even a short trip away from home, having people visit, etc. At such times, a terrible feeling of isolation and dread would come over her. She was certain that something awful was about to happen or that the world was about to collapse. She would struggle for breath, feeling trapped. Terror would grip her.

Doctors told her that it was "just nerves," and she was given tranquilizers. Despite the doctors' reassurances and the medication, the attacks did not stop and she became thoroughly convinced that she was really crazy and that one day she would stop functioning altogether. She waited in dismal anticipation for the next attack.

Tova was lucky. A friend dragged her to an EMETT group meeting. Although she felt that no one there could really understand how serious her problem was, she began to attend regularly. Slowly, she began to grasp that her anxiety was largely in her mind, and that she could calm herself down by thinking certain calming thoughts and doing specific positive actions.

Thus, the next time anxiety overcame her, she was prepared. She was unable to fall asleep. Suddenly she began to fear that something terrible was about to happen to her or one of her children. She began to panic, wondering how she would function the next day without sleep. She had visions of herself losing control, screaming, feeling totally alone and terribly sad. Instead of lying passively, obsessing about her fears, she commanded herself to get up and read one of her favorite books on the philosophy of the Torah. Although she was having difficulty concentrating, she knew from her EMETT classes that positive actions are essential for overcoming the mind's negativity. So she endorsed herself for each line she read and for each calming breath she ordered herself to take.

As she had been taught, she watched her feelings and sensations as if from a distance. She remembered to measure the intensity of the anxiety on a scale of zero to ten. She decided that this was only a six, a thought which had an immediate calming effect. She continued reading, waiting patiently for the anxiety to peak and fade on its own, while telling herself, "I have coping strategies and resources. I'm not the helpless child I once was. I can function with this discomfort. I don't have to be perfect. It's not dangerous to not have everyone's approval. I'm an adult now. No one is going to hit me. I can replace fear with acceptance of myself and others."

She commanded herself to breathe calming breaths, breathing out twice as long as she breathed in. She repeated her affirmations: "If I can breathe calmly, there must be no real danger. I do not have to get anxious about being anxious. *I refuse to attach danger to these symptoms.* My feeling of danger is a feeling, not a fact. This situation is distressing, but not dangerous. It will soon pass.

She remembered someone saying, "Lack of sleep doesn't make you crazy; it's the thoughts you have about not sleeping that do!" Though she did not yet fully believe these words, she told herself that it was true. She repeated to herself, "I am lovable and capable." As a matter of fact, she had the initials of this phrase - ILAC - embossed on a necklace and she touched it as she read. Mentally, she surrounded herself with a protective shield of Godly love.

Then she took out her xeroxed summary of EMETT tools, (*EMETT*, pp. 27-29) which she kept close by. She went over the "Eight Enemies of Mental Health," the "mental saboteurs" which constantly must be weeded out lest they destroy one's mental health. She monitored her thoughts to discover what might be keeping her in a state of panic. Yes, there was (1) gloomy extrapolation into the future, thinking that she was sure to go crazy some day. Yes, she was making (2) erroneous assumptions, such as thinking that panic attacks are a sign of craziness, or that she could not bear the discomfort of these moods. Yes, she was feeling (3) exceptional, positive that no one else suffered from anxiety as intense and painful. Yes, she had an (4) unrealistic, romantic demand that she should have a calmer nervous system and (5) an erroneous belief that she was not deserving of anyone's love or respect because she was not as confident, calm or together as her sister-in-law or many of her neighbors.

She noted that she was also not looking at the total picture, discounting all the times that she functioned at an average, or above average level. She smiled to herself as she realized that these were her old thinking patterns which needed to be weeded out daily, just as one must weed a garden. By this time, she knew that even if she did not have a full night's sleep, she would manage adequately the next day by thinking secure thoughts and keeping her actions positive.

How to cope with an anxiety-ridden person in your home

In order to overcome anxiety, certain spiritual exercises must be practiced. You can no more exercise someone's mind than you can exercise their bodies for them. If you live with someone who suffers from GAD, you must be like a physical therapist: you can be caring, enthusiastic and supportive, but you can only put forth effort to the extent that the other person is willing to do so, as well. Accept the person's high level of insecurity without judgment, with neutrality, as you would accept anyone with a handicap. But remember, a handicap is no excuse to behave irresponsibly.

It is extremely helpful to speak EMETT language in the home. To influence the person, show how you use this language to calm yourself down. For example, whenever you get nervous, say, "I'm nervous, but I can still demonstrate self-control." "I made a mistake, but on a scale of one to ten, with ten being a major catastrophe, this is only a one. It's a triviality. It's my choice to work it up into a major catastrophe or work it down into a minor disappointment." "This is distressing, but not dangerous, thank God." "I'll either fix it or ignore it. I refuse to get upset about something I have no control over." In time, these phrases will penetrate the other person's consciousness if you say them in an empathetic, non-judgmental manner.

The anxiety-ridden person must understand that starting an exercise program is most uncomfortable in the beginning. The "spiritual exercises," such as gratefulness, forgiveness, endorsing and detaching, all seem artificial and even silly at first. If you can help this person over his initial resistance, self-motivation will take over as soon as he sees the calming effect these exercises have. But do not take upon yourself the responsibility for this person's changing or you will actually retard his progress.

Harnessing the imagination to fight anxiety

A highly developed negative imagination is the main source of anxiety. But the imagination can be harnessed and disciplined for your benefit. Just as you have the power to arouse anxiety by thinking of anxiety-provoking situations, so too can you use your imagination to calm yourself down. To prove this, have someone read the following exercise to you:

"Close your eyes and think of an anxiety-provoking situation. Notice your anxiety like an outside observer. Yes, your body is tense, but note that you do not have to become frightened or ashamed about this fact. You do have the choice to stay objective and neutral. Good. Yes, you have some disturbing nervous symptoms and unpleasant feelings. This is due to a harmless outpouring of hormones which will fade away as you keep your thoughts and actions positive.

"Note where the tension is in your body. Use your breath to breathe into that place and release the tension. Now, take the remaining tension in your body and breathe it into a balloon. Let that balloon go up into the air, higher and higher, until it disappears. Wait patiently as the nervous sensations fade.

"Imagine yourself as a child. Now, imagine holding that child in your arms and saying, 'The *real you* is not any one thing. You are a composite of many traits, both positive and negative. I accept you as you are. You are precious to me as you are. Yes, you have imperfections, just like everybody else in the world. Like a caring orthodontist, we'll apply gentle pressure over the course of your lifetime to help straighten you out. Be patient. It is a lifetime of work. I am not ashamed that you are not smarter, calmer, more self-confident or successful. I am not ashamed that you are high-strung and deeply emotional. These are God-given characteristics, chosen for you because they fit your particular mission in life.'

"Many years ago, you lost contact with your *neshamah*. But like a child who is kidnapped and returned, you can contact it any time you want. Listen to your *neshamah*. Let it talk to you. It will tell you that you have a great, untapped reservoir of inner strength. Get in touch with that source of strength. It is like a tiny dot. Let it grow and fill you until it drives away all fear.

"Fear and shame prevent you from hearing the voice of your

neshamah. Allow love to push the fear from your heart, now from your head, now from your entire body. Listen. You are being told that you are lovable and capable.

"Each day you will have many opportunities to prove that you are no longer a frightened, defenseless child. You are grown up now. You have skills you didn't have before. You can define your needs and state your rights. You can handle stressful events adequately. You can know that God is with you, guiding you at all times. Feel His love for you."

After repeating this exercise for a few weeks, you will find yourself actually coping successfully with your everyday stressful events.

The only "good" anxiety

All emotions are meant to bring us closer to God. Even the positive side of anxiety is apparent when we realize that God gave us the capacity to feel anxious in order that we might experience fear and awe before Him. A GAD sufferer's particular spiritual work is to build a relationship with God, and to accept Him as the ultimate source of his security. Whenever he feels anxious, he can let it be a cue to take a calming breath and think, "God, I trust that You are here with me right now."

We are told that the secrets of the Torah cannot be conveyed "...except to one whose heart is anxious within him" (*Chagigah* 13a). In other words, anxiety over our *middoth* and the correct performance of mitzvoth is good and brings us closer to God. So we see that anxiety can be constructive, but only if used for this purpose.

The Chazon Ish, *z"l*, stated that faith in God has infinite degrees (*Art Scroll Bereshith*, p. 1748). Do not blame yourself if you are not at the highest level. Anxiety is a sign that you still have work to do. We all do!

CHAPTER 10:
Subtle Powerholism

Who is mighty? He who subdues his passions; as it says, he who is slow to anger is better than the mighty, and he that ruleth over his spirit than he that taketh a city. (AVOTH 4:1)

The Jewish home has always been known as a place of love and devotion to the highest moral and ethical ideals. This is because Judaism stresses the importance of self-mastery. However, when the drive for self-mastery is perverted into an excessive lust to control others, it changes into an addiction called powerholism, which destroys the home.

Powerholism is one of the manifestations of the condemnaholic personality, in which a person uses various manipulative tactics, such as constant fault-finding, prolonged punitive silences and angry explosions, in order to deprive others of independence and autonomy. While depressed or anxiety-ridden people are excessively self-conscious and approval-seeking, powerholics are characterized by their lack of self-awareness and lack of shame or guilt over their ill treatment of others.

There are two types of powerholics: the seemingly well-intentioned, over-protective, intrusive types who control others with subtle tactics and the more violent, outwardly abusive type. Both types have one goal: to decrease their anxiety through *domination and emotional distance.*

Powerholics feel compelled throughout the day to reestablish their position of dominance with smirks, grimaces or criticism, unsolicited advice or threats. Since they thrive on conflict, they will pick on something — anything — to feed their addiction.

It is essential to understand that it is not other people's behavior which causes powerholics to become anxious, critical and hostile. Rather, they are nervous, hostile and overcontrolling to begin with, and grab any excuse to indulge their compulsion to exert their authority over people. Whether it is an unwashed dish or an uneaten bit of food, the powerholic is sure to notice and punish others with a critical comment, and demand that it be set right, usually with a smirk, a snicker or a sneer. Ironically, it's the normal person who is apt to feel like he's wrong!

◆ EXAMPLE: "I know from experience that when I walk through the door, my wife is going to snap at me for something. I dread coming home. There's tension about everything — when and how we sleep, eat, dress, spend money... For a long time, I thought I must be stupid for not being able to figure out how to please her. Finally, I realized that no matter what I did, it would be wrong. In every interaction, she tried to make me feel guilty and ashamed of myself. Once I realized this, I refused to be dragged down. Then she got angry because she couldn't goad me to explode or seethe with resentment."

It is important to keep in mind that a disturbed person may have a grown up body and be quite intelligent, yet have the emotional level of a child of two or three years old who thinks he must bully people in order to get what he wants and punish them if they don't give in.

◆ EXAMPLE: "My social worker drives me up the wall. She makes me go from one office to another for unnecessary signatures and makes me bring certain forms each month which could be brought once a year. She digs into my personal life and constantly tries to prove that I am an unfit mother. It's useless to argue with her. She delights in showing me that she's got the power to run me ragged and break me down."

Although they are extremely touchy about their own feelings, powerholics think others should not be at all upset about their own rude, cruel behavior. It is as though they are surrounded by a dense wall which blocks any awareness of or concern about others' feelings.

◆ EXAMPLE: "After each birth, my mother-in-law invites herself to stay with us for at least six weeks, even though we have only a small two-room apartment. She criticizes me constantly, then blames me for being cold to her. She can't understand why I'm always finding excuses to leave the house."

It is not surprising that sensitive types who live or work with powerholics often suffer from digestive disturbances and ulcers as well as emotional distress.

◆ EXAMPLE: "My parents were very controlling. They read our mail, listened to our phone conversations and wanted to make all our decisions. I felt like there was always a fist in my face, telling me to 'Do more! Accomplish more! Be perfect! Get the best marks or you're nothing.' I was never accepted for who I was, which to me felt like being dead in their eyes. Not to accept someone is like having a death wish for that person. No wonder I had an ulcer by the time I was seventeen."

Such depersonalization is traumatic for any human being, but especially a child, whose self-worth is derived from his parents' attitude toward him. As an adult, the merest hint of depersonalization from anyone, such as a teacher, doctor, spouse or even a clerk, can reawaken all the rage which was stored during those childhood years when he was treated like an object. Those involved may have no idea why the person responds with such fury, for the roots lie deep in one's subconscious.

Because powerholics are so tense and so driven to change everyone around them, a person can never feel comfortable in their presence. One can never relax and just be oneself. They create the same atmosphere of tension and torment which they experienced as children, by forever complaining and provoking fights with people whenever they don't get their way.

Powerholics believe that their behavior is a perfectly healthy, legitimate response and is an appropriate way to take charge and express concern and even love for others.

The dominate and crush philosophy

Powerholics want unquestioning obedience as proof of others' love and respect. The idea of compromising, of making decisions democratically or respecting people's own needs and interests is completely foreign to them. In their minds, people are objects to be manipulated and coerced and turned into robots. There is only one way to do things — their way.

Powerholics view all their interactions with people as power struggles which they must win. There are only winners and losers, and the challenge is to find the tactics which will enable them to come out on top in any conflict. A conversation with them is like a highly competitive chess match, in which the powerholic's goal is to score points, not solve problems. They delight in pointing out how stupid and inept the other person is and gloat over his mistakes, If they make a "sacrifice" and give in to the other person once in a while, it is only in order to trap him later.

◆ EXAMPLE: "I'm so jealous of my friends whose husbands are their best friends. My husband and I never work as a team, because no matter what I do or say, he opposes me. Every conversation turns into a battle. Instead of a husband, I have a sparring partner who keeps knocking me to the ground."

◆ EXAMPLE: "My stepmother is impossible to deal with. For example, a day or two before every class trip, she has found some excuse to keep me from going, like I didn't talk to her right or didn't put my things away. Whenever my father promises to give me money for clothes or something, she'll make some demand that I must fulfill before I can get the money and then tell me that I didn't do it right, so I can't have it."

In the presence of a powerholic, the normal person is apt to feel as though there is a noose around his neck. He knows it is only a matter of time before he is bound to say or do something which the powerholic considers wrong, and then the trap door will open and in he'll fall. Sometimes the control tactics are so subtle and the contempt so disguised that the unsuspecting victim may not even realize why he feels so bad.

For example, powerholics exert control by implying that if a person doesn't agree with them, he must be selfish, unspiritual, abnormal, uncaring and stupid. It is common to hear them say: "If you really cared about me, you wouldn't go," "Any sane person would agree with me," or "A really spiritual person wouldn't feel that way." Since most people want to be pious, unselfish, loving and intelligent, they end up doing whatever the powerholic says in order to avoid being seen in a negative light.

♦ EXAMPLE: "When I told a relative that I was going to an EMETT group, she grimaced and said, 'You don't really need that, do you?' as if I must be abnormal for going. When I told her that all people need to work on their *middoth*, and that's what we do there, she said, 'Don't you think the Torah is enough?' as if I'm not really spiritual if I feel I need the fellowship of other women. When I said that I like the insights and understanding I gain, she said, 'You know how dangerous these psychological theories can be.' By then, I had such strong feelings of danger and self-doubt that I was ready to agree with her and never go back to my group. My self-trust was down to zero. It took me hours to get back to myself and feel that my opinions are also valid and that I have the right to make my own decisions and do what I feel is good for me."

The most minor difference of opinion will warrant a no-holds-barred power struggle, more from the powerholic's need to dominate, rather than from the actual realities of the issues involved. On the surface, they may appear to want a relationship, but what they really value is power. Their need to conquer keeps them from being sensitive to others' feelings.

♦ EXAMPLE: "A relative generously invited my whole family out to eat. We looked forward to the evening, but it turned out to be a disaster. First, she told us what food to order. If someone wanted something different, she smiled and said she knew what was best. Then, no matter what anyone said, she kept redirecting the conversation back to her topic of interest. If anyone said something which was not on that topic, she would ignore his comments and act as if nothing had been said. It was so strange. We had no real contact with her. By the end of the meal, we were all silent."

Since only the most highly respected, exceptional people are considered capable of measuring up to the powerholic's standards, he has no hesitation in letting most people know that, in his eyes, they're not worthy of his consideration or respect. Since he does not know what it means to bond positively to others, he does not do the things which would build a foundation of trust and love, such as taking time to develop emotional honesty or allowing others to share in the decision-making powers.

Powerholics will readily destroy a relaxed and happy moment with some critical remark, or make a major scene over the most minor mistake. It is common for them to suddenly stop talking to family members, sometimes forever, over some petty squabble. That is because they would much rather feel "right" and superior than feel loving or loved.

◆ EXAMPLE: "My little granddaughter came bounding into the house to tell her mother that she had won a prize in school. I felt so bad when my daughter-in-law yelled at her angrily for tracking mud onto the floor. The child ran away, and I don't think my daughter-in-law ever found out about the prize."

With their superior stance, insecure people are likely to agree that the powerholic's criticism is justified.

◆ EXAMPLE: "My spouse was forever saying that he criticizes only to improve me. It's a growth-through-torture approach. I believed him at first, because it really did seem that he knew what was best for me more than I did. I let him make all the decisions, and he gladly took control of my life. Soon I began to feel like the world's biggest failure. I lost confidence in my ability to make even the smallest decision on my own, because he was always telling me it was wrong. Since he kept saying that he just wanted to help, I didn't realize that he was completely undermining my self-respect. It took years for me to take charge of my life and build myself back up."

As with all addicts, powerholics get progressively worse as time goes on, with the people around them suffering emotional damage as well.

The either/or trap

Like other emotionally wounded people, powerholics see life in terms of a very narrow set of options, completely unaware of healthy alternatives in the middle. In their minds, it's either "control or be controlled; be a tyrant or a wimp." Their lack of trust in people is evident in their unspoken conviction that, "Either I maintain absolute control over people, or I will be seen as uncaring and weak." "I will sink into apathy and indifference." "I will be taken advantage of." "I will not be able to get people to satisfy my needs."

Denial and self-delusions

Powerholics usually have a positive self-image, thinking of themselves as merely ambitious and concerned parents and citizens.

They constantly feed their sense of being superior by making others feel wrong. By focusing on others' flaws, powerholics constantly reinforce their sense of rightness and justify their impolite or even abusive behavior. Yet powerholics deny having any emotional disturbance, despite constant proof of their inability to get along with people. They assume it is always the other person's fault. They excuse their behavior by saying,

> *"I don't have a problem; I'm just stubborn. I like to have things my way. That shows strength of character."*

> *"I only give constructive criticism. I want to help people improve. What's wrong with high standards? It's admirable!"*

> *"I have to take control because I can't trust the stupid, slow, unspiritual, insensitive people around me."*

Powerholics are always ready to attack. If someone mentions a mistake they have made, they will immediately shift the focus of attention away from themselves and retaliate against that person.

> ◆ EXAMPLE: "If I merely hint that I dislike something this relative is doing, she ignores the issue and, instead, attacks me personally, mentioning all the mistakes I've made. She keeps reminding me that since I lack certain academic credentials, I cannot possibly have anything of value to say, as though it's a waste of time to even listen to me. I always end up feeling like a worm squirming at the end of a fishing line, full of shame and guilt when I haven't done anything wrong!"

> ◆ EXAMPLE: "It's the strangest thing. I don't even know how it happens. But every time I try to talk to this particular relative, I end up feeling like a total idiot! I can't even put my finger on what she does, because she usually smiles and acts chummy, while implying that everything about my life is wrong, and that, therefore, I should let her make the decisions. Yet she always starts off by saying, 'Look, I respect your judgment and you don't have to take my advice.' It took me a while to realize that she didn't really mean what she was saying."

Two types of powerholics

The seemingly well-meaning, subtle powerholics often come on like "fixers" or "reformers" who just want to go around setting everyone straight and making them see the light. When they don't get their way, they tend to punish the guilty parties with silent hostility or endless complaints to others about those who have hurt them. Abusive types attack in more obvious ways. Subtle powerholics may take on the role of "big sister," "counselor," or "substitute parent," initially hiding their true intentions with a smile and assurances that "I only want to help." However, there is an underlying threat of rejection which surfaces as soon as there is any opposition to their will. They may say, "All right, have it your way," but they withdraw angrily, sometimes for years.

Aggressive powerholics openly admit their desire for control. Their insistence on having their way is usually accompanied by some immediate show of force or threats of violence if they even suspect that there is any opposition to their will.

Both types can be quite polite and charming when things are going well — i.e., when they feel in control. But their compulsion to control makes them unreasonably angry when people don't take their advice or things don't go their way.

Domination in the guise of service

There is a very thin line between healthy concern and unhealthy powerholism. Concern for others is a desirable trait, and we deplore the apathy and indifference which afflict many people. However, concern must be balanced by respect for others' autonomy and individuality, or it becomes destructive.

It is not always easy to distinguish between healthy and unhealthy involvement in others' lives. For example, the wife who pleads with her husband to stop smoking for the sake of the family's health and welfare is not a powerholic. But a wife who hounds her spouse day and night with criticism because he does not have the personality traits she had hoped for in a husband, is. To know when we have crossed the line, each of us must examine his own heart, for "The greatest service of God lies in the purification of motive" (*Strive for Truth!* vol. 1, p. 99). An outsider certainly cannot always be sure of another person's intentions.

Subtle powerholics dominate by appearing helpful. They often preface their remarks by saying, "Do it my way. It's for your own good. I want to protect you from immorality/obesity/poverty." The fact that they get so furious when their advice is not accepted proves that their helpfulness is really only a thinly disguised attempt to dominate.

Because powerholics deny that the ultimate motive behind their behavior is domination, not service, they have no compunctions about imposing their personal likes and dislikes on people, telling them what to wear, what to read, where to live, what to buy, what to eat and how to think, all the while seemingly oblivious to, or unconcerned about, the hostility they are engendering.

◆ EXAMPLE: "My parents generously offered to support us while I continued studying, but then wanted to make all the decisions, including where we should live, what to name their grandchildren, what food to buy, where we should go for the holidays, how to arrange the furniture, etc. There's always a big guilt-trip if we don't do precisely what they want."

◆ EXAMPLE: "A colleague came to my office and said that she wanted me to work with her on a project. When I told her that I was already overwhelmed with work, she said, 'But I'll help you.' The more I insisted that I didn't want to do it, the more she insisted that I must. Each reason I gave, she shot down as nonsense. I finally found the courage to insist that I had no interest in doing what she wanted. She got angry and accused me of being hostile to her! Then she stomped out. I felt like a fly who'd been trapped by a very crafty spider. The bullying is very subtle, but it's bullying just the same."

◆ EXAMPLE: "For months, I thought this neighbor, who had befriended me when we moved in, was simply concerned when she kept probing me for information about problems I was having with my work and certain family relationships. I was very open and honest, and she offered a lot of advice. But as the months wore on, I began to feel uncomfortable because she got upset that I didn't always do what she told me to do. I tried to relate to her as an equal, but whenever I asked about her life, she withdrew. So she always came out in the superior position, the one who had it all together and, therefore, could tell me how to run my life."

Powerholics also dominate in the guise of rigid service to their organizations and blind obedience to self-made, arbitrary principles.

◆ EXAMPLE: "The head nurse in the ward where I work is a powerholic who rules like a ruthless tyrant. Of course, she always says that she is only maintaining hospital discipline for the sake of the patients. But they are the ones who suffer the most from her gruffness and lack of flexibility."

Domination in the guise of love

Powerholics confuse love with domination. They think, "To love you is to change you." "If you love me, you will let me have control over your mind and body." Having never experienced genuinely loving relationships in their early lives, they do not realize that real love frees others to develop their individual strengths and talents. When a person really loves another, he is happy with him as he is, even if he hopes he will improve, and even if there are aspects of his behavior which he does not like. It is phony love which makes others feel stifled, ashamed and suffocated.

Many powerholics are extremely paranoid, convinced that others are out to exploit or betray them or alienate the affection of their mates, thus justifying their tight control.

◆ EXAMPLE: "My little sister and I were four and six when my mother died, and my father was very close with us after that. He waited until we both married before he remarried. His wife-to-be was very charming and friendly to us, and we expected to continue our close relationship with him after their marriage. However, a few days before the wedding, she made him sign a paper promising that neither of us would visit without calling first. She said she was doing this because she loved him so much that she didn't want anything to come between them. It seemed like a reasonable request, so my father agreed. But after the wedding, she kept making excuses for us not to come to visit every time we called. She was so critical and unpleasant to us that we eventually stopped even asking to come over. Our father was so afraid of her fits that he would only call us was when she was out of the house, which didn't happen too often. It was a terrible loss for us."

◆ EXAMPLE: "My husband says he loves me, yet whenever I'm feeling overwhelmed by all that I have to do, he puts me down with comments like, 'I just don't see why you can't manage, when other women are able to handle much more.' He's always comparing me to his older sister, who has more children than we have, but whose house looks like a dream. Once, when I said I wanted to get a job so I could get out of the house and be with people, he said I was too incompetent to do anything. When I got angry about that statement, he said he loved me and just wanted to protect me from failing. He's always telling me how poorly I manage. I begged him to go with me to a family therapist, but he insisted that since I was the sick one with no self-esteem, it was a waste of time for him to go. How can I believe he loves me when he's so unhappy with me the way I am?"

Abuse in the guise of religiosity

Judaism, the greatest power for good in the world, can be twisted and used to tyrannize people by depriving them of all autonomy, creativity and individuality. This is one of the most disturbing traits of powerholics who often use religious principles to justify their selfish lust for control while hiding beneath a mask of piety. Since every human being needs improvement, it is difficult to defend oneself against someone who insists that, "I only want you to be more spiritual."

Because they claim to be acting in the name of God, they provoke guilt and confusion among Observant Jews who, when disagreeing with them, are accused of being irreligious.

Rabbi Eliyahu Dessler spoke of such powerholics when he said, "They have to show that whatever *they* are involved in must be better than anything else in the world. Their apparent zeal for the mitzvoth simply means that their arrogance makes them intolerant of anyone who dares to go against their wishes. By influencing others...they are simply expressing their urge to dominate other people" (*Strive for Truth!* vol. II, pp. 81-82).

The strictness of powerholics is not rooted in a desire for Godliness, but in the need to punish and control others and to experience the perverse pleasure of feeling superior to those who are less strict.

One way to tell whether a *chumrah* [a stricter religious practice than what is required by *halachah*] is rooted in Godly or ungodly motives, is to look at the effect on the person and those around him. Those who are motivated by love of God become more tolerant and compassionate toward all mankind as time goes on. Their faces radiate warmth and love. Their patience with their family members is notable. In contrast, as powerholics become stricter, they become more arrogant, insular, intolerant, irresponsible and unbalanced. They may show off their piety in public, but they tyrannize family members in private.

◆ EXAMPLE: "My wife has turned us all into nervous wrecks with her hysteria about cleanliness. You'd think that the entire religion was nothing more than washing hands and keeping everything spotless. But no matter how hard we try, it's never enough...never. We can never be perfect enough for her."

◆ EXAMPLE: "My husband has become so strict about everything that I now feel like a prisoner. I rarely get out of the house to visit family or friends or even to shop, because he says that a proper wife stays home. He won't let me listen to the news on the radio, even though I like to know what is going on in the world. He says that if I were really religious, I wouldn't even have a desire to know about the outside world or even want to leave the house, but that I would be happy being home all the time. I want to do what's right, but I'm confused. As time goes on, the harsher his demands become. If I express any opposition, he accuses me of being a selfish feminist."

Charismatic leaders often attract insecure, dependent people who feel relieved to hand over control of their lives. Insecure people feel safe in the hands of these authoritarian figures who claim to have all the answers and who make all their decisions for them, thus relieving them of the "burden" of free will.

Suppression of initiative

Powerholics display a characteristic "polarity response," automatically doing the exact opposite of what others want. Whenever anyone takes the initiative or expresses an opinion, even on the most petty issue, such as what to eat or where to put a piece of furniture, they take the opposite view, just to create a fight that they can win. If someone states a desire, powerholics will shoot it down, saying that it is stupid, wasteful, dangerous, inappropriate or unrealistic.

This "polarity response" is due to the fact that powerholics interpret the taking of initiative as a threat to their position of superiority and dominance. Of course, powerholics always have a list of reasons as to why they cannot allow a person to do what he wants, but these reasons are mere excuses to maintain control.

◆ EXAMPLE: "It's really sad that no matter what a child asks for, my husband shoots it down. It doesn't matter whether a child wants to sleep over at a friend's house or learn a new skill, he's bound to say that the idea is stupid and refuse permission. His contempt is crippling them."

◆ EXAMPLE: "I am in charge of a project, but must submit all my plans to my boss before they can be implemented. When I show him my ideas, he gives me a list of reasons as to why they are ridiculous. Then he makes a few minor changes and signs his name to what I gave him in the first place. If I want to keep my job, I have to keep my mouth shut."

The no-win situation is also common:

◆ EXAMPLE: "My mother invites us all over for the holidays. If we refuse, she won't talk to us for months. If we come, she complains about how much money she has to spend and how hard she works. I lose no matter what I do."

Childhood roots

The powerholic's inability to relate to others in a healthy manner has its roots in early childhood when he felt so powerless. He now tries to control people in a desperate attempt to feel safe. But the opposite happens; he constantly recreates the same level of tension and trauma he was used to as a child, so he never feels really secure or loved.

Some powerholics were spoiled by parents who indulged them in a desperate effort to get their children to provide the love that they could not get from each other or had not gotten from their own parents. In doing so, they ignored their children's need for firm boundaries and discipline. Seeing how easy it was to get what they wanted by tyrannizing their parents, they kept up this behavior as they got older.

Most powerholics suffered from childhood neglect or abuse, much of it so subtle that it didn't even seem like abuse.

◆ EXAMPLE: "My wife's parents laugh when they tell about the time when she was two years old and she wouldn't finish her scrambled eggs. Her father was determined not to allow her to waste food, so he made her sit at the table until she finished them. They say she kept those eggs in her mouth for two hours, refusing to swallow.

They didn't see themselves as abusive. They thought they were teaching her not to waste food. But what they really taught her was not caring about people's feelings. She still has tremendous anxiety about food and is very controlling of what we eat."

Fixer types were often forced into premature adulthood by having to take care of emotionally disturbed or sickly parents at an early age. Later, they could not abandon their sense of excessive responsibility which was thrust upon them so early. They feel safe only when they are overfunctioning and relating from a one-up position as another person's caretaker.

Aggressive powerholics learned early in life that abusive behavior is excusable, because they saw one or both parents getting away with it. When parents discipline only with violence, the children learn that screaming and hitting are legitimate reactions to frustration. The children suppress their desire for love because they know they won't get it. To them, "strong" means "not feeling and not connecting." When hit, they proudly say, "It didn't hurt."

These events teach them that it is legitimate to punish those who cause them pain. Such people enjoy being feared, taking out their anger on those they consider to be inferior to themselves. This makes them feel powerful, thereby lessening their feelings of helplessness and vulnerability.

Although this helps us to understand why powerholics act the way they do, it certainly does not eliminate the pain of being with such people.

Characteristics of powerholics

Other identifying signs include:

Lack of self-awareness. Because they deny their shortcomings, powerholics never think that they may be the cause of interpersonal conflict. Whenever something goes wrong in the relationship, they blame others. If someone merely hints that they are lacking in any way, they become enraged. Since they deny that they have a compulsion to control and do not see themselves as critical people, they expect others not to be upset by their criticism or other control tactics. No one can penetrate the thick psychic armor which keeps them from seeing that their behavior is destructive.

Extreme sensitivity to any snubs or slights to their honor.
Though very touchy about their personal honor, powerholics are
unconcerned about their abuse of others. They have "selective
amnesia," quickly forgetting their own harmful doings, but forever
remembering and exaggerating the hurts, imagined or otherwise, that
others have done to them.

Emotional stinginess. Powerholics are stingy with their time,
compliments and attention. Any request to give makes them feel
diminished, used, exploited.

Since powerholics are uncomfortable with emotional closeness,
they are attracted to theories of childrearing which spout the positive
benefits of parental indifference. They look for excuses not to give
children affection, citing that this will make them independent. They
demand obedience in a ruthless and inflexible manner. These parents
pride themselves on never giving in to a child and on their ability to
stick to rules, theories and schedules even if they are irrational in light
of human needs.

Financial stinginess. When powerholics do give — and some of
them are very generous donators to charity — the purpose is public
approval and to prove to others that they are not stingy. However, in
private, powerholics tend to be unbelievably stingy, unless they have
initiated the purchase and decided what to buy and how much to
spend. They maintain tight control over family members by making
them beg for every penny and then criticizing them for being wasteful
no matter how they spend it. They may go through the garbage can to
see if someone threw out something which could be used, or go
through the dirty laundry and pull out items that could be worn one
more day, thereby saving water and electricity.

The long, drawn-out process of getting anything from a
powerholic is so humiliating that many family members prefer to lie,
sneak, or do without what they want, rather than have to go through
the agony of the begging process.

Arguments about the use of money, electricity and gas are
continuous. Powerholics are forever growling, "You forgot to turn
off the light!" "Turn the heat off!" "Don't use so much hot water."
"Don't waste the batteries." "How did your shoes wear out so fast?"
"Don't waste gas by driving the guest home."

Paranoia. Powerholics' inner isolation and fear of closeness makes them think that their own present family members are also deliberately out to exploit, cheat, and manipulate them. Even small babies are seen as "manipulators" or "tyrants." People who do not carry out their commands immediately are accused of having hidden desires to hurt, rather than simply having their own needs or interests.

Projection. Like Korach (*Bemidbar* 16:3), who thought that Moshe was as power-hungry as he was, the powerholic projects his own weaknesses onto others, accusing everyone else of being immoral, selfish and arrogant because he cannot face that he himself has these faults.

Lack of remorse. Powerholics feel no remorse for the pain they cause others, justifying it as deserved, since the other person did not behave properly. If you tell a critical powerholic, "You hurt my feelings," she gets insulted and attacks back. Then she insists that you apologize.

Vengefulness. In retaliation for a small, unintentional slight to their honor, which the guilty party may not even be aware of, they will hit back a hundred-fold or may carry on a hate campaign for months and years.

Perfectionism. Perfectionism is a form of abuse, a way of humiliating others by demanding unrealistically high standards, and then punishing them for failing to achieve them. Those who don't achieve are losers and failures in their eyes.

Moodiness. Powerholics keep others on edge with their unpredictable moods. They blame others for making them unhappy. When their desires are frustrated, they can go into an autistic mode, becoming detached and withdrawn. Or, they can become hysterical, depressed or violent.

Secretiveness. They are secretive about themselves, their past, their feelings (except anger) and their finances. However, they feel justified in intruding on others' privacy.

Isolationism, jealousy and possessiveness. While some powerholics are quite friendly on the surface, they often isolate family members from any friends and relatives who might be sources of love and inspiration. They criticize everyone who visits, except the chosen few who won't see through their external image of niceness. They may cut off phone privileges and visiting rights from friends and relatives, with the excuse that this one is too religious and that one isn't religious enough; this one talks too loud and that one is a bore, etc. These excuses are just smoke screens to hide their real goals of dominance, distance and control.

Marriage

Powerholics usually marry naive, people-pleasing types because they are the easiest to manipulate. Insecure types are often attracted to domineering, take-charge powerholics, who promise to provide protection and security.

Before marriage, powerholics seem to want nothing more than to establish the closeness they never received as children. They can be the most charming people imaginable. However, the battle of wills usually begins with the wedding arrangements. Typically, the nonpowerholic side keeps backing down and giving in so as not to appear petty, cheap or argumentative, while the powerholic side will get its way, perhaps giving in on one or two issues just to keep from appearing too obviously controlling. The nonpowerholics who suspect that something is amiss usually remain silent, fearful of speaking *lashon ha-ra* and anxious to be decent and not endanger the wedding plans.

After the marriage, powerholics show their true colors, sulking angrily, becoming dictatorial or cruelly silent as soon as they meet with any opposition. Yet because they refuse to acknowledge their compulsion, it is impossible to talk to them about it. Instead, they project their defects onto their spouses, blaming them for being pushy, immoral and manipulative, because that is what *they* are. These accusations usually make the nonpowerholic confused, ashamed and guilt-ridden, and even more anxious to please than ever.

Emotional blackmail: the "prove it" trap

One way the powerholic gains control over people is by telling them to prove their love by giving up their money, favored activities, friends and, finally, their entire identities. Anything less than total submission is likely to be met with statements such as, "If you don't do what I want, you don't really love me." This is emotional blackmail.

Spouses are often seduced into believing that if they just try harder or give in one more time, the powerholic will finally act normal and loving. They think: "I'll prove that I'm not selfish, materialistic or uncaring by doing everything that person wants. I'll be the thriftiest, most submissive, most self-sacrificing, tolerant and undemanding person alive. I'll always be available and agreeable. I'll give up all my personal desires. When I prove myself, then I'll be loved."

But no proof is ever enough. No one can please a seriously disturbed person.

Invalidation

One of the most frustrating aspects of dealing with powerholics is that it is impossible to get them to listen or understand another point of view. They are so determined to have their own way that trying to have a normal conversation with them is an exercise in futility because, no matter what you say, you will be invalidated or opposed. If you tell them you need something, you are told, "You don't really need it." If you get upset, you are told, "Stop making mountains out of molehills." If you say you are sick, you are told you are a sicko or a faker. If you say you are hurt by their criticism, they attack you back even more. Frequent phrases are:

"I didn't hurt you; you're the one who hurt me!"

"You're imagining things. I never said (or did) what you're accusing me of having said (or done)."

"You're crazy, hysterical and overly emotional."

"I didn't hurt your feelings. You're just too sensitive."

"Who's been putting these ideas into your head?"

To powerholics, emotional closeness means loss of control.

That is why they feel anxious when someone tries to draw them into a closer relationship. The very act of trying to communicate with powerholic people will usually intensify their abusive behavior! Thus, they are driven to sabotage the best efforts of rabbis, therapists and family members to repair their home situation.

Why stay?

Just as in repressive regimes, where the populace lives under constant threat of imprisonment or even death, those who live with powerholics feel similarly threatened. They will not dare challenge the powerholic if doing so might result in a hostile fit, the loss of a job or worse. Family members are forever weighing the desirability of honest communication against the severity of the hostile response it is likely to draw. It is not easy to stand up to someone whose response is, "Do as I say or I'll never speak to you again," or "You won't get any grocery money for the rest of the month."

Divorce from a powerholic can be worse than staying married to one, as the powerholic becomes even more abusive after the separation. Powerholics thrive on conflict, and will enjoy devoting their time to vindictive activities, including long, drawn-out court battles. The powerholic is in his element, excited and energized by the fight and the opportunity to match wits with unscrupulous lawyers in figuring out what torment to spring on his estranged spouse next and crush her spirit even further. Meanwhile, the normal spouse suffers both psychologically and physically from the added aggravation. When a wife breaks down, as sometimes happens, the husband and legal personnel involved may think that she really was to blame all along and may even recommend taking the children away from her.

Powerholic men, being stubborn and vindictive, are the ones most likely to refuse to give their wives a divorce, thus keeping the latter in the status of *agunah* for years. They see themselves as loyal and loving and the wife as being cold and totally to blame. To them, a forced, loveless marriage in which both parties are locked in a bitter battle feels normal and comfortable. They thrive on the tension and torment, this being the atmosphere they grew used to from childhood. Even if they do agree to a divorce, powerholics do not let go their desire to control a former spouse. Kidnapping is common. So the torture never really ends.

Effect on family members

Codependents, i.e., those who feel responsible for other people's negative behavior, believe that if they just keep trying harder to please the disturbed person, they will eventually win the love they crave. People-pleasing and excessive care-taking are the typical ways that codependents attempt to control others. They blame themselves when powerholics gets angry and try to figure out what they did wrong. They are always apologizing for the powerholic's behavior because they think that they could have somehow prevented it. When all their attempts to get the powerholic to change end up in failure, they feel they have failed and are certain that someone prettier, more patient, more obedient, smarter or more spiritual could have succeeded. Codependents do not realize that their dreams of reforming someone else are doomed from the beginning, because no one can win a powerholic's love, at least not for long.

Children of powerholics tend to have low self-esteem and have problems with self-control, either overcontrolling or undercontrolling themselves where matters of food, sex, money, health and cleanliness are concerned. In an attempt to prove that they have some control over their lives, they may become anorexic, obese, turn away from religion or run away from home. Stealing is a common symbolic way of trying to steal the love that is lacking. These actions give the child some sense of power, even if it is only the power to hurt themselves or others. Digestive disturbances are frequent.

Less sensitive children usually become cold and cruel, while more sensitive types become depressed, anxiety-ridden and may threaten suicide.

♦ EXAMPLE: "The only way I could protect myself was to turn cold to my powerholic mate. But the effect is that I feel frozen in general. I've turned off to life. I used to love life and reach out to people with such enthusiasm. Now I feel like I'm freezing to death inside. It's so lonely."

Even the lowliest bug flees frantically from any attempt to restrict its freedom of movement. So it is no wonder that human beings feel just as frightened and frantic when trapped by a hostile and threatening powerholic, and either attack back or crawl into their shells to die.

Can powerholics change?

Anyone can change — if he wants to. But powerholics rarely change on their own initiative, because they don't think anything is wrong with them. Even if they are dragged to therapy, they usually lie about or deny their role in order to maintain their superior position. Only long-term therapy will change the way they think or relate to the people around them.

It is essential to remember that no matter what you do to please them, powerholics will maintain their position of superiority by saying or implying "It's not enough. You still don't measure up." The sooner you realize that it is impossible to escape their contempt or satisfy their insatiable demands, the sooner you can take steps to distance yourself emotionally or physically, thereby minimizing the emotional damage. Sometimes, this detachment helps.

> ◆ EXAMPLE: "When I married, I was very insecure and weak, which fed my spouse's desire for absolute control over me. The criticism was leading to violent episodes. Everything was falling apart. Finally, I decided to demonstrate some act of self-control, usually over my mouth, whenever I felt hysterical or hopeless. The more disciplined I became, the less reactive I was. The relationship is still basically empty and cold, but I've learned to honor myself, even if no one else does."

One way to maintain emotional distance is to refuse to bend over backwards to please powerholics just to avoid their accusations of being selfish, unspiritual or uncaring. You will be accused of having these traits no matter how hard you try to please them. Don't deny the emotional pain you may be feeling. But to stay in control, keep reminding yourself of the reward you get for not returning the insults, for when one refrains from causing pain to someone who has hurt him, his sins are forgiven (*Rosh Hashanah* 17a).

Some powerholics can only be influenced by being threatened with separation, but you must be prepared to go through with the threat or it will be ineffective.

The worst advice to give family members is to tell them to be even more submissive and give up all those friends and activities which give them a sense of confidence and emotional nourishment. Giving more control to the powerholic is like giving alcohol to an alcoholic. Powerholics respect power. They are more likely to respect someone who relates to them from a position of confidence. The more time that family members spend in confidence-building activities, the less they will be susceptible to the powerholic's attacks.

> ◆ EXAMPLE: "Having been hit a lot as a child, I became a compulsive people-pleaser and approval-seeker to avoid rejection. Disapproval filled me with panic. I was sure I'd get crushed if I

asserted myself. But once I decided to overcome this negative pattern, I almost welcomed opportunities to calmly assert myself because I knew that that was the only way I would ever stop feeling like a defenseless child. For example, last week when I had to face an intimidating person, I was so terrified that I could hardly breathe. However, I looked him in the eyes and calmly said, 'I appreciate your advice. Tell me what you want and then I'd like to give you my ideas.' What a victory! I walked out of his office feeling like I had defeated a childhood bogeyman. I had been assertive and I didn't die. Later, I told a teacher I work with who is also quite pushy, 'No, I will not go along with that.' Now, instead of allowing myself to be terrified by these types, I take the attitude that God wants them in my life so that I will grow by dealing with them from a place of love and confidence instead of fear. And, you know what, these people are usually not as awful as I thought they were! I find that if I'm self-respecting, people usually are respectful toward me."

◆ EXAMPLE: "My mother-in-law used to criticize everything I did, from how I sliced carrots to what I fed the kids. It got to the point where I was physically ill before and after each visit. Finally I told my husband that he had to tell her to stop criticizing me. Well, she was very hurt and stomped away angrily. It was very hard on our marriage, because my husband was also terrified of her disapproval. In fact, we were both prisoners of that fear. But we stuck to our guns. After two months, she called to say that she wanted to visit. Now she controls herself. Too bad it took twenty years to get up the courage to take control of our lives and protect ourselves."

◆ EXAMPLE: "A year before my son's Bar Mitzvah, my husband's family was already putting pressure on us to make a big affair which would have put us in tremendous debt. Also, I am an introvert and don't like big, fancy affairs with hundreds of people. Usually I am a very meek person and just go along with what others want, but this time I was determined to take control and not let them dominate me. I told them that we would have a modest affair and were not going to compete with wealthier people. They tried to lay a guilt trip on me, telling me how selfish I was and how unhappy my son would be. I just kept repeating, like a broken record, that since there was no *halachic* issue involved, there was no reason to feel guilty or ashamed of our decision. I was surprised at how forceful I could be when I stopped feeling that I had to make the whole world happy at my own expense."

The family member who is used to thinking of himself as a helpless nothing and the powerholic as the overriding power in his life, must learn to do the opposite: to give greater value to his own fulfillment and to shrink the significance of the powerholic's opinions and needs dramatically.

Although powerholics demand obedience, they are actually contemptuous of those who give in to them, seeing them as weak, stupid pushovers. When family members make independent lives for themselves and find work which makes them feel confident and worthwhile, powerholics sometimes treat them with greater respect. Hence, when others improve their own self-esteem, powerholics may become more respectful in reaction. If the powerholic cannot succeed in starting the fireworks he is used to creating so easily, he may gradually give up.

When powerholics refuse to seek help, those who must live with them can only try to make the best of a very stressful and tragic situation.

CHAPTER 11:
The Abusive Personality Syndrome

Without a sense of personal power, a person sinks into apathy and depression. However, like any force, power can be used for good or for evil. It is good only if one is motivated by love for God and man and a recognition of God as the true Master of the universe. Without this balance, the healthy drive for power becomes an unhealthy compulsion.

Cruelty is the extreme form of powerholism. It is so foreign to the Jewish people, that a cruel person's Jewish ancestry is to be doubted (*Shulchan Aruch: Even HaEzer* 2:2). Yet such people obviously do exist in our midst. They have little capacity to connect in any meaningful way to other human beings. Whatever caring they do express is sporadic and unsustained, and is usually a manipulative tactic aimed at getting something in return.

It is important to recognize the signs of the abusive personality syndrome in order to be self-protective, for abusive people are often very charming on the surface, adept at hiding their dishonesty and cruelty. Pathological liars, skilled at deceiving people, they hurt without shame or remorse. Many outsiders cannot believe that a person who acts so charming in public can behave so abominably in private.

Ironically, for the same reason, a person may not realize he is abused because he may be so naive and forgiving that he assumes, "These explosions are just flukes. He isn't really disturbed. He's really good underneath it all." In the meantime, the abused person's self-respect and self-confidence is slowly eroding away.

Because abusive people are so overcontrolling, they often polarize family members into becoming undercontrolling and underfunctioning. Outsiders will then look at the abused one and say, "Look how depressed she is. She's just a doormat and a *shmateh*. No wonder she gets pushed around!" They do not realize that depression is the most common response to an oppressive situation in which a person feels deprived of love and hope.

The tactics which promote healthy relationships, such as honesty and trust, are counterproductive when applied to abusive people. They only respect power and become even more abusive unless met with tough assertiveness, or, when that is impossible, cold indifference, self-protective silence and wary distance.

Abusive people use two main methods to hurt others: (a) bullying people with violent physical and verbal explosions, and (b) psychological torture in the form of ridicule, constant criticism, emotional coldness, moodiness, miserliness, secretiveness, unpredictability, etc. Powerholics will start law suits at the drop of a hat, and often win them because they thrive on conflict and have no compunctions about lying and cheating.

The abusive person gradually undermines others' sense of self-worth and sanity, often to the point where they lose their will to live. However, they also have just enough moments of humor and niceness to keep others confused as to what their true nature really is.

Public frauds, private bullies

A depressed or anxiety-ridden person usually admits to being depressed or high-strung. But tell a cruel person that he is cruel and he will vehemently deny that there is any truth to the accusation. Unlike depressed people, who have an unreasonably low self-image, abusive people usually have a high regard for themselves, justifying their outbursts as anomalies or flukes. Many think of themselves as paragons of piety and, therefore, cannot understand why others get upset with their behavior. Others are aware of their mean nature, but excuse themselves by saying that they are impelled by forces beyond their control or justified by external circumstances. They note only the Jekyll side of their Jekyll-Hyde behavior.

Abusive people don't take responsibility for their behavior. They excuse and justify their cruelty. For example, abusive teachers pride themselves on their high academic standards and obedient students. Abusive bosses pat themselves on the back for their efficiency, productivity and determination. Abusive parents defend their meanness as being necessary for the education of the child.

When abusive people need to impress someone, they can act so friendly and helpful that outsiders are often duped into believing this facade is real. Their most abusive behavior is usually reserved for close family members, neighbors, students or workers, when there are no witnesses whom they consider important enough to impress.

Sadly, when victims complain about being abused, they are likely to be invalidated by those who try to deny or minimize the problem by saying, "This can't possibly happen in our group of friends!" They not only deny the existence or complexity of this problem, they often think that by applying Band-Aids to the cancer, the problem will disappear. They'll advise, "Just communicate and I'm sure he'll understand." "It's so easy to have a good relationship!" "Bring her a gift once in a while." "Just be more respectful and everything will work out." They'll reassure the victims that, "He's just hot-tempered, but he really loves you." "She seems so nice; you must be exaggerating. It can't possibly be as bad as you think." Or, the victims are told to fight back, when doing so might bring terrible consequences.

It is a commonly held myth that abused people, battered women in particular, come from abusive backgrounds and, therefore, unconsciously provoke the abuse because that is what they are used to and want. No one wants to be abused. The vast majority are like the victims of any crime — they are normal, trusting people who got caught in a web of evil and are too terrified to assert their rights. To say that abused people want to be abused because of some personality defect is to blame the victims and leave the perpetrators of the crimes free of responsibility and blame.

Many outsiders believe that all problems can be resolved with honest communication. They do not realize that abusive people lie, ridicule, attack or ignore those who try to relate to them. Furthermore, if you get the courage to tell an abusive person that you don't like a specific behavior, the person will repeat that behavior more often!

Even when neighbors overhear the screams of children or mates being physically abused, they are likely to justify, excuse or ignore the incident by assuming that the abuser was provoked, that s/he really does love the abused ones underneath it all, and that, since it doesn't happen often, it must not be so serious.

◆ EXAMPLE: "It's not the physical beatings which cause so much damage. That doesn't happen so often. It's the constant terror which is so crippling. I'm always terrified that someone will get sick or that something unexpected will occur and then that will be an excuse for him to terrorize us. He'll swear at me and the kids, calling us every nasty name imaginable. Then he'll break things and get physically violent. Then there are weeks of stony silence. That's what I face if I don't give in immediately to his wishes."

Outsiders' lack of understanding magnifies the victims' pain. Victims are not only ashamed of being abused, because they feel they are somehow to blame for it, they are shamed by people who blame them for not being able to handle the situation more successfully, as if it were easy to do so. When, as is typical, the victims undergo severe psychological changes such as depression, numbness, hysteria and regression, they are often accused of being emotionally unstable and, therefore, deserving of the abuse they receive.

Like a drug, the lust to control every aspect of the victim's life increases in time, as does the abused person's capacity to bear the abuse. What was outrageous, abhorrent and unbearable yesterday becomes tolerable today. The mind protects itself from ongoing trauma by becoming numb. Like people who numb themselves to the horrors of war, the victims of abuse in the home become numb, suppressing the rage which normally accompanies abuse. Thus, shame, terror and emotional paralysis often keep the victims from speaking out or seeking help.

Abusive people are also in a kind of emotional coma. If they read this chapter, they will not admit that they are reading about themselves. They are extremely resistant to seeking therapy, for they do not think they are sick. They are convinced that if they just get enough control and things go smoothly enough, everything will be fine. If they do apologize for their destructive behavior, their remorse is shallow and they remain essentially unchanged, although they may try to convince others that they have "seen the light" and will never lose control again.

The key: self-loathing

A sense of self-respect is the foundation of mental health. Abusive people are arrogant and self-centered, not at all self-respecting or self-nourishing. Their sense of self-importance is achieved by robbing others of theirs. They adopt a facade of superiority because they cannot bear to face how empty and weak they really are.

The key to understanding abusive people is to be aware of the profundity of their unacknowledged self-loathing. It is for this reason that they avoid emotional intimacy and resist counseling. This also helps explain their obsession with the external trappings of power and piety, including wealth, beauty, fancy possessions and public honors. It also explains why they are so demanding of obedience and respect, and why they are so keenly aware of who is and who is not giving it to them. Of course, being addicts, they never feel they are getting enough. They conceal their self-loathing by feeding their compulsion to be adored and in control. If a family member merely looks at or talks to someone else, or buys the most insignificant, unauthorized item, this may be enough to provoke an explosive, jealous rage and accusations of disloyalty and disobedience.

Abusive people treat others like objects. They experience a pleasurable, highly addictive thrill in being able to dupe, dominate, shame and punish those they consider inferior to themselves, which includes just about everyone. There is an added pleasure in being able to kick the person again once he's down.

> ◆ EXAMPLE: "We have tried everything to have friendly relations with our neighbors, but they just seem to get some thrill out of making our lives hell. They'll throw garbage in our garden, park in our parking space, play loud music late at night, and so on. And their children call us crazy whenever they see us. We tried talking to them in the most respectful manner possible, but they got even worse! They've brought out a vicious, vengeful side of me I never even knew I had. The hardest thing is not to respond in kind."

Abusive people want to be feared. It makes them feel powerful. They enjoy the process of breaking people down, of driving them crazy or turning them into self-effacing non persons. They strive to erase the individuality of their mates, children, students or employees, and make them mute, servile puppets whose minds are mere carbon copies of their own, and who surrender quickly to the will of the "master" without opposition or delay. And they feel no shame, regret or guilt about the abusive tactics they use to achieve these aims, such as icy indifference, incessant criticism, and an awesome variety of strange personal habits and oppressive ideologies which are hotly defended and clung to with stubborn insistence.

Good rulers vs. bad rulers

A good ruler is one who, like Moshe Rabbenu, is a giver and sees himself as a servant of those he leads. In contrast, abusive people see themselves as masters of those they dominate and are only concerned with taking. Ironically, they see others as takers from whom they must defend themselves.

The act of giving makes abusive people feel demeaned and diminished, unless it is at their own initiative. They feel threatened, even panicky, whenever asked to give of their time, money or power. They also resist giving in to emotional demands, such as for understanding, appreciation and support. Abusive teachers find it difficult to give a high mark to any but the most brilliant student, and may derive pleasure from flunking others. Abusive parents are quick to criticize and slap, but find it painful to part with the most meager allowance or even to take the time to listen to a child. They constantly provoke fights with close relatives or neighbors, yet may be nice to distant ones. They even twist lofty religious or educational principles to prove that their motives are worthy and their behavior justified.

Abusive people often appear extremely charming and helpful when they are in pursuit of a goal, such as a marriage partner, job, financial deal or public recognition. However, once they have what they want, they revert to their true selves. They can act as if they care, but it is only a pretense. After a loving courtship, for example, the abuse begins soon after the wedding, with a sudden refusal to communicate or with devastating criticism of the new spouse's body, manners, habits, relatives, etc.

Abusive people want to dominate and maintain distance because they are emotionally autistic, unable to form a lasting attachment of love and respect with anyone. Locked in a prison of loneliness, they may seem friendly on a short-term basis, but easily betray, abandon and forget friends, relatives, and family members without regret or sorrow since there was never any true attachment in the first place.

The hot-tempered, violent powerholic is described in *The Path of the Just* (p. 161):

He is angered by any opposition to his will and becomes so filled with wrath that his heart is no longer with him and his judgment vanishes. A man such as he would destroy the entire world if it were within his power to do so... He can easily commit any conceivable sin to which his rage brings him, for he is bound by nothing but his anger and will go where it leads him.

◆ EXAMPLE: "I knew that my daughter's husband suffered from the Abusive Personality Syndrome when, a few days after they were married, she confided that she already had to lie about how much she spent to keep him from exploding, and that he kept using the words 'garbage dump' to describe their home whenever the smallest thing was out of place. Typically, he demanded that she produce a child every year, hold a job and keep a noise-free, spotless house. He is a very dependent type who wants to be taken care of by others and refuses to work for a living. He monitors every move she makes. When I told her that she would only be encouraging his stranglehold over her if she gave in to his insane demands, she told me that she was too terrified to oppose him, and that he was so nice at times that she was sure he would change. Then he forbade her to speak with me, so she cut me off. She has a high-strung nature to begin with, so there was no way she could cope with such pressures. She kept denying the extent of the problem until she became suicidal and all her children were showing signs of severe emotional disturbance."

Such people are in love with power. And giving in to them only increases their lust for more.

Emotional underdevelopment

The mark of a Torah-true Jew is that he is "kindhearted, modest and charitable" (*Yevamoth* 79a). These three qualities are interrelated, for they all require a degree of self-nullification, i.e., the ability to give up the self-centered mentality which is the mark of an immature personality and to put others' needs first. Unfortunately, this is something which abusive people find almost impossible to do, for they are stuck at an infantile stage of emotional development, keenly aware of their own needs, but oblivious to the needs and feelings of those around them and unconcerned about the impact of their behavior on others.

Lack of compassion is the most striking characteristic of the abusive personality. No matter how much their victims may plead and cry, the abusive person remains stone-hearted in the face of their pain, if not more so because of it.

> The cruel person feels no pain at the troubles of his companions...
>
> (THE WAYS OF THE RIGHTEOUS, p. 145)

Abusive people are so self-preoccupied that there is no room in their hearts or minds for anyone else, including God, though they may appear superficially pious and caring. They give only to get, or to cover up their underlying desire to control and deceive. Even giving a compliment is impossible, unless, of course, they want something from the other person. They may justify and excuse their reluctance to compliment by saying that they refuse to engage in flattery, but the truth is that they do not want to share their feeling of self-importance with anyone else. They are afraid to give because they are terrified of connecting with people. They are afraid of connecting because they do not want anyone to discover who they really are or be forced to give. They are afraid to give because they feel so empty and so needy themselves.

We emulate God when we give. Empathy is the purest form of giving. But empathy requires that one momentarily ignore oneself in order to experience another's reality as if it were one's own. Abusive people are unable to do so. They place themselves at the center of their universe, and they think that they are the only important being in it. Others exist as peripheral planets, only to provide service and adoration. People have no lasting or intrinsic value to them. Such egocentricity is in stark contrast to humility, for

> The essence of humility is in a person's not attaching importance to himself for any reason whatsoever.
>
> (THE PATH OF THE JUST, p. 283)

It is almost impossible to penetrate the protective wall of self-importance and irrationality which surrounds the abusive person. Real contact is impossible because they are secretive, rewrite or deny past events, ridicule people's feelings and attack angrily unless others agree with them instantly. Numerous subjects are taboo, and they explode if those subjects are mentioned. Without mutual honesty and trust, a healthy relationship cannot exist. But how can you be honest with someone who is a pathological liar, who forgets or distorts the past and denies having any problems?

Love dies unless it is nourished. In a relationship with an abusive person, one cannot but feel terribly alone, hurt, misunderstood, unappreciated and, at the same time, burdened by the endless demands of an easily enraged individual whose needs are insatiable.

Are they really abusive?

Not all people who engage in occasional acts of violence are abusive. Many basically good people lack the self-discipline and communication skills which would enable them to express their frustrations in a respectful manner. However, if they are normal, they are aware that what they are doing is wrong, feel ashamed of what they've done and seek help. Once they learn how to discipline themselves and communicate properly, such people make steady progress. But abusive people remain rigidly stuck in their negative patterns no matter how much others try to help.

◆ EXAMPLE: "My husband and I had a good relationship until he stopped learning in order to support our growing family. When he couldn't find a job, he became nervous and critical. He's very intelligent and ambitious, from a well-educated family, and he suddenly felt like a nothing. He lost all sense of self-respect and turned his frustration against me and the children. Thankfully, our rabbi kept reassuring me that he is a basically good person who felt like a failure and didn't know how to express his pain. He found him a job in an institute where he could use his talents. We also took a communications course which taught us how to talk to each other in a respectful manner even when we're upset. Since then, things have been much better."

◆ EXAMPLE: "My wife was the sweetest person you could imagine when we first married. She adored our firstborn and took very good care of him. Then we had three more children very quickly, and our world became a nightmare. She became hostile and violent toward me and the children. Thankfully, she joined a mothers' support group where she learned to focus on self-control and solutions. She realized that she wasn't crazy, just so tired and overwhelmed that she lost touch with the nurturing part of herself. In time, she became more self-respecting and loving toward us. I also saw the importance of giving her a lot of encouragement and help."

These examples are quite different from what occurs with basically abusive people, who do not acknowlege their problems, or if they do, refuse to do anything about them.

Recognizing the abusive syndrome

Because many abusive people are extremely dynamic, gregarious and charismatic, even those closest to them may not realize that they are abused, since there are moments of good humor, affection and no external confirmation of their feelings. The following checklist can help a person decide if someone has a truly abusive personality. In general, abusive people:

* Insist on controlling every aspect of your life, such as what you buy, what you wear, how and what you eat, what you think, whom you befriend, etc., and become highly agitated and angry when you do not comply immediately.

* Accuse you of being all the things they are: selfish, untrustworthy, unfaithful, cold, cruel, crazy, unspiritual, incompetent, deceitful, stupid, vengeful, etc.

* Manipulate you into trusting them, then turn cold or attack you as soon as you begin to get close.

* Lie and betray your trust, then get angry and accuse you of being untrusting.

* Have amnesia about their own destructive acts, but never forget the most minor mistakes you have made.

* Are petty-minded, becoming constantly enraged over minor upsets and furious when things do not go smoothly.

* Create an atmosphere of chaos and tension, but insist it's all your fault.

* Ignore, invalidate or ridicule you when you express your feelings, then tell you that you're overly-sensitive, overly-emotional and crazy for being upset by their behavior.

* Expect you to be self-sacrificing, patient and forgiving no matter how moody or cruel they are.

* Say you are incapable of accomplishing anything of value or importance.

* Scream, throw things, hit people or smash possessions when upset, then blame it all on you.

* Hurt you indirectly by hurting the people you love, such as children, parents, siblings and friends.

* Use religion to subjugate, punish and shame you.

* Disregard or abuse others sexually.

* Think you're crazy for being upset at their behavior.

* Expect you to give up the activities and people which bring you the most pleasure.

* Induce shame and guilt by making you think you can live up to their impossible "shoulds," such as, "You shouldn't be upset by how I act," "You should make me happy" and "You should be perfect."

How the victim feels

Emotionally abused people often feel:

"I'm a failure. I can never satisfy her demands."

"Nothing I do is right. No matter what I do, it's criticized. I've lost faith in myself and my ability to make decisions or function in the world."

"I feel totally unvalued and unappreciated. If I died, he wouldn't notice or care."

"I feel invisible, not seen or heard."

"I feel crazy."

"I squirm with shame, as if I'm the guilty one."

"I feel constantly hounded, harassed and tense. I'm so used to being on guard that I can never relax. There is always a threat of violence, even when it's relatively calm."

"I must give in to him or he'll get enraged."

"I lie about where I've been, how much I've paid and what I think, always afraid of being found out and punished."

"I feel that I'm the one who's doing all the work to try to improve the relationship."

"I'm embarrassed to invite guests to our home because he has no qualms about being rude, crude, indifferent or abusive to friends or family members."

"I feel like an object, a thing which provides certain services but is basically a useless pest."

"I dread the holidays because it means spending more time with her. She gets hysterical and critical whenever there is a break in the routine or added expenses."

"I feel violated, alone, misunderstood, unappreciated, ashamed, hurt, hopeless, scared, trapped and helpless."

"I think about death (his or mine) as the only way out."

"I feel like I live a secret life, unable to reveal the truth to anyone because no one would believe me."

"I feel that my children are being scarred for life."

"I feel that it's my fault that I'm abused."

"I feel numb much of the time. I think I've adjusted, that it's good that her destructive behavior no longer bothers me. I'm not even upset that I've become deadened."

Abuse is always a matter of degree, determined by its frequency, intensity and duration. However, if you answered "yes" to many or most of the above items, you are in an abusive relationship. By facing the truth, you can then figure out how to minimize the damage.

Gaslighters

Psychologists call one of the most insidious, yet subtle forms of abuse "gaslighting." Gaslighters engage in emotional torture, but in a seemingly loving manner. For example, a gaslighter may make subtle changes in the position of the furniture while the spouse is asleep. When the spouse comments on the changes, the gaslighter will say, "Dearest, I never moved the furniture! I feel so bad for you. You must be losing your mind." The gaslighter will make promises, such as to meet the spouse at a certain time or buy a certain item. When the spouse complains that these promises were not kept, the gaslighter says, "Poor thing. I never said anything of the sort. You must see a psychiatrist right away. Something is seriously wrong with your mind." Inevitably, abused partners begin to lose confidence in their ability to make even the simplest decision and to feel that they are, indeed, insane.

Just words?

A popular children's saying states that, "Sticks and stones may break my bones but words can never hurt me." This is a terrible lie.

Humiliating put-downs have a cumulative effect, harming body and soul. Contempt cripples the spirit and can trigger numerous nervous ailments which may defy medical treatment. The pain of being unloved is one of the greatest of all emotional wounds. To crave love, security, understanding and appreciation, and receive nothing but coldness and contempt, is nothing short of emotional torture.

> An abusive person can also affect one spiritually: If a man has a bad wife — conceited and self-centered — she may remove from his heart the desire to fulfill the commandments.
>
> (THE WAYS OF THE RIGHTEOUS, p. 99)

Failure to achieve a loving relationship with one's spouse can make a person feel completely isolated, from both man and God.

Abusive thinking

Abusive people see the world differently from mentally healthy people. For example, their paranoia stems from the fact that they view people as actual threats. They are hyper-alert to signs of betrayal or rejection, which they always manage to find or imagine they have found. They see people as takers, against whom they must defend themselves. Thus, the most innocent request is viewed warily, as an attempt to drain or deprive them of their limited time, money or power. Yet they commonly feel that they are the victimized ones and talk constantly about how others are out to take advantage or exploit them. Whenever a family member makes a mistake, they attack, saying, "I was right! I knew I couldn't trust you!"

As parents, they treat their children as objects to be controlled and used. They are so needy themselves that the constant demands of a family make them feel inadequate, which enrages them. To them, to give is to be diminished and demeaned. Abusive parents interpret normal expressions of emotion — even a smile or a legitimate cry of pain — as a sneaky attempt to manipulate them. An abusive mother will interpret a child's bedwetting, clumsiness or refusal to finish his food as a deliberate attack and feel she must protect herself by attacking him back or pushing him away. An abusive teacher may see a difference of opinion or a failure to finish an assignment as a deliberate act of insolence and insubordination and respond accordingly.

Abusive people are quick to hit others with their verbal "sledge-hammer" and may also accompany their critical remarks with threats or physical violence as well. In their minds, these attacks are justified because they think:

"I must not trust people because they will betray me."

"I must punish people who make me feel bad."

"People deserve respect only if they live up to my standards and expectations. Anyone who is uncooperative, incompetent in some area, slow, insensitive or unspiritual deserves to be abused."

"I can't control myself."

"Force is the only way to get what I want."

"My unhappiness is other people's fault. They deserve to be hurt because they're not making me happy."

"All emotions, other than anger, are signs of weakness."

"If I feel hurt, I have the right to hurt back."

"Lack of obedience means lack of respect. I must hurt those who don't respect me."

"If I hurt someone, it's his fault for provoking me."

"I can't respect anyone who loves me, because anyone who could love me must be too stupid to see who I really am."

"If I succeed in deceiving someone, he deserves to be deceived because he was too stupid to detect the deception."

Because these beliefs seem like the truth to abusive people, they feel justified in being abusive. When others react with hostility, the abusive person then thinks that his beliefs are accurate and that he is justified in being abusive.

Sadly, abusive people often marry doormat types who believe: If I make demands, assert my rights and say no, it means I'm a bully type. In order not to have people reject me, I must be a doormat and always give in.

Childhood roots

We are all driven unconsciously to repeat the negative patterns of the past and fulfill the unhealthy messages we absorbed during childhood. This drive is overpowering and irresistible unless we gain insight into these patterns and messages and work hard to break them. Nowhere is this more true than in the case of abused children, who are likely to become abusive adults, filled with hatred toward themselves and those closest to them.

Recently, two authors, acting independently, attempted to find some common link among people who voluntarily risked their lives to help others, including Gentiles who helped Jews during World War II. Both found that these heroes included people who were both self-confident and insecure, the deeply religious as well as the nonreligious. The one common trait they shared was an upbringing free from corporeal punishment, where instead the parents reasoned with them (*The Compassionate Beast and The Brighter Side of Human Nature*).

In contrast, in an abusive atmosphere, the ability to care about the welfare of others is stifled. When children are abused, they feel like objects, not like people. In future relationships, they will depersonalize others, treating them as objects just as they were treated, constantly accusing others of disloyalty and disobedience, as they were accused in the past.

> ◆ EXAMPLE: "My husband's parents were terribly ashamed of his poor learning skills and they let him know it. They criticized him constantly and often hit him for getting poor grades. How can someone turn out normal if he spends all his formative years feeling like a total failure both at school and at home? After we got married, all that shame and suppressed rage got displaced onto me. He treated me the same way he'd been treated and was as impossible to get through to as his parents had been."

In an abusive environment, the children feel worthless because their needs and feelings are not respected. Inevitably, they conclude that, "Anyone who could love someone as despicable as me must be stupid and not worth respecting." Thus, not only can they not bond positively to others, they cannot respect anyone who tries to be loving toward them. To them, "Being loved means being abused," and "Being loving means being abusive."

Abusive people find it much safer and more exciting to hate than to love. Hating provides a "high," and an illusory sense of power and security, whereas loving makes them feel weak, vulnerable and stupid.

Abusive parents have unrealistic demands for a level of cooperation and maturity which small children cannot possibly meet, thereby making both their children and themselves feel like failures. It is common for such children to be heavily shamed and harshly punished for everything from their failure to be toilet trained early enough to their inability to sit still or cooperate instantly.

Abused children cannot express the anger they feel toward their parents because they will only be ignored, ridiculed or punished. So they displace their anger onto those they consider weaker or inferior to themselves, such as younger siblings or weaker classmates, animals, or the handicapped. Their feeling of inadequacy is manifest in a compulsion to tear others down.

Abusive people come from homes where they saw people getting their way by bullying others. Sometimes, the mother was a cold, dictatorial type who bullied both her husband and children. More commonly, it was the father who bullied the wife and children. When a mother fails to protect her children from an abusive father, the children usually turn their anger not against the father, but against the passive mother and all women in general, because women are seen as safer targets, since they usually do not fight back. In general, girls from abusive homes have a greater tendency toward depression, turning their anger against themselves, while boys tend to turn their anger outward in aggressive acts. However, when these girls become mothers, they are likely to vent their suppressed rage on their helpless children, as do men from abusive homes.

Emotional autism

Despite their superficial friendliness and charisma, abusive people do not bond normally to others. As soon as others start to form attachments to them, they do something to destroy the bonds.

Abusive people alternate between periods of explosive rage and autistic withdrawal, in which there is no attempt to connect at all. If they aren't criticizing, they have nothing to say, no way of connecting. Or, their talk is impersonal and superficial, not talk which would strengthen and deepen bonds of affection and understanding. Often, they act as if they don't need relationships and don't care whether anyone likes them or not. When they refuse to reach out to others and remain unaffected by others' needs or feelings, they feel powerful, thereby lessening their sense of vulnerability and insecurity.

While abusive people may have insatiable demands for physical contact, true closeness is absent. They can be cold, critical or cruel one minute and then expect the spouse to be warm and affectionate the next. For them, physical intimacy has more to do with conquering than with connecting. They may act as if they own their partners' bodies, disregarding all proper boundaries, including those of *halachah*.

Other abusive people shun even physical relationships with their partners, sometimes because of an abnormal attraction to children or members of the same sex. Such a person will blame the spouse for not being attractive, exciting or intelligent enough, but this criticalness merely hides the truth, i.e., that the abusive person cannot sustain normal bonds of love.

Marital disasters

Tragically, those married to abusive people may never know what it is like to feel loved, for their mates avoid the emotional honesty and unselfishness which build nourishing relationships and treat their spouses as objects to be used for their own selfish purposes. Furthermore, their harmful impulses are not held in check by the fear of rejection, which keeps normal people from hurting others.

Nothing is more terrifying than being attacked by a violent, irrational person who is impossible to get through to and who is bent on destroying someone because he thinks that person is the source of all his unhappiness. Unless the healthy partner stands up for himself and demands the elementary fundamentals of polite behavior (which is the most one can hope for in such a relationship), abusive partners will keep escalating their demands, criticism and violence. Unfortunately, few newlyweds do this for fear of appearing selfish or demanding, and because a normal person is so sure things will soon get better if he just gives in and appeases the other one.

◆ EXAMPLE: "This isn't a marriage. It's a war. She is either cold or exploding. I was so sure she would soften up with time, but it only got worse, no matter how I tried to please her. There is no way to get through. She is very demanding and very exacting. It's like living in a mine field. One wrong move and I get blown up. In the beginning, I kept thinking I should leave, but I kept hoping things would change. Now I'm trapped because of the children. I must stay so that they will have some positive input in their lives."

Rabbi Chaim Vital stated, "A man is measured by the way he treats his wife" (*Guide to the Jewish Marriage*, p. 104). The same can be said for a woman.

The mark of a mature person is that he wants to give to others for the sheer pleasure of giving. The mark of an immature person is that he only wants to take. The abusive spouse is utterly selfish, constantly demanding proof of love, yet never satisfied that what he gets is adequate.

When demands begin, love departs.

(STRIVE FOR TRUTH! vol. I, p. 133)

Rabbi Shmuel D. Eisenblatt identifies the six major ingredients of a successful marriage as: mutual understanding, empathy, combined and coordinated efforts, appreciation, patience and love (*Fulfillment in Marriage*, vol. II, pp. 118-119). In contrast, marriage to an abusive person means isolation, misunderstanding, lack of sympathy and appreciation, constant criticism and hostility.

Unfortunately, "leaky roof syndrome" often prevents abused people from seeking help. When things are going smoothly, everyone wants to forget what happened or they fear bringing up the issue and enraging the person again. Then, when things are bad, the abusive person is so irrational and terrifying that it is impossible to communicate. Abusive people are so self-delusional that they do not want to admit their problems to themselves, let alone reveal them to a counselor.

People who suffer from Borderline Personality Disorder are often attracted to sadistic types because on the surface, these people appear to have everything they lack: they seem so self-assured, protective, decisive, unemotional and in control. They admire the unresponsiveness, rigid boundaries and take-charge attitude of the abuser. Because Borderlines suffer from such a fragile sense of self, they think such a "strong" person will give them an identity and provide them with the control, structure and security they need. Because they suffer from such overwhelming feelings of helplessness, they hope to be taken care of. Because they feel so painfully alone, they think,

"Better to be abused than alone." Because they suffer from intense self-loathing, they believe, "I deserve to be abused," and do not take measures to protect themselves from verbal, sexual or physical abuse. In fact, they may have learned in childhood that "love hurts," or "being in pain makes me feel alive and real."

Because Borderlines think in black/white terms and live in the present, there is no continuity from one day to the next. During moments when they decide another person is really all good underneath it all, they forget about the past and don't think it is necessary to take any action to correct the situation.

It doesn't take long before abused Borderlines feel more helpless, misunderstood and alone than before the marriage. Then their blind rage bursts forth, directed at themselves in self-mutilating acts or suicidal attempts, or directed at their children or the abusive person. However, their fury is so aimless and chaotic that no positive changes can take place.

Why they "take it"

Those involved in abusive relationships are often condemned for being stupid, masochistic or deserving of whatever they are getting because they don't try hard enough to please the abuser. In the school system, parents unwittingly encourage this belief by telling the child who has an abusive teacher; "It's all your fault. You must have provoked him." This makes children think that violence is permissible, that the recipient should feel guilty, and that it is useless to complain about it.

Outsiders often compound the problem by saying, "You're stupid if you don't stand up for yourself," or "You look fine, so it can't be all that bad." When victims blame themselves for the abuse, they become paralyzed by shame. And they often avoid seeking help because they fear being told, "You deserve it", or "You're to blame."

Abused wives have a particularly difficult time because they are almost always in a state of total economic dependency and paralyzing fear of physical brutality. Even if a woman does get divorced, abuse continues in the form of nefarious legal maneuvers, threatening phone calls and attempts to kidnap the children or brainwash them into hating her. There are continuous efforts to break her emotionally and financially, and to drive her insane in order to prove to the world that she was to blame all along. After a divorce, abusive men usually remarry quickly, while their wives are still left to deal with poverty, shame, social isolation and the fear of not knowing when the next bomb will fall.

> ◆ EXAMPLE: "A hundred times a day, I tell myself that I must get out, that I cannot take it anymore and that I'll die if I have to go on enduring the endless cruelties inflicted on me and the children. I feel like a married widow, living without love or communication. Yet divorce would be worse because I'd not only be impoverished, I'd also be ostracized socially. He'd do everything to take the children away. In my world, divorced women are outcasts, looked down upon as if they have committed a terrible crime, even if everyone knows they were abused. Many husbands won't allow their wives to associate with a divorced woman or let their children play with her children. If I were a widow, I'd be an object of pity. But a divorcee is seen as a threat to marriage, a home wrecker. People think women should endure abuse no matter how bad it is, just to keep the family together. They think that if my husband is unhappy, it's because I don't try hard enough to please him. Even if I left, he'd go on tormenting me. Whether I stay or leave, he'll hurt me."

The choice of whether to stay or leave is never an easy one, especially when children are involved.

The provocationist theory of abuse

Outsiders often blame the abused person for provoking the abuser by being overly demanding, overly emotional or having a victim mentality, the implication being, "If you would just act right, your spouse/teacher/boss/parent would be nice to you." Such people excuse the abuse by implying, "You're at fault because you provoked him by talking on the phone, not having his food ready and not keeping the children quiet and the home completely spotless." Or, "You don't make enough money, don't bring her enough gifts and don't help enough with the household chores." To a child, they will say, "You provoked your parents [or teachers] by making noise and not cooperating."

Blaming the abused one is like accusing the victim of a robbery of "asking for it" by wearing an expensive watch. Such thinking excuses the thief's behavior and absolves him of responsibility. Furthermore, even if a person is not highly intelligent, is overly talkative, emotionally needy, unorganized or high strung, does this justify abusive behavior? Sadly, many people think so.

What such people do not realize is that the abuser abuses, not because of anything the victim does, but because the person is addicted to abuse and experiences a sense of pleasure in being able to hurt others. The fact that the wife left dirty dishes in the sink or the child failed to do his homework are merely excuses to indulge in the addiction. The event merely triggers the underlying compulsion to crush.

Thus, it is futile to tell the victim not to provoke abusive people since abusive people are provoked by the very existence of other human beings! Anything and everything can arouse their compulsion to control. Even if others try to keep things neat and clean, try not to make noise or make demands, some bit of dust, a delayed meal, some bill, loss or mistake will be used to justify and excuse an explosion. Merely feeling hungry or nervous is enough reason to lash out and make others feel inferior.

"Don't provoke him" advice is counterproductive because it is impossible to avoid doing so. In addition, it makes the abused one feel that he is to blame for being abused.

Irresponsibility is encouraged when one excuses those who claim, "I threw things because I just couldn't stand seeing those dirty socks under the bed," "I slammed him up against the wall because it's the only way to knock some sense into his head," or "I just couldn't keep from exploding when she served those leftovers again. How else is a hungry person supposed to react to such an insult?"

Abusive people just don't accept the truth that they are responsible for their actions. They don't accept that *middoth* are independent of the events and people which they encounter. They think that those who display good *middoth* in difficult circumstances are somehow lucky or don't have the financial or emotional burdens which make them explode.

The Torah states that we have the inherent ability to control our thoughts and act with dignity no matter how abominably others behave. A person who does not acknowledge this freedom of choice denies one of the most fundamental principles of the Torah (*Guide for the Perplexed*, p. 261).

Spotting potential abusers before marriage

Since the consequences of a bad choice can be so tragic, it is of utmost importance that people try to spot the signs of a potentially abusive spouse before marriage. A few essential questions which can be asked are:

* Did they suffer maternal deprivation during the first few years of life? Were they abused or neglected by their mother or father? If so, connecting to people may be impossible and abuse will seem normal.

* Were they known as bullies in their youth?

* Did they do poorly in school and suffer humiliating scoldings or beatings for not getting top grades?

* Are they overly fastidious about external appearance, e.g., looks, clothing and other possessions? Such people will put things and their public image before human needs.

* Do they boast about how wonderful they are, or the opposite — how inadequate they are?

* Are they jealous of your close relationships with family members or friends?

* Do they have numerous prejudices toward groups which differ in thinking or cultural background from theirs?

* Are they vengeful, always talking about getting even with people who have hurt them?

* Are you afraid of their anger and do you lie or withhold information in order not to enrage them?

* Are they unusually nervous?

* Do they seem "too good to be true," almost saintly and not quite honest or aware of their deficiencies?

* Have they threatened suicide if you don't go through with the marriage?

All too often, friends and relatives assure the prospective bride or groom that the disturbed person's problems are minor or nonexistent, and that everything will work out after the marriage. If one decides to go through with the marriage despite one's doubts, counseling should begin immediately and the couple should focus on developing good communication techniques and uncovering the irrational beliefs which allow the person to justify abusive behavior.

The merry-go-round syndrome

To maintain dominance and distance, abusive people often use a merry-go-round tactic which prevents the abused one from developing any sense of security or maintaining the momentum necessary to continue therapy. Typically, what happens is that (1) the abused one bears the physical and emotional blows with stoic forbearance for months or years. Finally, the situation becomes so unbearable that (2) the long-suffering spouse finally blows up and seeks to separate or divorce. (3) The abusive one is surprised, having no inkling that anything is wrong. He promises to improve or even go to therapy. However, in therapy, he is either so resistant that nothing can be accomplished, or, (4) he acts so loving that the therapist thinks all is well. If so, things may change for the better temporarily, so that the couple discontinues therapy after a few sessions, sure that these changes are permanent. However, (5) as soon as the healthy one starts to feel close and trusting, the abusive one begins having more frequent explosions. Disillusioned, the abused one goes back to stage (1) of stoic forbearance. But, once again, (2) the situation becomes unbearable. The healthy one sees that nothing has really changed. Once again, they (3) have an emergency session with a rabbi or counselor, after which there is (4) a period of temporary improvement and renewed hope, which is (5) dashed as soon as the abuse intensifies.

Is there hope?

> I will remove the stony heart from out of your flesh, and I will give you a heart of flesh.
>
> (YECHEZKEL 36:26)

Can this stony heart become human? Anyone can do *teshuvah*, but the prognosis for improvement depends on the severity of the problem and the person's willingness to accept responsibility for his behavior. *Teshuvah* requires that a person feel guilt and shame over what he has done and be determined to change. Powerholics are the least likely of all types to even realize that they need to change. If an abusive person reads this chapter and sees himself in it, this is an indication of hope.

As for those who must deal with violent people, it must be realized that the average person has no more expertise in dealing with abusive people than he has in performing brain surgery. Strategies must be learned: particularly communcation techniques and assertiveness tactics. It is essential to reject the commonly given advice to "do what he wants." The more passive the victims are, the more everyone will suffer.

Because abusive people are so afraid of exposure, the oppressed one takes a major risk when speaking out and going for help. But this must be done. Hiding the problem only makes it worse. After hearing that the spouse or child has gone for help, abusive people will often become even more threatening and violent or withdraw into autistic silence. Yet the oppressed ones must continue knocking on every door possible and continue getting the help they need. They might not find anyone capable of influencing the abusive person, but they are at least creating a support group for themselves, which makes the isolation and pain a little more bearable.

In the presence of a bully with superior physical strength, one must usually apply the rules of oppressed people everywhere, i.e., obey immediately; don't challenge their authority openly; be emotionally dishonest — don't show that you are hurt, sad or sick, because weakness enrages them and they enjoy kicking those who are down; keep a low profile — pretend you are a nonentity, because that is less threatening to their ego; don't talk, but if you must, don't communicate anything of importance, for anything you say will be used against you, ridiculed or invalidated; maintain your dignity in the face of the countless indignities by developing emotional and spiritual strengths.

◆ EXAMPLE: "During the early years, I stood by passively, paralyzed by horror and indecision. Finally, I realized I had to be strong and try to keep the atmosphere as positive as possible. The kids all have their disturbances, even though I tried to emphasize their good points. They all feel rejected, which has left scars. I live a schizophrenic life — cold, withdrawn and on guard when she's around and then warm and loving when she's not. It's very difficult."

◆ EXAMPLE: "Once I understood that most of my pain came from feeling depersonalized, I was able to do things to maintain my personal sense of dignity and worth during difficult times. I learned to feel like a worthwhile person no matter how others were treating me, and this has helped me deal with other emotionally disturbed people as well."

Whenever possible, pressure tactics or threats should be used to get the abusive person to restrain himself because this is the only language they understand. For example, therapy can be required in lieu of a prison term or fine or as a condition to staying married. Insistence on polite behavior, even if it is superficial and phony, can sometimes bring about change because disturbed people must first force themselves to act healthy in order for the act to ever become real. The false act is the first step to health, whether the person is a tyrannical bully or a depressed grumbler. School principals should not wait patiently for abusive teachers to "soften up." They should remove them from their jobs, since they encourage abusive behavior in some children and build tolerance for cruelty.

Abusive people respond best to group therapy with other abusive types who are not fooled by the phony facade or excuses which they use to justify abusive behavior. Being with other abusive people who are struggling to control their own violent impulses provides the encouragement which gives newcomers hope that they, too, can succeed in doing the same. Most important, seeing others open up and reveal their deepest fears and feelings provides a model for them to do the same. They learn to listen, to be emotionally honest and to take an interest in others. This creates the foundation for forming healthy attachments. It is only then that there is hope of breaking down the isolating walls and overcoming the emotional crippling which began so early in life. There should be no illusions about the time it takes to heal — the healing process is a life-long struggle.

To avoid feeling like a helpless victim, it is essential for family members to avoid blaming themselves for the abuse and to know that their *middoth* must be independent of the abusive person's behavior. They must resolve not to be dragged down to the abusive person's level by engaging in name calling, vulgar language or acts of violence. In time, abusive people may come to respect the fact that, no matter what they do, they cannot drag the other one down. That may awaken a small spark of trust and respect on their part. If not, then these demonstrations of self-discipline under such trying circumstances will strengthen the self-esteem of the healthy one.

◆ EXAMPLE: "To teach my children coping skills, I shared the phrases which I was using to stay calm, such as: 'We need to solutionize, not emotionalize,' 'I'm proud of myself for not losing control right now,' 'My worth is determined by God, not man,' 'Here's an opportunity to demonstrate the values of Torah,' 'He's doing the best he can with the tools he has,' etc. When all else fails, I hum sayings from *Tehillim*. I may live in an abusive situation, but I'm the one who has gained true strength, while my partner, who seems to have all the power, is the weak, pitiful one, the one who can't reach out, the one who has no consciousness of God."

Family members must have fulfilling interests, loving friends and pleasurable activities, which may have to be kept secret, since abusive people often find excuses to sabotage these outlets.

One must forget about being a husband, wife, child or parent in the usual sense of these terms, and instead, adopt the role of a strict teacher. Disturbed people need firm limits, guidelines and instructions. They must be taught to be polite and responsible just as one would teach a young child, repeating over and over again in a calm but firm voice, precisely what is and is not acceptable behavior. In this way, abusive people can sometimes be taught to restrain their compulsion to hurt. Even if they never achieve much depth of self-awareness or real concern for others, superficial good manners is a step forward.

It is especially important to find an insightful rabbi who takes a personal interest in helping the person apply Torah principles to resolve daily conflicts. This relationship can also bring about a "reparenting" process which is necessary for the one who was abused during childhood and never developed enough trust to be able to form stable emotional attachments. Unfortunately, abusive people often refuse to consult or accept the advice of a counselor, because they think they know more than anyone else. They also tend to think that there is nothing wrong with them, that therapy is a waste of time and money, that all therapists are crazy, and that only emotional cripples need counseling. Such people don't change. Those who think that a miracle will take place without the person putting forth tremendous effort to become more disciplined, will be sorely disappointed.

CHAPTER 12:
Coping with Disturbed People:
Turning Darkness into Light

Our Sages teach us that just as an olive must be crushed before it brings forth its oil, so is Israel often persecuted before its light shines forth.

(SHEMOTH RABBAH 36:I)

How do people live with disturbed people? The same way people live with muscular dystrophy, cancer or other serious physical illnesses. It is essential to learn coping strategies. The most important is the choice of attitude. A person can either curse his bad luck and allow rage and despair to overwhelm him, or he can practice the disciplines necessary to maintain his own sanity. Mental health is essentially a matter of imitating God's attributes in whatever circumstances one finds himself. The challenge is to do so even if others don't.

There is no sense of victimization if one feels that one's spirit is free, that the inner light shines forth not only despite the darkness, but because of it. The coping strategies in this chapter may or may not have a positive affect on others. But they will liberate your spirit from fear and hatred. They are the steps to your own healing journey.

To hope or not to hope? That is the question

No matter how long one lives with a disturbed individual, there is always the hope that somehow things will change and the person will turn into a loving, responsible human being. One always wonders, "Should I continue to hope?" Just as a doctor cannot say for sure if a person will ever awaken from a physical coma, we do not know if certain people will ever emerge from their emotional comas.

Since disturbed people often act quite normal, family members waver between hope and despair. They see progress and think, She's being so nice. She must really be all right. Then suddenly, the person slips back into her old abusive patterns, especially in close family relationships, where emotional problems express themselves more frequently.

Hope is a double-edged sword: it can bring joy or sorrow. On the one hand, people say, "Where there's life, there's hope. No one is a lost cause. Never give up." On the other hand, false hopes delay one's acceptance of reality, keeping one from detaching physically or emotionally, or from dealing assertively with the disturbed person. Unrealistic hopes can fill one with bitterness if one waits passively for change.

> Hope deferred makes the heart sick, but a desire fulfilled is a tree of life.
> (MISHLEI 13:12)

Is there hope? Yes — if (and that is a big "if") the disturbed person diligently and courageously fights for health. Obviously, the situation is most hopeful for those who recognize that they are at least partially responsible for their pain and want to change. The prognosis for those with more serious character disorders is worse, since they do not think they are disturbed and, therefore, take no responsibility for their behavior or the pain they cause others. In fact, they often think they are quite pious and caring. The more severe the disturbance, the more massive the denial.

Whatever the outlook, hope is what the emotionally healthy person needs for himself most of all — hope that he will grow in strength and wisdom and not be dragged under.

The challenge: to sanctify the experience

The key to living or working with a disturbed person is the development of a strong faith in God and a disciplined will. It takes incredible strength of will to withstand the tension which disturbed people create.

In commenting on the words of the Mishnah (*Avoth* 5:23), "The greater the suffering, the greater is the reward," the Maharal states that a person gets the greatest reward for doing those mitzvoth which are most difficult for him (*Tifereth Yisrael*, ch. 61). This is different for each person, depending on his particular nature. Each encounter with a disturbed person gives us an opportunity to strengthen the *middoth* in which we are weakest:

> *"If I didn't have such a hot-tempered spouse, I don't think I ever would have learned such self-control, because the only way I can keep things calm at home is for me to be incredibly self-disciplined."*

> *"I learned to practice gratefulness every minute of the day. It was the only way to keep my spirits up."*

> *"I never would have had such compassion for others if I hadn't experienced what it's like."*

> *"I learned to rely on God, because there was no one else to turn to. Terrible loneliness returned me to Him."*

It is gratitude which allows us to bloom spiritually in whatever situation God plants us.

The Chazon Ish, *z"l*, was reported to have said concerning children with Downs Syndrome that they do not come into this world in order to do *tikkun* (healing of their character defects), because they lack the awareness to do so. Instead, by bringing out the best or the worst in others, their very existence allows others to reach greater spiritual heights if they deal with the situation in a positive way.

Therefore, to deal positively with disturbed people, the most important thing is to focus on our own *middoth*. When confronted with their fault-finding, laziness, cruelty or irresponsibility, do we get sucked into a whirlpool of rage, fearful withdrawal or despair ourselves? Or, do we maintain our faith, determination, self-respect and integrity in the face of their negativity? This is our spiritual test.

The Gemara speaks of Rav Chiya, whose wife caused him to suffer greatly. Despite this, he brought her gifts, explaining that she deserved it because she raised his children and protected him from sin (*Yevamoth* 63a). There is no mention of any improvement on her part. But Rav Chiya certainly exemplified the highest level of having respect for others, and in so doing serves as a role model for all those who come in contact with disturbed people.

Remember, God brings certain people into our lives because He deems that they are necessary for *our* growth. When we trust that the encounter will elevate us, if we act in an elevated manner no matter how badly we feel, we are soon lifted to a whole new level of spiritual consciousness. God promises us that, "Those who sow in tears will reap in joy" (*Tehillim* 126:5). That is a real promise. Each person we encounter is part of our own healing journey.

Helplessness aggravates the worst stress

Researchers have found a positive correlation between certain personality types and the development of cancer and stress-related illnesses. It is not so much the stressful events themselves which weaken people's immunological systems, but the feeling of having no control over these events which does the damage (*Superimmunity*, p. 34-60). Thus, the people most likely to develop malignancies are those who feel:

(1) *Unloved and inadequate* — those who are unable to satisfy their desire for emotional closeness or achievement and who feel crushed by this loss.

(2) *Nonexpressive* — those who are unable to express their deepest feelings, such as anger, fear and anxiety, to those closest to them.

(3) *Self-denigrating* — those who habitually put themselves down and feel like failures.

(4) *Helpless and hopeless* — those who acccept their situation passively, who feel that they are incapable of coping with life, are unassertive, overly nice, overly-patient and tend to avoid conflict by giving up and giving in.

People who feel that they have some control over a stressful situation suffer less physical and emotional trauma than those who do not. Therefore, one should do everything possible to avoid feeling powerless and inadequate. One cannot control another's hostility, but one can achieve a sense of power by gaining control over one's own attitudes and taking responsibility for getting one's own needs satisfied.

The difficulty of remaining sane

With the pure You deal purely and with the perverse You deal crookedly.   (MEGILLAH 13b)

Those who must live with an abusive person cannot avoid being affected physically, emotionally and spiritually as well. In fact, we are told that during the time that Avram was with Lot, the word of God departed from him (*Bereshith* 13:14, Rashi).

People tend to get stuck emotionally at the age when their most severe traumas took place. You may be dealing with someone who is emotionally at the level of a six-month-old or a two-year-old, and is just as demanding, self-centered and possessive, but without the child's charm and infinite capacity for love.

The worst part about living or working with disturbed people is that they tend to bring out the worst in everyone. How do you deal with a powerholic who has cheated you out of all your money or a depressed person who lies around and does nothing all day? Not only is there physical wear and tear from the stress of living with someone who is moody, demanding, dishonest and volatile, but there is also the stress of having to protect oneself psychologically by adopting defenses which may, in themselves, be harmful. For example, one may lie to avoid being screamed at by an explosive person or protect oneself by turning off one's feelings and becoming emotionally numb. These protective habits of dishonesty, mistrust and withdrawal can spill over onto one's other relationships, so that one often finds it difficult to relate normally even to normal people. One may lose the spontaneous warmth and enthusiasm which is characteristic of healthy relationships. Thus, the walls one builds to protect one's spirit may end up destroying it.

Someone who is distraught about having to live or work with an abusive person is actually exhibiting a sign of emotional health, because it means he has not yet numbed himself to the pain. To lose one's ability to feel outrage over abusive behavior or grief over the waste of human potential is to lose one's humanity. A normal person does not want to turn himself into a rock in order not to feel the pain. He wants to be honest and loving with those who are trustworthy, yet protective and untrusting around the disturbed person. This requires living simultaneously in two very different worlds. Since it is impossible to build walls and bridges at the same time, the healthy person sometimes hurts those he loves by being in a "wall mode" when he should be in a "bridge mode."

Furthermore, assumptions which apply to healthy people cannot be applied to those who aren't. For example, in a healthy relationship one assumes that one will be comforted and supported in times of distress and that the other person will not deliberately hurt you, or that he will feel sorry and apologize if he does. But disturbed people are ruled by unrestrained passions and irrational fears. They are often deliberately vindictive and abusive. When their help is needed most, they can usually be counted on to attack, withdraw or run away. So it is not surprising to find a change for the worse in the normal person's behavior over a period of time:

◆ EXAMPLE: "In order to stop feeling so much pain, I deadened myself emotionally. I don't even know what I feel anymore."

◆ EXAMPLE: "I used to be a nice person. But after living so long with someone who sleeps half of the day, won't bathe or go to work regularly and is so grouchy, demanding, lazy and irresponsible, I've become a bitter, mean, screaming witch."

It is easy to blame others for making us feel so awful. But the truth is that they merely evoke negative qualities in us which we need to overcome, particularly the tendency to be wishy-washy complainers, critical condemnaholics and childishly demanding and dependent. Yes, they bring out the worst — so that we can see where we need to work.

Survival skills: liberating your spirit

We who lived in concentration camps can remember the men who walked through the huts comforting others, giving away their last piece of bread. They may have been few in number, but they offer sufficient proof that everything can be taken from a man but one thing: the last of the human freedoms — to choose one's attitude in any given set of circumstances, to choose one's own way.

In reality, there was an opportunity and a challenge. One could make a victory of those experiences, turning life into an inner triumph, or one could ignore the challenge and simply vegetate, as did a majority of the prisoners (*Man's Search for Meaning*, pp. 65, 72).

It is an enormous challenge to deepen one's faith in God and strengthen one's ability to remain loving in such difficult circumstances. How does one bear the contempt, the loneliness and stress? Strength of will is the key to sanity. The following disciplines will help.

(1) *The power of love.* Love heals and transforms — if not the other person, then certainly oneself.

> I command you this day to love the Lord thy God, to walk in His ways, and to keep His commandments and His statutes and His ordinances that you shall live...
>
> (DEVARIM 30:16)

Just as there are infinite degrees of faith, so too are there infinite degrees of love, the highest being unconditional acceptance of the person as he is. But love cannot coexist with a desire to control or change the loved one. One must accept the person with his present level of consciousness in order to have a positive influence. Often, this works wonders.

> ◆ EXAMPLE: "Having been abused as a child, I was very insecure and anxious when I got married. I had lived with so much terror as a child that I was afraid to love or be loved. But my husband was so consistently caring during the lengthy period during which I tested his love, I finally learned to trust that he was not going to hurt or abandon me as I had been. I am a different person today because of his love."

Disturbed people are starved for love. But they are so accustomed to rejection that they often ignore, ridicule or resent your efforts to be kind and loving, as if you are trying to hurt. Even if they accept your love today, they are sure it will end tomorrow, just as it did when they were children and were constantly disappointed and betrayed by others.

To remain emotionally healthy, you must retain your ability to love life, to love friends and to love yourself. Try loving gestures, even if they are insincere at first, for "A person comes to love the one to whom he gives" (*Strive for Truth!* vol. 1, p. 130). If you cannot arouse a true feeling of love for the disturbed person, you can be polite and respect him as a creation of God and for whatever good qualities he does have, unless, of course, he is truly evil. And you can work to develop your love for God by trusting that He is with you in this difficult experience.

Loving someone does not mean always being submissive or passsive. The opposite is true! It means being fiercely protective of your mental health and often tough and demanding, doing everything possible to help the other person:

◆ EXAMPLE: "When my daughter first started losing weight, I didn't take much notice. We barely had a relationship as it was. But as she got thinner and thinner, I grew more frantic. I'm generally quite passive and I thought that I had to let her struggle with her own problems. My husband is a very distant person and the doctors I consulted about her anorexia could not offer me any help because she wouldn't cooperate. Finally, I decided to take charge. I quit my job and stayed by her night and day. I slept in the same room. I made her eat and I watched to see that she wouldn't throw it up. I discovered an inner determination I never knew I had. Little by little, the urge to destroy herself lessened. We became closer. I think we healed each other, for both of us had wounds which we had ignored."

Your criticism of others is a reflection of your own lack of self-acceptance.

◆ EXAMPLE: "Almost from the day I married, I complained about my wife's weight, cooking and housekeeping abilities. I was hypercritical, yet I demanded that she be loving to me. When I complained about her to my rabbi, he said that very critical, demanding people treat whomever they marry with contempt because they are afraid of contact. He said that every time I started to criticize, I should remember that my nonacceptance of others is really my own nonacceptance of myself coming out. Since then, I've worked hard to be less critical and to give what I never received. It wasn't easy to make loving gestures when these things didn't come naturally! At first, I felt stupid and demeaned and awkward. I thought I would die. A part of me did. The sick part."

The one thing disturbed people never got as children was unconditional acceptance. If they get it as adults, there may be some gradual improvement in their ability to bond. However, psychopathic types are usually resistant to all such efforts. In such situations, your attention should be focused on protecting yourself and your other family members from abuse.

(2) *The power of acceptance.* Faith is best expressed in the acceptance of God's will as if it were our own will (*Pirkei Avoth* 2:4). In commenting on the verse (*Tehillim* 118:24), "This is the day which God has made, we will be glad and rejoice in Him," as interpreted by *chazal* in *Yalkut Shimoni*, *Yeshayahu* 505, Rabbi Ya'akov

Kamenecki, *z"l*, said that this means to rejoice no matter what the day brings because it is all from God and, therefore, all good even though we may not apprehend that good with our limited understanding. This is the key to inner serenity. The degree of our emotional pain is equal to the degree of our resistance to His will. Peace comes when we surrender to God whatever is beyond our control.

Acceptance means different things to different people. For example, one says, "Because I accept my condition, I will live with it and reject further treatment." Another says, "Because I accept that I have a serious problem, I will try any treatment that anyone can propose!"

Accept that you will not always know what to do. Should you ignore their hostility, irresponsibility, insensitivity and cruelty? Should you make demands? If so, which demands are appropriate, which not? No one knows for sure.

Accept that you will never be able to satisfy disturbed people's demands. They are insatiable.

Accept that these people are crippled to some degree, but you do not cripple yourself with feelings of failure because you cannot get through to them or heal them.

Accept your feelings. Before acceptance comes grief. Allow yourself to grieve, but don't let it paralyze you. In his lectures, Rabbi Zelig Pliskin, author and counselor, often tells people who ask him how to deal with painful emotions, "Feel the pain, but don't get stuck in it."

Accept that you are powerless over other people's wills. People heal only if they develop their ability to be loving and self-disciplined. You cannot force change; you can only demonstrate the values of the Torah yourself and hope they will be influenced. Whenever you feel yourself getting tense, visualize yourself letting go of the desire to control the person. See yourself accepting God's will.

Accept that you will not function well all the time. Functioning with a broken heart is like walking with a broken ankle. Do the best you can; don't heap shame and blame on yourself for not doing better or your spirit will be crushed.

Accept that acceptance is a lifelong struggle. It is as difficult to accept a handicapped mind as it is to accept a handicapped body. You think you're over the pain, and then suddenly it's back again in full force. Acceptance is something you do over and over again, day in and day out.

(3) *The power of surrender.* When you were a child, you wanted to control the entire universe. Maturity means recognizing that the most you can ever hope to control is your own thoughts and impulses. Everything else is in God's hands. So, let go. Put forth maximum effort, but surrender the results to God. Turn over to Him the past and the future, your anger and resentment, your grief, loneliness and your impatience to make yourself and others perfect. Give over your impossible dreams and your impossible demands. Let go of your passion to control anything other than your mind and muscles. Relax your grip. God is in charge.

Each time you get tense, angry or frightened, let this be a cue that you need to relax your grip and let go of control over anything except your thoughts, speech and deeds. Each time you do this, you'll calm down because you're connecting to Him. Thus, every stressful event carries an inner blessing, because you're using it as a cue to connect.

More than anything, let go of your condemnations of yourself and others. Trying to function with condemnations popping into your thoughts is like trying to run with two heavy suitcases. One suitcase consists of your judgments against yourself. The other is your judgments against others. Keep reminding yourself throughout the day to drop those judgments. They only make you more tense and irrational.

(4) *The power of avoiding harmful control tactics.* Your desperate need to get the disturbed person to change by getting angry, sad, sick and crazy hasn't worked. Instead, you've gotten stuck in these negative states. To extricate yourself from them, you must learn to identify, define and communicate your messages directly. For example, fear and anger can be healthy, protective emotions which say, "Danger! Be alert! Stay away!" As a child, fear and anger were your only means of defending yourself against abuse. But you're an adult now. You don't need to protect yourself with fear and anger. You can just stay away from those people who might hurt you! And if you can't, you can surround yourself with God's holy light and ask for His protection. Similarly, depression was your childhood way of numbing yourself to the pain of not getting what you wanted. But you don't need to get depressed anymore. You're an adult now. You have

the power to do the things which will make you happy. You can take care of yourself.

◆ EXAMPLE: "I was always in a state of chronic anxiety, shame and resentment around my parents. I'd get upset in order to get them to accept me as I am. In my support group, I learned that I first have to accept myself and them as we are and be forgiving and compassionate. They may never love me as I want them to, but I am an adult now and can give myself what they couldn't. Torturing myself with shame and guilt or trying to control them with anger won't change reality."

◆ EXAMPLE: "I thought I had to be angry all the time about my son's behavior or he'd think I was satisfied with him as he is and never change. But anger didn't bring change, only distance and hatred. To stop being so critical, I had to face the grief that he may never be all I want him to be. Yet I found that by loving him as he is, I can apply 'parental orthodontics' far more effectively. Before, I was pushing him around to satisfy my needs for approval and closeness. Once I put him in God's hands, the atmosphere became more loving."

To extricate yourself from negative emotional states, ask yourself, What underlying message am I trying to get across by being so tense, hostile, fearful or depressed? [It is helpful to have a compassionate person to listen to your answers.] For example: I'm trying to say:

"Love me as I am! Appreciate me! Value me!"

"Don't hurt me! Stop trying to control me!"

"Respect my needs and feelings!"

"I must protect myself by staying distant from you!"

"I'm not heartless or selfish. I have to go on with my life because that's the only way I can stay sane."

There is nothing wrong in wanting appreciation, approval and safety. But trying to get these messages across by staying in a chronic state of unhappiness doesn't work. Either forget about getting through to that person or get your messages across directly.

Now ask yourself, What positive things can I do to nourish myself instead of depending on another person to satisfy my needs? A new job? A friend? Fulfilling activities?

Give up the childish dream of being able to control people with unhappiness. Give up the neurotic habit of trying to reach people who have no desire to be reached.

You can love people to the extent that you love yourself. If you cannot accept another, it's because of your own self-hatred. By accepting others, you heal yourself.

(5) *The power of forgiveness.* Acceptance brings forgiveness, and forgiveness clears away the poisonous bitterness from your heart. However, forgiveness does not mean forgetting, condoning or ignoring deliberate sins or abusive behavior. There is no obligation to forgive abuse until such people have repented of their sins and asked for forgiveness.

Wounded people try to protect themselves from rejection by hurting others. Don't be so forgiving that you forget to protect yourself or make excuses for abuse.

Forgive normal mistakes and failures by acknowledging, "This person is doing the best he can with his present level of consciousness." By assuming that people really are doing the best they can at this present moment, you immediately calm down somewhat and become more objective and rational. Forgive for the sake of your own mental health, because hatred hurts you. It ties you to the disturbed person and brings you down to his level. Thus, we pray each night,

> Master of the universe, I hereby forgive anyone who has angered or vexed me or sinned against me, either physically or financially, against my honor or anything else that is mine, whether accidentally or intentionally, by speech or deed...
>
> (PRAYER BEFORE RETIRING AT NIGHT)

Even if you cannot say the words sincerely at first, say them anyway. They will become true eventually.

You may be afraid to forgive, fearing that, If I forgive, then I'll forget, then I'll get close and get hurt again. Hatred is a child's major protective emotion, a signal to stay away from certain people. However, as adults, we can simply validate our desire for distance. We no longer need to sustain a state of chronic anger in order to remind ourselves to stay away. We can forgive, yet remain protectively distant and wary.

Forgive yourself for not always responding positively. You are an average person trying to cope with a very great difficulty. You won't pass all the tests.

Forgive God for putting you in this situation. In this world, we must bless God for both the good and the bad, but in the World to Come, we will see clearly that there is only good (*Pesachim* 50a).

Warning: If there is actual danger to your physical or mental health, being too forgiving can make you passive and keep you from taking assertive action. Do not be forgiving out of cowardice, apathy or denial of the severity of the problem. This is especially true if you live with dishonest, violent powerholics.

Finally, forgive those who do not understand what you are dealing with. People only truly understand what they have experienced themselves.

(6) *The power of neutral detachment.* At times, you feel like a yo-yo, yanked up and down by the disturbed person's unpredictable moods and insatiable demands. To minimize the emotional trauma, you can train yourself to respond like an emergency room doctor, with neutral detachment to the person and his various control tactics, such as whining and criticism. Remember to detach with love, not hatred.

◆ EXAMPLE: "Like most women, when I got married my husband was the center of my life. I was preoccupied with his moods, his feelings, his stomach, his ego and his opinions. I wanted nothing more than to please him. But he was like a tyrannical child, demanding more than I could possibly give. I became so hateful and bitter, obsessing about him night and day. Finally, I forced myself to focus my attention on other people and activities. It was like surgery, very painful! Plus, I crave emotional closeness and have to repeat this detachment process each time I start to get depressed. When he's in a bad mood, I imagine myself in a mental helicopter, watching the whole thing from above. That way, part of me stays calm and distant even though another part of me feels pain. I walk away, get busy, repeat *Tehillim*, and recount all the things I have to be grateful for. This keeps me from being dragged down. Real control means staying calm, not spending my time trying to get him to be what I want."

◆ EXAMPLE: "Much as I tried to bend over backwards to please my mother-in-law, she still hates me with a vengeance. I learned to survive by fake indifference to her comments and chilling looks. Her remarks hurt, but I treat them like bad weather which will soon pass. She was love-starved as a child and this is the result. I pity her from afar. It takes an iron will to keep my thoughts about her from taking over my life. I think of my life as a piece of paper. She takes up a small, corner portion. When I begin to obsess about her, I push my thoughts back to the corner, like a lion tamer with a whip. I refuse to tie my self-worth or happiness to her."

You have a life to live. Bending over backwards and putting on a performance to please won't make people love you any more. People who can love will love you for who you are. Those who can't, won't, no matter what you do. You do these people a favor when you perform that "surgery," become self-sufficient and make your life as fulfilling and pleasant as possible. This is healthy behavior. If change is possible, your loving self-discipline and neutrality will influence the person to take responsibility for his own happiness. If not, you have managed to maintain your dignity and strengthened yourself spiritually.

(7) *The power of joy.* When a person is in a state of joy over the performance of a mitzvah, the *Shechinah* rests upon him (*Shabbath* 30b).

> Taste and see that God is good; happy is the man who finds refuge in Him.   (TEHILLIM 34:9)

Disturbed people have little *simchath chayim* [joy in life]. Not wanting to be alone in their misery, they try to pull everyone else down with them. By keeping yourself in a state of joy, they are deprived of their sense of power over you. If you, too, are addicted to pain, you'll have to train yourself to look for things that bring you joy. Bitterness is a cancer which you have the power to control only in yourself.

Just as you can make yourself anxious and angry by thinking certain thoughts, you can arouse a state of joy by singing passages from *Tehillim*, finding something pleasurable to do right now and planning happy events for the future.

Remember, you choose what to do with your own mind. Even faking happiness can help, for it provides a feeling of self-control. At first, the disturbed person may become even more angry and abusive in an attempt to gain control over you. Don't react in kind. Your ability to be joyful despite your pain is the most powerful tool which might possibly influence the disturbed person and eventually win his respect.

◆ EXAMPLE: "Because our home life is so tense, I decided that I had to work extra hard to keep things positive. It wasn't easy, because I am high-strung and tend to get depressed myself. But I saw how much it frightened my children to see me sad. I knew that joy would give us strength to face life's difficulties. So I made joy a major goal. When I walked in the door, I put on a smile. I studied Torah or went out for walks with the children when I was down. When I felt hostile, I made an extra effort to say *berachoth* out loud with a joyous spirit of gratefulness and gave the children extra hugs. Little by little, I stretched my capacity for joy and I actually did become a happier person. My self-discipline also began to influence my mate. It takes two to fight. When she saw that she couldn't drag me down, she stopped being so explosive."

◆ EXAMPLE: "In order not to react with hostility to certain critical relatives, I imagine the spiritual reward I earn for not returning their insults and for giving them the benefit of the doubt. I also imagine that their grimaces and comments are little darts which fly right out the window instead of getting stuck in my brain. Also, I thank them for bringing out my compulsive need for approval so that I can work on tying my sense of worth only to God. This attitude brings me a measure of real joy, because it means that I am growing from these experiences, painful as they may be."

Humor is impossible and inappropriate, of course, during times of real crisis or danger. But at other times, humor is your best friend. Even in the concentration camp, Frankl revealed, "Humor, if only for a few seconds, was another of the soul's weapons in the fight for self-preservation" (*Man's Search for Meaning*, p. 42).

(8) *The power of assertiveness.* It is very difficult to know when to be in a stoic mode and when to be demanding and even aggressive. Do you confront the powerholic and demand that he return the money he stole, or let the incident go for the sake of your inner peace? Do you confront a depressed person and make demands, or withdraw and go on with your life? Sometimes assertiveness works; at other times it merely intensifies a war-like atmosphere. We don't know until we try.

Assertiveness is a learned skill. If you are shy and insecure, the thought of stating your needs firmly and directly and standing up for your right to be treated with respect may be terrifying. Growth involves stretching your capacity to act differently from how you have acted in the past. You won't grow unless you have the courage to stretch and bear the anxiety involved in changing. The first few times you change a pattern, it may seem terrifying. But you don't die. What you find is new inner strengths and a greater delight in living.

You must assert your right to have friends and creative outlets, to have decent food, medical care, sleep, heat in the winter and other necessities, or you may be denied even these basics. If you cannot speak directly to the person, find a rabbi who may be able to influence the person.

Although some people may scoff at your efforts, the following statements may be helpful with others:

> *"I know you can control your urge to put me down."*
>
> *"Tell me two practical things you feel I can do to improve our relationship. Then I'll make the same request of you. I'm sure our relationship will improve if we do this once a week. Let's try it right now."*
>
> *"Because I care about you, I'm cancelling our charge accounts to help you get control of your impulsive spending."*
>
> *"Let's focus on solutions. Just tell me what you want."*
>
> *"I am leaving the room so that we can both calm down. Let me know when you are able to talk without putting me down."*

Since many people feel insulted if told that they need therapy, it might be best to say, "Let's go to someone who can help us improve our communication skills."

> ◆ EXAMPLE: "I noticed how selfish and self-centered my oldest son was. So one day, I calmly but firmly told him that if he wanted to live at home, he would have to help with the household chores and do some regular *chesed* work for the community. I took a big risk. I kept telling myself that the results were in God's hands. My son was angry at first, but he eventually learned to be more caring and considerate of other people."

Assertiveness only works if you can state what you want without hatred or a demand that the outcome be the way you want it.

(9) *The power of private therapy and support groups.* One of the problems of living with a disturbed person is that you often have to hide your true feelings so others won't feel uncomfortable around you or try to avoid you. Silence and secrecy are terrible burdens, especially in a community where there might be difficulty marrying off one's children if the truth were known. While therapists cannot work wonders, they can help you understand yourself better, help you to recognize your options and help you to feel less alone. A therapist can also help you break negative patterns which you have adopted in response to the disturbed person's behavior or which prompted you to form this unhealthy relationship in the first place.

In a support group, you receive unconditional love, which is what you need most. By talking openly and honestly, you retain your ability to form healthy relationships. A support group can provide you with the comfort of knowing that your situation is quite common. You feel, If they can cope, so can I! Because EMETT members are extremely careful to avoid *lashon ha-ra*, they discuss tactics to keep their spirits up without mentioning precisely who is being talked about. The friendships formed in these groups are tremendously healing to those who feel so alone with their pain. Furthermore, when you are able to help others with similar problems, you feel that your suffering is not in vain, for it has given you the insight which can lessen others' pain.

Do not think of the need for counseling as a sign of weakness. On the contrary! It is a sign of courage and good emotional health to seek contact. It's the weak ones who prefer to stay stuck in isolation.

(10) *The power of adopting the role of teacher.* We have an obligation to try to help others improve whenever possible (*Shabbath* 54b). You cannot have a normal relationship with a disturbed person, but you can sometimes teach elementary principles of polite behavior and good communication techniques, explaining exactly what is acceptable and unacceptable in the same neutral, yet stern voice which teachers use with uncooperative children. To teach, you must not only have a loving heart and infinite patience but well-defined rules and achievable goals. Books on behavior modification may help you learn how to set up a structured situation which will train the disturbed person to behave in a more responsible manner.

◆ EXAMPLE: "I used EMETT phrases with my children not only to calm us down but also in the hope that my spouse would overhear and absorb them. I was always saying to the kids, 'I'm endorsing myself for staying in control'; 'This discomfort is distressing, not dangerous'; 'We don't get upset about trivialities'; 'I'm sure you didn't hurt me on purpose'; and 'Remember, put-downs are *traife.'* Over the years, things have calmed down considerably because I learned to stay calm."

(11) *The power of silence.* We are told, "Do not answer a fool, lest you become like him" (*Mishlei* 26:4). Many times, the best you can do is to grit your teeth in stoic silence. It is often preferable not to share personal thoughts or feelings with a disturbed person, because this information will be used against you at some future time.

◆ EXAMPLE: "I became so resentful of my husband that every time he said or did something, I wanted to say how stupid, wrong or insensitive it was. I was totally out of control. I knew I had to get control of my mouth or the family would be destroyed. I decided to say no more than three or four words at a time and only what was absolutely necessary in order to get something done. At first I was silent, but the hostility still burned inside. But after a few months, I gained a quiet acceptance of him. I'm more forgiving of him and of myself. I'm not so bitter or angry anymore. I made many mistakes which I'm trying to correct now."

You may have to play the role of a mute nonperson in order to keep the atmosphere calm. However, do not allow yourself to wallow in silent hostility. Be "positively silent" — i.e., keep busy endorsing yourself for your inner victories, such as for the self-discipline it takes to remain silent, your patience, courage, *emunah* and *bitachon.* Endorse the most when you feel most hurt and most likely to lose control.

The whole world exists in the merit of he who restrains himself during a quarrel.   (CHULLIN 89a)

A prolonged period of silence will also help you determine whether or not the other person cares about having a relationship at all. If your silence is very upsetting, it may provoke the disturbed person to seek help in order to get you to communicate again. However, if the person welcomes the silence, you can then face the reality that she doesn't really want a relationship. Warning: The person may only want to talk so that she can start fighting and put you down again.

Make a firm rule not to talk when you are hostile, because anything you say will do more damage than good. It is a myth that an angry, explosive outburst will clear the air and make you feel better by getting things off your chest. You may feel better for a few seconds, but in the long run, your loss of control will lead to an increase in the number of outbursts.

Silence is also important in most social relationships. You may think you will win sympathy when you tell others how awful things are, but it is more likely that people will blame you, ostracize you socially, or offer inappropriate advice. Prospective employers may refuse to give you a job.

Be especially careful for your children's sake. If word gets around, other children may ridicule them for having a "crazy" relative. Also, don't talk to others about your "difficult person" in front of your children. They are ashamed enough as it is without feeling that their secrets are known in the community. On the other hand, it may be appropriate to give visitors a brief warning about what to expect. You don't have to go into detail, but you can tell them in a neutral tone of voice, "This person has a problem. If you are not treated politely, don't take it personally. It's not your fault."

(12) *The power of staying healthy.* You may have the fantasy that the disturbed person will suddenly become kind and attentive if you get sick. It is more likely that he won't believe you, will still make the same demands, or will be angry that you cannot serve him as usual. Others may actually want you to be ill so that you can be more easily controlled. You need to be strong and healthy in order to keep the unbalanced person as calm as humanly possible and to give your children the attention they need.

(13) *The power of separation.* Minimize the time you spend with this person. For example, you may have a romantic ideal of a family sitting down to a peaceful dinner while everyone shares and listens attentively to each other. But if your spouse is critical, it may be better to eat separately. Some husbands should be encouraged to come home only after the children are asleep. It may be helpful to take separate cars to events to avoid nasty confrontations and even separate vaca-

tions. Fun activities with the children can be planned for times when the person is away. If the person is violently abusive, complete separation is probably a necessity.

(14) *The power of perspective.* In the concentration camps, people were given numbers instead of names. This was part of an attempt to erase all sense of personhood in the inmates. Disturbed people will often try to do the same thing to you. Do not accept this depersonalization process. You retain your sense of personhood by maintaining your inner freedom. This means not adopting the disturbed person's perspective of you. Make the focus of your self-worth internal, not external. You *are* worthwhile, even if this person is too blind to his own Godliness to see Godliness in you.

Keep your perspective with outsiders as well. Many people will minimize your difficulties or deny the problem. They will tell you, "It can't be that bad." Only you know the truth — that things may look fine on the outside, yet be very unhealthy on the inside. Also, many people will advise, "Don't let it bother you," as though you are to blame for being in pain. You would have to be a stone wall not to feel heartbroken at the loss of a normal family life. Few people can imagine how stressful your situation is or how courageous and disciplined you have to be in order to remain functional. They cannot really sympathize because they cannot understand.

(15) *The power of outside confirmation of your normalcy and intrinsic value.* Endless criticism can make you feel like a total failure. You need appreciation and respect in order to be healthy. It is important to be around normal people so that you don't forget what that is like! Volunteer work, even for one hour a day, can bring the appreciation and respect you need. An outside job can put you in contact with people who see you as competent and likeable. Since disturbed people will often try to prevent you from feeling successful and competent, you may have to keep many arrangements secret.

(16) *The power of a hopeful message to the children.* In an abusive home, children inevitably have lower self-esteem and fear closeness. When "traumatic bonding" takes place, the children seek love most from the parent who is least able to give it and cling to and imitate that parent in an attempt to win his or her love. Also, they may always feel like failures for not getting that love, having been incapable of pleasing that parent no matter how hard they tried. A

parent, friend or relative who provides a model of love and stability can often strengthen the children's self-esteem and help them exercise their power to choose healthy thoughts and actions.

> ◆ EXAMPLE: "As my grandchildren got older, I often reminded them, 'In order to strengthen steel, it is placed in a fire and then hammered. Your difficulties at home have put you through the fire and made you stronger. You have understanding and strengths which other children do not have. You will be more sensitive and compassionate toward those with emotional handicaps. You'll be better parents because you will know how important it is not to hurt people's feelings. You don't have to live there forever. You can leave home when you're eighteen. You will marry someone who treats you well.' I was very honest with them. I told them of the many reasons why parents stay married despite their problems, such as to keep the family together, to avoid the machinations of unscrupulous lawyers and the court system, which might not award custody wisely. My openness with them made us very close."

(17) *The power of leading a secret life.* Keep your friendships, thoughts, plans and many of your feelings secret in order not to give the disturbed person ammunition to put you down or deprive you of the things which give you pleasure.

(18) *The power of the "insincere gesture."* An "insincere gesture" is what you use when you feel awful and yet realize that it would only make matters worse to express your real feelings. You pretend to be loving, confident, calm or happy when you don't feel it, not because your are trying to fool yourself, but because you are striving for an ideal which you know you can eventually reach. An insincere gesture of love, sanity or confidence generates true feelings eventually.

> ◆ EXAMPLE: "My children became very frightened whenever I yelled that I was going crazy and couldn't cope anymore. When I fell apart, they became more hostile and aggressive. For their sake, I learned to calm my panicky feelings by pretending to be strong. I'd tell them that everything was going to work out, even if I was terrified that we couldn't pay the bills or that I'd have a breakdown. The mask of self-control also helped remind me that I really could stay in control. By trying to create a more secure world for them, I ended up generating true feelings of confidence, which I never had before."

◆ EXAMPLE: "After a violent clash with her father, my daughter took her anger out on me and spoke to me meanly. My natural impulse was to react in kind, but I knew that this would only escalate the hostility. Though I was afraid of being hurt by her, I pretended to be loving. When we were praying together in *shul*, I put my arm around her. It felt insincere at first, but after a minute, she put her arm around me and started to cry softly. I did too. We both hugged each other in mutual caring. I was so glad that I didn't give in to the impulse to return her hostility with my own."

When the great Sage, Shammai, said, "Greet every man with a cheerful countenance" (*Avoth* 1:15), he was certainly aware that we do not always feel cheerful. But he knew the power of the "forced gesture" to lift our spirits. He knew that "A man is influenced by his actions" (*Sefer HaChinuch* #16).

(19) *The power of endorsements.* To counteract the disturbed person's negativity, it is essential to *flood* your home with positive feedback for any act of self-control and *chesed*, no matter how minor. Program your children to think positively about themselves by endorsing them whenever they are being caring, self-disciplined, patient, reliable, independent, flexible and creative. Let them know that, "What you did was very responsible." "That showed good judgment. You know how to make good decisions."

Keep the Endorsement Principle in mind: When you endorse yourself for any step, no matter how small, which you take to lead a healthy, disciplined life today, you will take bigger steps tomorrow. But if you crush yourself for your mistakes and failures today, you will do even less tomorrow.

You can plant positive seeds in the disturbed person's mind by saying, "I know you didn't really mean to hurt me." "I know you really love the children." Write down positive acts on a piece of paper attached to the refrigerator, such as that he mailed a letter or she gave a small amount to charity. Appreciation for these small steps is the first step to change.

Warning: Many disturbed people respond to praise with hostility. So be prepared for such a response. However, many emotionally wounded people eventually become more positive and trusting if fed a daily diet of endorsements.

(20) *The power of self-respect.* Engage in activities which build self-respect. Turn every encounter into a success experience which

you can endorse yourself for, even if "success" only means being silent, speaking calmly about your feelings, getting a meal on the table, getting out of the house when you feel you are losing control, or smiling even though your heart is breaking. Keep repeating to yourself: I am loved and capable. And, God loves me. As your sense of worth becomes firmly established within your consciousness, you will be less influenced by others' judgments:

> What is meant by whole-hearted devotion to God? It means that in every act, public and private, the aim and purpose should be service of God for His Name's sake, to please Him only, without thought of winning the favor of human creatures...It should be the same to one whether his fellow-creatures praise or depreciate him.
>
> (DUTIES OF THE HEART, vol. II, pp. 11-13)

(21) *The power of imagination.* Your imagination is your most powerful tool! Use mental imagery (see the P.E.P. exercise in *EMETT: a step-by-step guide to Emotional Maturity Established Through Torah*, p. 197) to program yourself to remain calm, confident and self-respecting, and to respond constructively in stressful situations. During quiet moments, imagine a stressful situation, such as when someone is critical or indifferent, and visualize yourself being detached, self-respecting or calmly assertive.

◆ EXAMPLE: "I knew my son would storm out the door when I refused to give him the loan he wanted. Anger is his control tactic, and I usually give in to avoid upsetting him. The night before his visit, I imagined myself calmly but firmly refusing his request and him leaving angrily. I imagined myself then going about my work, knowing that I was really doing the best thing for him, and waiting patiently for my physical and emotional distress to fade away on their own."

◆ EXAMPLE: "Before visiting my disapproving relatives, I took a few seconds to imagine myself sitting with them and thinking, 'I refuse to shame myself or them. I accept and honor myself and them as we are.' This visualization helped me stay calm during the actual visit. I feel myself stretching, stretching my ability to love."

◆ EXAMPLE: "I used to scream at my kids when they were uncooperative or insolent. I believed that I really could not control myself. Then, one night before going to sleep, I visualized myself responding calmly yet firmly to them. The next day, I was actually able to do what I had imagined myself doing. Whenever I do this at night, the next day is calmer. I stay in control for my own sake, because when I'm out of control, I lose respect for myself."

Researchers have found that visualizations produce actual changes in the brain cells, since the brain can be programmed by an imagined experience, as well as an actual one. Anything you can imagine yourself doing you are more likely to actually do (*Psychofeedback*, p. 62).

(22) *The power of doing double.* Give yourself and your children double doses of love. You'll get it all back tenfold.

(23) *The power of a pleasant home atmosphere.* Keep the house decorated with pictures of *tzaddikim* and uplifting quotations. Fill your home with plants and music as well. Plan celebrations when the disturbed person is away. Plan outings with friends and other family members.

(24) *The power of knowledge.* Learn as much as you can about mental illness to help you understand the problem.

(25) *The power of prior planning.* With all the tension and chaos in your life, you need to keep things as predictable as possible. Tensions which can be handled in a normal household, such as getting ready for the Sabbath, create explosions in a dysfunctional home. Keep things as scheduled as possible. That means doing whatever can be done ahead of time, like setting the Sabbath table the night before, making Pesach early and having extra cooked food for emergencies. Keep a calendar, make lists, and stick to schedules. Go to sleep and get up at normal hours. Attend classes at scheduled times, because nothing else in your life might be predictable. You might even schedule times to exercise or visit friends just to make sure that you don't neglect yourself. Being responsible to yourself will give a measure of stability to your life.

(26) *The power of physical exercise.* The nervous system has the ability to secrete natural substances called endorphins, which, when released, alleviate pain and produce a natural "high" feeling of well-being and power. Two natural ways to get these calming endorphins flowing are vigorous physical exercise for at least twenty minutes and physical stroking, such as hugging. Since the body and spirit are so intimately connected, any positive physical act will have a positive effect on your entire state of being.

...just as zeal can *result* from an inner burning so can it *create* one... If, however, he is sluggish in the movement of his limbs, the movement of his spirit will die down and be extinguished.

(THE PATH OF THE JUST, p. 89)

You may feel very depressed and sluggish at times. That is when you need to forcefully create an inner zeal through exercise. It will keep your spirit from dying!

(27) *The power of avoiding inappropriate shame and guilt.* Disturbed people will blame you for their unhappiness, and accuse you of being unspiritual, selfish, disloyal and insensitive. If you have a codependent personality, you will tend to think the abused person is right, that you are to blame for not trying hard enough. You will be filled with unnecessary shame and guilt, while the disturbed person has neither. If you accept blame or think you deserve to be punished for not doing enough, you will not have the courage to become self-respecting, because you won't really believe you deserve it.

(28) *The power of knowing your limitations.* You will not always be in control, always be compassionate and forgiving or always know what to do. Trying to be perfect will only intensify your feelings of failure and abnormality. Give yourself permission to be average. Stop thinking that if you would just be more pleasing, pious or self-sacrificing, the other person would become happy and loving. Going overboard to please people is the worst thing you can do because it reinforces their belief that you're to blame for their unhappiness, and that the only way they can be happy is to control you and force you to cater to their needs.

◆ EXAMPLE: "My wife is frequently depressed. I tried to prove my love by rushing home from work whenever she was 'in crisis.' She ended up being 'in crisis' so often that I lost my job. No matter how much time I spent with her, she still complained that it wasn't enough. I now accept that I cannot fulfill her demands, and needn't feel ashamed of it."

◆ EXAMPLE: "I tried everything I could think of to not let my boss's criticism get to me. Finally, as I got sicker and sicker, I accepted that I just don't have the personality to withstand such abuse. Perhaps a colder type can, but not me!"

(29) *The power of gratefulness.*

The true service of God is built on a foundation of gratitude.

(STRIVE FOR TRUTH! vol. I, p. 153)

Our ability to thank God for what we have, no matter what the external circumstances, has been the secret of our strength as a Jewish people. But gratefulness is a habit which must be cultivated vigorously, day in and day out, or the weeds of bitterness take over.

Gratefulness and love feed on each other. So do bitterness and hatred. The more bitterly you complain, the more bitter and deprived you feel. The more you practice gratefulness, the more grateful you will actually feel! In order not to go through life feeling deprived, keep a daily list of things for which you are grateful or that bring you pleasure, such as inspiring words of Torah, your own little successes, caring people, etc. You can even fake gratefulness! It will soon become a habit if practiced throughout the day.

(30) *The power of realism.* Trying to get love from a rock does the same thing to you that sucking on an empty bottle does to a hungry baby. It's a neurotic habit which can be overcome. Denial means thinking that everything would be just fine if only there were more money, a different job, more children, less children, no pressures, etc. Denial means thinking you can be rational, open and honest with an irrational, closed, dishonest person. Denial means waiting impatiently for momentous personality changes to take place.

Realism means accepting that the person is emotionally crippled, that you will not get the depth of communication or the consistency of caring that you want, and that you must be satisfied with less than you hoped for. Realism means working toward realistic goals, such as a polite, if superficial relationship and a reasonable sharing of responsibilities.

(31) *The power of a diary.* Keep a detailed log of both the person's destructive behavior as well as his positive acts. This is important for future counseling sessions as well as to enable you to properly evaluate the severity of the problem. For instance, the situation might not be as bleak as you think. On the other hand, it might be worse.

When you go to a counselor, you might be so flooded by pent-up feelings that you cannot provide a clear picture of the situation. The counselor may then decide that it's not that bad, or that *you* are the one with the problem, since you are so upset, while the disturbed person may be absent or sitting calmly. A list will keep you focused and logical.

(32) *The power of financial independence.* Money is always an issue with disturbed people: they overspend, hoard, are secretive and stingy, or refuse to work but expect you to and to give your paycheck to them. If you can't take full control of the budget, at least put aside as much as you can for your own needs. Open a secret bank account if necessary. Money enables you to have greater independence, creative outlets, and the possibility of getting away when things are rough.

(33) *The power of reading uplifting material.* Start with the Torah. Note how our patriarchs and matriarchs struggled with their difficult situations. Whatever your circumstances, know that you are not alone. Your heartache has echoed throughout history. King David said, "...every night I drench my bed, with my tears I soak my couch" (*Tehillim* 6:7), yet his poetry is full of joy and faith. Could we understand his words if we never suffered? Would we stretch our arms out to Him if we were never crushed?

Throughout Jewish history, our people have endured great losses. What kept us strong was our sense of having a mission in life — to maintain our moral integrity and help build the Jewish nation. This goal will draw you like a magnet, helping you to transcend your personal pain and to do something meaningful with your life.

(34) *The power of self-nurturance.* In a non-nurturing relationship, you must be extra careful to nurture yourself. That means keeping up your appearance, eating healthy foods and engaging in activities which nourish your spirit.

(35) *The power of knowing the secret of happiness.* The most difficult lesson to learn in life is that happiness is not determined by other people and external events, but by your attitude toward them. Ultimately, happiness comes not from getting what you want, but appreciating what you get.

◆ EXAMPLE: "A certain official was very nasty to me. Normally, I would have felt like an absolute worm. But I remembered my resolution to avoid shaming myself or anyone else in nonhalachic matters and to think of every event as being sent by God for my ultimate good. As soon as I thought of her as providing me with the opportunity to practice the ideals of Torah, I felt free of fear and hatred. She couldn't get to me! I simply ignored her comments, looked her in the eyes and focused on getting the information I needed. I actually felt happy, even though my guts were in turmoil, because I saw that I could cope successfully with a kind of person who had always intimidated me in the past. I had changed a negative pattern. I had confronted her quietly yet assertively instead of wallowing in self-pity or running away. I saw that this incident was rooted in God's love for me. He sent this person to give me the opportunity to heal the wounds of my , past. That's when I understood that the source of happiness is within me, inside my own mind, and that I can use any situation for growth. I wanted to shout this message to the whole world, to teach people that by seeing everything as a gift from God, we can use the same events which used to get us down to elevate ourselves spiritually. This is a whole new level of consciousness!"

(36) *The power of faith.* The next time you feel hurt, say the following words, even if they are completely insincere at the time: "I bless God for this event. I make His will my will. I don't really like what's happening, but I trust that God has brought me this pain out of love. I trust that this is true, even if I do not feel the love at this moment."

The miracle of faith is that by repeating these words, you will establish a strong connection with God and will eventually come to actually bless the event as having refined and sensitized you and brought you to a higher level of faith.

We are told, "A righteous person lives by his faith" (*Chavakuk* 2:4). Faith alone takes away fear, bitterness and hatred and allows us to experience love and joy.

> There is no blade of grass that has no spirit above...
>
> (BERESHITH RABBAH 10:6)

If a blade of grass has a "spirit above," then surely we, who are connected with the Source of all spirits, do as well. Faith requires that we actively strengthen that connection throughout our interactions.

No one is born knowing how to cope with pain. To be able to bear discomfort without endless complaining and bitterness, and to keep moving forward despite the pain, is a sign of courage, maturity and faith. It is something we all must learn — the hard way.

These thirty-six disciplines must be repeated countless times each day, even when they seem quite futile and insincere. If you do practice them, especially when you are in the most pain, you, too, will experience the miracle of faith and will reap in joy what you sowed in tears (*Tehillim* 126:5).

CHAPTER 13:
The Healing Journey:
A Summary of Coping Tactics

In the midst of a painful encounter with a difficult person, or when feeling discouraged about your own ability to cope, it is essential to focus on thoughts which will put you in a state of hope, faith and love. No matter how badly you have behaved, you can always do *teshuvah*. No matter how badly others treat you, you can still honor yourself. You can use every stressful event as an opportunity to achieve a higher level of self-discipline and awareness.

The following list will provide some measure of "first aid" in a crisis. Each one is a kind of "stretching" exercise which expands our ability to think and behave according to the ethics of the Torah. It takes countless repetitions to integrate these thoughts into our lives. If you repeat the phrases which are most relevant, no matter how insincere they may feel at the time, and take some positive action, no matter how minor, you will eventually achieve a heightened sense of awareness and attachment to God. Promise! (Duplicate this list and keep it in convenient places so that you can reread it during difficult times.)

(1) *Permission to feel*: I choose to allow myself to grieve. It is normal to feel alone, hurt, helpless, misunderstood and unappreciated around disturbed people. However, I will avoid the excessive shame which produces chronic anger and anxiety.

(2) *Hashgachah pratith*: I choose to let God control the universe. I choose to make God — not my personal desires — King. Since God meant my life to be this way, I choose it to be this way, too, for my growth. By working to see the good in every situation, I will eventually see His guiding Hand in all that happens to me.

Every time I feel tense, I choose to use the tension as a reminder to reconnect to God and fill my heart with love, not fear.

(3) *No right or wrong*: I choose to avoid the judgement of right and wrong except as it applies only to matters of *halachah*, and not to matters of personal taste or opinion.

(4) *Priorities*: I choose to focus on my goals of doing God's will, loving others and protecting my mental health by doing whatever brings me closer to Torah. Everything else is secondary.

(5) *Choices*: I choose not to anger or upset myself by thinking there is immediate danger to my physical or mental health, or that people are deliberately out to hurt me (*davka*). By removing the *davka* and the danger, I automatically calm down and can think more clearly.

(6) *Avoid approval seeking*: I choose not to be a marionette who must dance when others pull the strings. My needs and feelings are important. I can bear the pain of rejection. Disapproval is merely distressing, not dangerous. People who can love, will love me; those who can't, won't, no matter what I do. My worth is determined by God, not man.

(7) *Nisayon*: I choose to focus on the *berachah* in this situation, in that it helps me to grow spiritually by forcing me to develop acceptance, assertiveness, compassion, cheerfulness, *chesed*, courage, decisiveness, detachment, diligence, honesty, *emunah*, flexibility, forgiveness, *gevurah*, gratefulness, humility, love (for self or others), patience, self-discipline, silence, self-sufficiency, etc.

(8) *Average*: I choose to consider myself average, not exceptional. Averageness means I can handle the situation. I give myself permission to be human and make mistakes, to be average, not superhuman.

(9) *Benefit of the doubt*: I choose to think, "They're doing the best they can given their present level of consciousness, their skills, the pains and passions of the present and their conditioning and upbringing of the past."

(10) *Distressing, not dangerous*: I choose to think that I can bear this discomfort with dignity and good will. Comfort is a want not a need. I choose to believe that I can face these disappointments and frustrations and cope adequately.

(11) *Ignore and depersonalize*: I choose to adopt a neutral "Oh... response", like an impersonal reporter, in order to achieve emotional distance. I choose not to be dragged down to other people's negativity.

(12) *Pleasure*: I choose to nurture myself and make my life pleasurable.

(13) *Seek peace, not power*: I choose to act from love, not the desire to control. Ego victories are empty victories.

(14) *Total view*: Although I feel bad right now, I choose to take the total view of my life as positive.

(15) *Part acts*: I choose to bear the discomfort one minute at a time, one day at a time.

(16) *No comparisons*: Since I am unique, I choose to avoid competing or comparing with those who manage better or have more. God has given me what I need to accomplish my specific mission in this world.

(17) *Gratefulness*: Although some aspects of my life aren't so great, I choose to be grateful for all I do have (e.g., health, children, financial security, an intact family unit, an on going incentive to connect to God and work on myself). Gratefulness will bring joy into my heart.

(18) *Humility*: I choose to accept my limitations humbly and humbly accept the limitations of others. I accept that I cannot control anything other than my own *middoth*. I have the humility to know that I can not judge because I do not know what is in another person's heart or mind.

(19) *Temporary*: I choose to consider minor distresses easy to manage or overlook because they are temporary.

(20) *The mask*: I choose to make an insincere gesture of love, hope and confidence, because it is better than a sincere gesture of hatred and despair. The mask will generate sincere feelings eventually.

(21) *Humor*: I choose to find humor whenever I can. Humor is my best friend; bitterness and hatred my worst enemies. Negativity cannot penetrate my soul if I am in a state of joy. I choose to take myself lightly so that I can soar.

(22) *Resourcefulness*: I choose to believe that my inner strengths and the wisdom of Torah will pull me through.

(23) *Courage*: I choose to face this distress bravely and go on living with love despite it.

(24) *Realism vs. romanticism*: I choose to give up romantic demands for perfection from myself and others, for approval and appreciation from everyone, and the need to cure, control or communicate with everyone. No amount of honor, control, attention,

approval, food or pleasure can satisfy my deepest needs. Only God can fill my deepest needs.

(25) *Patience*: I choose to have patience during my own and others' growth and to stop expecting quick cures. Impatience means I'm trying to control the universe.

(26) *Do the difficult*: I choose to discipline myself to do the things which bring me joy and self-respect. I choose to be assertive when I am afraid, loving when I feel hateful, polite when I feel vengeful, disciplined when I feel out of control and take risks to build courage when I feel anxious.

(27) *Drop condemnations*: I choose to avoid condemning myself and others for not being perfect and to avoid condemning God for not giving me all I want in life. I choose to drop my judgments against God, myself and man for the sake of my mental health and inner peace.

(28) *Feelings do not always reflect facts*: I may feel that I cannot cope or control myself, but I choose to recognize the truth that I really can. I may feel that I am worthless, but I can choose to believe that I am a being of infinite Godly value. I may feel that I am going to lose my best friend or die if I give up my bad habits, but I choose to believe that when my addictive self dies, I will have much more love in my life. When I feel that I am unlovable and incapable, I chose to think I am both lovable and capable.

(29) *Solutions, not theatrics*: I choose to ignore what I can't fix. I choose not to dwell on what I can't change.

(30) *Forgiveness*: I choose to forgive myself and others for the sake of my own inner peace.

(31) *Endorse*: I choose to endorse myself. The more I endorse, the more I grow. I endorse for effort, not success. If I make a mistake, I can endorse for having learned. Every act of self-discipline increases my self-respect.

(32) *Trivialities*: The situation as a whole is not trivial, but many of the incidents surrounding this matter are trivialities when compared to my mental health goals in life.

(33) *Freedom of choice*: I choose to avoid blaming others for my actions. I choose to take responsibility for choosing my own thoughts and actions. I allow others the freedom to be who they are, instead of trying to dominate and control.

(34) *Attachment to God*: I choose to realize that the purpose of this pain is to help me forge an internalized awareness of God as King.

The eight enemies of mental health to be avoided

(1) *Erroneous beliefs*. Ask yourself, "Am I holding on to childish beliefs?" E.g.: "I must mold myself to be as others want me to be." "I must be all things to all people." "The only way I can get what I want is by acting angry, sad, bad, sick or crazy." "I cannot control myself." "I deserve respect only if I'm successful." "Disapproval is disastrous." "Mistakes are unforgivable." "I'm basically defective." "I have to punish people who don't live up to my standards." "My happiness is produced by external events and people." "My worth is tied to people's judgments of me."

(2) *Romantic or unrealistic demands*. Ask, "Am I making impossible demands of God, myself or others?"

(3) *Exceptionality*. Ask, "Do I believe that I am the most unlovable, that I have the worst problems, the greatest sensitivities and the least abilities to cope."

(4) *Exaggeration*. Ask, "Am I exaggerating the danger or discomforts involved in trivial situations and awfulizing the molehills?"

(5) *Extrapolating negatively into the future*. Ask, "Do I think that the future holds only doom, gloom and disaster?" When my children misbehave, do I think, No one will want to marry him/her. She'll end up immoral, irreligious or insane. Do I fear ending up crazy, isolated and unfulfilled?

(6) *Excessive responsibility*. Ask, "Do I take excessive responsibility for others' happiness or mental health? Am I trying to control others' growth?"

(7) *Evading responsibility*. Ask, "Am I running away from my responsibilities? Am I failing to take assertive action?"

(8) *Eclipsing the good*. Ask, "Do I fail to see the good in myself, other people or in my life, and focus only on the negative?"

Three truths which may seem like lies when we first say them

(1) *To strengthen love for and faith in God*: "Since God has chosen that I experience this situation, it must be perfect. Therefore, I choose it to be this way for my *tikkun*."

(2) *To strengthen love for others*: "I bless you for giving me the opportunity to demonstrate Torah values."

(3) *To strengthen love of self*: "I am a being of infinite value. I am lovable and capable."

Constant repetition of these phrases throughout the day, especially over minor inconveniences and losses, will build a firm foundation of love for God, man and ourselves.

Empowering exercise

Recall the last time you felt strong, hopeful, happy and connected to God. Recall the scene. What were you doing? Visualize the environment, the sights, sounds, smells and feelings you were experiencing at the time. Make the picture brighter and more powerful. Identify the thoughts which you were thinking at the time, thoughts which made you feel successful and hopeful. Take time to feel the happiness, the joy at feeling God close to you, protecting you. Feel the warm glow of security and safety which surrounds you. Now, transfer that feeling of resourcefulness and security to some problem you are having right now in your life. Realize that you have inner resources to cope and that there are numerous people around who can help you figure out the strategies for dealing with any problem.

You have created this scene and these positive feelings with your own mind. That is a power you can exercise any time you want, to create either a positive or negative state of consciousness.

Bibliography

English

Adahan, Miriam. *Appreciating People,* Feldheim Publishers, in conjunction
with Gefen Publishing House, Jerusalem-New York, 1989.
EMETT, Feldheim Publishers, Jerusalem-New York, 1987.
Raising Children to Care, Feldheim Publishers, in conjunction with
Gefen Publishing House, Jerusalem-New York, 1988.
Art Scroll, *Bereshith,* Mesorah Publications, New York, 1978.
Art Scroll, *Haggadah,* Mesorah Publications, New York, 1979.
Rabbi Bachya Ibn Paquda. *Duties of the Heart,* Feldheim Publishers,
Jerusalem-New York, 1962.
Cohen, Seymour J. *The Ways of the Righteous,* Ktav Publishing House,
New York, 1982.
Dessler, Eliyahu. *Strive for Truth!* Feldheim Publishers, Jerusalem-New
York, vol. I, 1978, vol. II, 1985.
Eisenblatt, Shmuel. *Fulfillment in Marriage.* Feldheim Publishers,
Jerusalem-New York, 1987.
Rabbi Eliyahu ben Shlomo Zalman (Gaon of Vilna), *Even Sheleimah,*
English translation by Rabbi Chayim Dovid Ackerman and Rabbi Yaakov
Singer, entitled *The Vilna Gaon Views Life,* Jerusalem, 1974.
Rabbi Israel Meir Hacohen (The Hafetz Hayyim), *The Stories and Parables
of the Hafetz Hayyim,* Feldheim Publishers, Jerusalem-New York, 1976.
Kitov, Eliyahu. *The Book of Our Heritage,* Feldheim Publishers,
Jerusalem-New York, 1968.
Lopian, Rabbi Eliyahu. *Lev Eliyahu,* translated by Rabbi B.D. Kelin,
published by Rabbi Kalman Pinski, Jerusalem, 1975.
Luzzatto, Rabbi Moshe Chaim. *The Path of the Just,* translated by Shraga
Silverstein, Feldheim Publishers, Jerusalem-New York, 1966.
Maimonides, Moshe. *Guide for the Perplexed.* Dover Publications, New
York, 1956. *The Book of Knowledge,* edited and translated by Moses
Hyamson, Feldheim Publishers, Jerusalem-New York, 1974.

Pliskin, Zelig. *Gateway to Happiness*, The Jewish Learning Exchange, Jerusalem, 1983.

Raz, Simcha. *A Tzaddik in Our Time*, Feldheim Publishers, Jerusalem-New York, 1976.

Sefer haHinnuch. Ascribed to Rabbi Aaron HaLevi of Barcelona, translation by Charles Wengrov, Feldheim Publishers, Jerusalem-New York, 1978.

Teherani, Rabbi Eliyahu Porat. *Peace of Mind*, Bnei Brak, 1988.

Rabbeinu Yonah of Gerona, *Sha'arei Teshuvah*, ed., Levin, Epstein, English ed., Feldheim Publishers, Jerusalem-New York, 1968.

Rabbi Zalman, Shneur. *Likutei Amarim*, Kehot Publications, New York, 1973.

Hebrew

Rabbi Eliyahu de Vidas. *Reishith Chochmah*, ed., Lubin, 1888.

Rabbi Yehudah Low (The Maharal). *Tifereth Yisrael*, Bnei Brak, 1972.

Rabbi Eliezer Papu. *Pele Yoetz*, Kushtandia, 1824.

Zaitchyk, Rabbi Chayim. *HaMeoroth HaGedolim*, Jerusalem, 1969.

Author Unknown

Ahavath Yisroel, Kehot Publications, New York, 1977.

Alei Shur, anonymous, Jerusalem, 1987.

Chayei HaMussar, Hotzaoth Chochmah U'mussar, Bnei Brak, 1963.

Kuntres Ahavath Yisrael, Kehot Publications, New York, 1977.

The Ways of the Righteous, translated by Seymour J. Cohen, Ktav Publishing House, New York, 1982.

Yalkuth Shimoni, classical anthology of *Midrashim*, *Yalkuth Hoshea*, earliest known edition dated 1308 in Bodlian Library, ed. Vilna, 1898.

Secular Books

Ayres, Jean. *Sensory Integration and the Child*, Western Psychological Services, 1979.

Frankl, Viktor. *From Death Camp to Existentialism* (also known as *Man's Search for Meaning*, Beacon Press, Boston, 1959.

Hunt, Morton. *The Compassionate Beast*, William Morrow & Co., New York, 1990.

Kohn Alfie, *The Brighter Side of Human Nature*, Basic Books, New York, 1990.

Kreisman, Jerold, M.D., and Straus, Hal. *I Hate You — Don't Leave Me: Understanding the Borderline Personality*, Avon Books, New York, 1989.

McCullough, Bonnie and Susan Monson. *401 Ways to Get Your Kids to Help Around the House*, St. Martin's Press, 1981.

Pearsall, Paul. *Superimmunity*, Fawcett Publishers, New York, l987.

Thomas, Paul. *Psychofeedback*, Prentice Hall, New Jersey, 1979.

Secular Articles

"Unipolar and bipolar depression," *Archives of General Psychiatry*, Nov. 1988.

"Increased acetycholine sensitivity and depression," *The New England Journal of Medicine*, vol. 311, #4.

"Learned helplessness in humans: Critique and reformulation," *Journal of Abnormal Psychology*, vol. 87, #1.

"Interaction of drug therapy and therapy in depressive patients," *Journal of the American Medical Association*, vol. 252, #4.

Glossary

AHAVATH CHINAM: (literally, baseless love) love which one gives to
another even though the person does not seem to be deserving of it.

ALIYAH: (literally, going up) to grow spiritually.

ATZVUTH: sadness.

AVODAH: work, spiritual effort.

BEITH HAMIKDASH: The Holy Temple.

BEN MELECH: son of the King (God).

BERACHAH: a blessing.

BITACHON: trust in God's personal involvement in one's life.

BNEI YISRAEL: the Children of Israel.

CHESED: kindness.

CHILLUL HASHEM: desecration of God's name.

CHUMRAH: an extra-strict religious practice beyond what the Law requires.

DAVKA: on purpose.

EMUNAH: faith in God.

HECHSHER: the rabbinic approval given to a product which has been
certified as kosher.

HOD NAFSHO: the Divine glory of one's soul.

KLIPAH: (literally, outer shell) the various psychological barriers which keep
us from experiencing Godliness in this world.

KASHRUTH: food which is permissible for a Jew to eat.

KAVOD: respect.

KORBAN: (literally, to come close) a sacrifice.

LASHON HA-RA: evil tongue, gossip.

MAMALASHON: (Y.) mother tongue.

MIDDAH (MIDDOTH): character trait(s).

MITZRAYIM: Egypt.

MITZVAH: a religious commandment by which one binds oneself to God.

NESHAMAH: the Godly soul.

NISAYON: a test.

PASUK: a brief phrase from the Torah.

SEFER TORAH: a Torah scroll.

SHALIACH: a messenger.

SHALOM BAYITH: peace in the home.

SHIUR (SHIURIM): lecture(s) or study group(s) on some Torah subject.

SHMATEH: (Y.) a rag.

SIMCHAH: joy.

TEHILLIM: Psalms.

TESHUVAH: (literally, return) repentance, to show how sincerely one regrets one's past actions by changing one's future behavior.

TIKKUN: improvement, repair.

TZADDIK (TZADDIKIM): righteous person(s).

TZAV: an order, a bond.

TZELEM ELOKIM: the image of God.

TZITZITH: the four-cornered fringed garment worn by males over three years of age.

YERIDAH: going down, descent.

YETZIATH MITZRAYIM: going out of Egypt.

Index